PostgreSQL Mistakes
and How to Avoid Them

T0400846

Get the eBook FREE!

(PDF, ePub, Kindle, and liveBook all included)

We believe that once you buy a book from us, you should be able to read it in any format we have available. To get electronic versions of this book at no additional cost to you, purchase and then register this book at the Manning website.

Go to https://www.manning.com/freebook and follow the instructions to complete your pBook registration.

That's it!
Thanks from Manning!

PostgreSQL Mistakes and How to Avoid Them

Jimmy Angelakos
Foreword by Gianni Ciolli

MANNING
Shelter Island

Manning Publications Co.
20 Baldwin Road
PO Box 761
Shelter Island, NY 11964

Development editor: Katie Sposato
Technical editor: Simon Pane
Review editor: Radmila Ercegovac
Production editor: Andy Marinkovich
Copy editor: Alisa Larson
Proofreader: Mike Beady
Technical proofreader: Frank Moore
Typesetter and cover designer: Marija Tudor

ISBN 9781633436879

For Elpida Anastasiou, my beloved partner, who has brought joy to my life over the past decade. Without her constant support, this book would not have been possible.

Dedicated to the memory of
My father, Giannis Angelakos, who sparked my lifelong passion for computing in 1984 by bringing home a Sinclair ZX Spectrum. He was always supportive and believed in me.

Simon Riggs, my mentor, colleague, and friend, who gave me my start in the professional PostgreSQL world. His trust and guidance were an invaluable gift to my growth.

brief contents

1 ■ Why PostgreSQL matters—and why talking about mistakes does too 1
2 ■ Bad SQL usage 12
3 ■ Improper data type usage 43
4 ■ Table and index mistakes 58
5 ■ Improper feature usage 75
6 ■ Performance bad practices 98
7 ■ Administration bad practices 124
8 ■ Security bad practices 142
9 ■ High availability bad practices 153
10 ■ Upgrade/migration bad practices 167
11 ■ PostgreSQL, best practices, and you: Final insights 180

appendix A ■ *Frogge Emporium database 191*
appendix B ■ *Cheat sheet 196*

contents

foreword xi
preface xiii
acknowledgments xv
about this book xvii
about the author xxi
about the cover illustration xxii

1 Why PostgreSQL matters—and why talking about mistakes does too 1

1.1 Why learning about PostgreSQL matters 1

1.2 Why talking about PostgreSQL mistakes matters 2

1.3 What you will learn 3

1.4 Typical kinds of PostgreSQL mistakes 4

*Coming with expectations from other databases 4
Misunderstanding PostgreSQL 4 • Misunderstanding the
documentation 5 • Using relics from the SQL Standard 5
Not following best practices 5*

1.5 How this book works 5

Mental models 6 • Example mistake 7

1.6 Sample database: Frogge Emporium 11

2 Bad SQL usage 12

2.1 Using NOT IN to exclude 12
  Performance implications 15 • Alternative 16

2.2 Selecting ranges with BETWEEN 17

2.3 Not using CTEs 19

2.4 Using uppercase identifiers 22

2.5 Dividing INTEGERs 24

2.6 COUNTing NULL values 27

2.7 Querying indexed columns with expressions 28

2.8 Upserting NULLs in a composite unique key 30

2.9 Selecting and fetching all the data 33

2.10 Not taking advantage of checkers/linters or large language models 35
  Code checkers/linters 36 • Large language models 39

3 Improper data type usage 43

3.1 TIMESTAMP (WITHOUT TIME ZONE) 43

3.2 TIME WITH TIME ZONE 46

3.3 CURRENT_TIME 47

3.4 CHAR(n) 47

3.5 VARCHAR(n) 49

3.6 MONEY 51

3.7 SERIAL data type 53

3.8 XML 55

4 Table and index mistakes 58

4.1 Table inheritance 58

4.2 Neglecting table partitioning 62

4.3 Partitioning by multiple keys 66

4.4 Using the wrong index type 68

5 Improper feature usage 75

5.1 Selecting SQL_ASCII as the encoding 75

5.2 CREATE RULE 81

5.3 Relational JSON 83

5.4 Putting UUIDs everywhere 86

5.5   Homemade multi-master replication   89

5.6   Homemade distributed systems   94

6 Performance bad practices   98

6.1   Default configuration in production   99

6.2   Improper memory allocation   101

6.3   Having too many connections   104

6.4   Having idle connections   108

   What is MVCC? 108 ▪ The problem with idle connections 108

6.5   Allowing long-running transactions   110

   Idle in transaction 110 ▪ Long-running queries in general 112

6.6   High transaction rate   113

   XID wraparound 113 ▪ Burning through lots of XIDs 114

6.7   Turning off autovacuum/autoanalyze   115

6.8   Not using EXPLAIN (ANALYZE)   117

6.9   Locking explicitly   118

6.10   Having no indexes   119

6.11   Having unused indexes   121

6.12   Removing indexes used elsewhere   121

7 Administration bad practices   124

7.1   Not tracking disk usage   124

   *Deleting the Write-Ahead Log 126 ▪ What can eat up your disk
   space? 126 ▪ What can you do? 127*

7.2   Logging to PGDATA   127

7.3   Ignoring the logs   130

   *Bad configuration 130 ▪ Performance issues 131
   Locks 131 ▪ Corruption 132 ▪ Security 132*

7.4   Not monitoring the database   133

7.5   No tracking of statistics over time   135

7.6   Not upgrading Postgres   137

7.7   Not upgrading your system   139

8 Security bad practices   142

8.1   Specifying psql -W or --password   143

8.2   Setting listen_addresses = '*'   144

8.3   trust-ing in pg_hba.conf   145

8.4   Database owned by a superuser   146

8.5   Setting SECURITY DEFINER carelessly   149

8.6   Choosing an insecure search path   150

9 High availability bad practices   153

9.1   Not taking backups   154

9.2   No Point-in-Time Recovery   156

9.3   Backing up manually   158

9.4   Not testing backups   160

9.5   Not having redundancy   162

9.6   Using no HA tool   164

10 Upgrade/migration bad practices   167

10.1   Not reading all release notes   167

10.2   Performing inadequate testing   171

10.3   Succumbing to encoding chaos   174

10.4   Not using proper BOOLEANs   176

10.5   Mishandling differences in data types   178

11 PostgreSQL, best practices, and you: Final insights   180

11.1   What type of user are you?   180

*The dabbler 181 ▪ The cautious steward 182 ▪ The oblivious
coder 182 ▪ The freefaller 183*

11.2   Be proactive: Act early   184

11.3   All right, so you inherited a bad database   185

*"Historical reasons" 185 ▪ What now? 185
First things first 186*

11.4   Treat Postgres well, and it will treat you well   187

appendix A   *Frogge Emporium database*   *191*

appendix B   *Cheat sheet*   *196*

index   *203*

foreword

This book definitely contains what its title promises: there are many examples of mistakes, and there are also suggestions on how to avoid them. The interested reader, however, will find much more than that.

Examples are written in a clear and factual way, and represent scenarios that can really happen. This is not a surprise: I have known Jimmy for many years, and we worked together on many real-world projects, helping customers address the challenges that they faced. At some point, we were both part of the solutions architecture team, which focuses on combining technologies into consistent solutions. That kind of work provides a wide-angle viewpoint, driven by tangible outcomes and by how these outcomes impact the customer's business, but it also requires attention to detail and top-level hands-on skills. While working in that role, technical skills are gradually reinforced, and you are exposed to a valuable variety of demanding production environments.

While reading *PostgreSQL Mistakes and How to Avoid Them*, you can recognise the eye of the solutions architect, using theory to filter facts and organize them, while being always ready for a technical deep dive to whatever level of technical detail and practicality that the problem requires.

This book is a recommended read for whoever needs to work with PostgreSQL in production. Job roles such as system administrator, DBA, application developer, application architect, etc., are clearly different from each other in terms of goals and skills required, but they all share the common tract that a detailed PostgreSQL knowledge does help, as, in my experience, many customers have learned over the decades.

Chapter titles clearly refer to relevant topics such as SQL, data types, tables, and indexes, but also more generally to topics such as high availability, performance, administration, security, upgrades, and migrations. One can start from a chapter that they feel more familiar, and then extend the reading to the other chapters, not necessarily in the order presented in the book. More general conclusions are drawn in the last chapter of the book, and to reaffirm its nature as a work tool, the book ends with a few pages ("cheat sheet") providing a compact summary of the entire book.

I am sure you will find this book very interesting and useful, as I did when I read it. I am grateful to Jimmy Angelakos for the effort he undertook in writing it, which admittedly is a little bit easier in his case, as he could use his experience as a popular speaker at PostgreSQL conferences to explain complex things clearly and pick the right selection of details.

—DR. GIANNI CIOLLI, VICE PRESIDENT,
PRACTICE LEAD FOR HIGH AVAILABILITY AT EDB

preface

PostgreSQL (or Postgres to its friends) is a general-purpose database management system (or DBMS) that has over 25 years of development behind it and a thriving, active community. We call it "general-purpose" because it is not specialized toward a particular use case. Rather the opposite: the many design choices spanning its long development history have tended to favor balanced behavior so that Postgres can offer equally good performance in many scenarios. This strategy has panned out over time, resulting in an extremely varied user base spanning many application areas, often complemented by specialized extensions.

According to the Stack Overflow 2024 Developer Survey (https://survey.stackover flow.co/2024), PostgreSQL is the most admired and desired database among developers in general, and professional developers in particular, for the second year in a row. It took over the top popularity spot from MySQL the previous year and shows no signs of slowing down. This popularity is a testament to its growing impact and signals that Postgres is a disruptive force that continues to evolve to meet the demands of the modern database market and software development industries.

I had been aware of PostgreSQL as a fully fledged DBMS with a good reputation since the late 1990s and started experimenting with it in the early 2000s. I started using it professionally around 2008 after being prodded by a friend and colleague. I've never looked back or used another database system since.

"PostgreSQL's biggest mistake"

Let's talk about the elephant in the room—the name. After Ingres, an older database created by Michael Stonebraker, came Postgres (*Post-Ingres*). The addition of SQL capabilities to Postgres brought along a name change to PostgreSQL, pronounced "post-gress-cue-ell." Many contributors and community members recognized that this name became an impediment but felt it was too late to change the project's name. As far as everyone's concerned, though, "Postgres" is perfectly acceptable and completely equivalent, so we're going to use both names interchangeably in this book.

Oh, and it's never "Postgre."

acknowledgments

I'd like to thank Jonathan Gennick, acquisitions editor, who approached me with the idea to transform my experiences into this book. His encouragement and insight provided the foundation for this project, and his support throughout has been invaluable.

Katie Sposato, development editor, deserves my heartfelt thanks for her expert guidance and thoughtful advice. Her ability to steer me in the right direction with practical tips and constructive feedback has greatly enhanced the clarity and structure of this book.

I am equally indebted to Simon Pane, technical editor, whose sharp eye and technical expertise ensured the accuracy and reliability of the content. His meticulous attention to detail and deep understanding of PostgreSQL have been instrumental in shaping this work. My thanks also go out to Frank Moore, technical proofreader, for his careful review and attention to detail, which further strengthened the book.

Thank you to all of the reviewers, Adam Wan, Alex Elistratov, AJ Bhandal, Amit Sharma, Andres Sacco, Andrew Eleneski, Anuj Tyagi, Bassam Ismail, Bill Mitchell, Cornel Ghiban, Daniel Vásquez, Dirk Gomez, Fernando Bugni, Frank Moore, Gregorio Piccoli, Harsh Ranjan, Henrietta Dombrovskaya, Ihsan Akin, Iyabo Sindiku, Jeremy Chen, Jose Alberto Reyes Quevedo, Joseph Pachod, Kiran Krishnamurthy, Luca Ferrari, Marcus Geselle, Manohar Sai Jasti, Mikael Dautrey, Milorad Imbra, Nadir Doctor, Naga Rishyendar Panguluri, Paul Snow, Potito Coluccelli, Prabhu Patel, Rani Sharim, Regina Obe, Ruben Vandeginste, Serge Smertin, Sergio Britos Arevalo, Simone Sguazza, Viktoria Dolzhenko, Wes Shaddix, and William Jamir Silva. Your thoughtful feedback helped improve this book.

A special thanks to SomaFM (https://somafm.com/), and specifically their Synphaera channel, for providing the perfect soundtrack necessary for concentration and deep focus.

Finally, I would like to reiterate my gratitude to the open and generous PostgreSQL community and the open source world in general. Your collaborative spirit, willingness to share knowledge, and enduring support have been an inspiration throughout my journey.

Thank you all for making this book a reality.

about this book

In February 2023, I gave a talk titled "Don't Do This" at the annual FOSDEM (https://fosdem.org) conference in Brussels, Belgium. The talk explored some of the common mistakes, pitfalls, and misconceptions that PostgreSQL users can face and discussed possible ways to undo them or work around them. The talk was well received, and I gave it at two further conferences. Afterward, I was left with the impression that there was much more to talk about on this subject. However, the volume of material was such that I no longer felt it fit the conference talk format well. The search for a better medium for this content is what spurred the discussions that eventually led to the writing of *PostgreSQL Mistakes*, my first book.

Spoiler alert: there are more mistakes than those listed in this book! I like to think that there is literally nothing that you cannot get wrong. But these are the most common or most dangerous mistakes that you are likely to encounter.

This book is a medium to explore the subject, which I feel is more suitable than a single-purpose website, disparate blog posts, answers to forum questions, or a series of conference talks. It can concentrate my thoughts on the proper way to do things in Postgres in a single place, and at the same time, it can dive deeper and go further than any of the aforementioned media. Needless to say, a book doesn't require the time needed to sift through all related Internet posts or the perseverance to sit through hours of live or awkwardly recorded talks.

The mistakes described in this book have been identified through experience with the PostgreSQL database and its software ecosystem. I have benefited from my daily involvement with Postgres in various capacities while working for two of the foremost PostgreSQL database companies, which has given me insight into how end-user systems are utilized, configured, and maintained, with use cases including both good practices to be followed and bad practices to be avoided. Through many years of deploying, observing, and fixing Postgres systems in the field, I have gained the necessary perspective to write this book.

Of course, no one is an island, and none of this would have been possible without the mentoring, knowledge sharing, and guidance that the PostgreSQL community has so generously provided to me over the years.

Who should read this book

To benefit fully from this book, you should have a general knowledge of relational database system operation and a working grasp of the SQL language. This means being able to design a rudimentary relational database using SQL DDL with a basic understanding of data modeling. Consequently, you should be able to write SQL queries with WHERE clauses and understand the concepts behind indexing.

A basic knowledge of PostgreSQL usage is also expected. You should be able to install and configure a PostgreSQL environment (just the basics; don't worry about things like performance tuning). What also helps is familiarity with the UNIX command line (specifically Linux). You will find it helpful to be able to run command-line utilities, with an understanding of piping and output redirection.

How this book is organized: A road map

This book is divided into 11 chapters and 2 appendices, each focusing on a critical aspect of PostgreSQL usage, pitfalls, and best practices. The chapters cover a variety of topics, from foundational concepts to advanced topics, while the appendices provide practical resources to support your learning.

Here is a brief overview of each chapter and appendix:

- *Chapter 1: Why PostgreSQL matters—and why talking about mistakes does too*—Provides an overview of PostgreSQL and highlights the goals of this book, including how to identify, categorize, and learn from common PostgreSQL mistakes
- *Chapter 2: Bad SQL usage*—Discusses common SQL pitfalls, ways to ensure the correctness of queries, and techniques for improving the performance of complex queries
- *Chapter 3: Improper data type usage*—Explores the implications of choosing the wrong data type, issues with time zones and daylight savings, and data types that are best avoided
- *Chapter 4: Table and index mistakes*—Covers advanced table features like inheritance, the importance of partitioning, and selecting the most effective keys and indexes for your tables
- *Chapter 5: Improper feature usage*—Examines the challenges and risks of misusing PostgreSQL features, such as encoding choices, creating rules, and using NoSQL features inappropriately

- *Chapter 6: Performance bad practices*—Highlights mistakes like using default configurations in production, mishandling connection limits, and mismanaging transactions, indexes, and autovacuum settings
- *Chapter 7: Administration bad practices*—Focuses on administrative oversights, including uncontrolled disk usage, ignoring logs, inadequate statistical analysis, and failing to upgrade PostgreSQL properly
- *Chapter 8: Security bad practices*—Identifies security risks, such as careless handling of passwords, granting excessive access, exposing the database to vulnerabilities, and insecure function usage
- *Chapter 9: High availability bad practices*—Discusses common issues in ensuring database availability, including neglecting backups, misusing recovery features, and failing to prepare for database failures
- *Chapter 10: Upgrade/migration bad practices*—Highlights potential pitfalls during upgrades or migrations, such as skipping versions, inadequate testing, and underestimating differences between database types
- *Chapter 11: PostgreSQL, best practices, and you: Final insights*—Summarizes the lessons learned, offers guidance on proactively avoiding technical debt, and suggests approaches for improving inherited PostgreSQL databases
- *Appendix A: Frogge Emporium database*—Provides a sample schema and data set for hands-on practice with concepts discussed in the book
- *Appendix B: Cheat sheet*—A quick reference for PostgreSQL tips and best practices to help you avoid mistakes and work efficiently

About the code

This book contains many examples of source code both in numbered listings and in line with normal text. In both cases, source code is formatted in a `fixed-width font` `like this` to separate it from ordinary text. Sometimes code is also **in bold** to highlight code that has changed from previous steps in the chapter, such as when a new feature adds to an existing line of code.

In many cases, the original source code has been reformatted; we've added line breaks and reworked indentation to accommodate the available page space in the book. In rare cases, even this was not enough, and listings include line-continuation markers ( ). Additionally, comments in the source code have often been removed from the listings when the code is described in the text. Code annotations accompany many of the listings, highlighting important concepts.

You can get executable snippets of code from the liveBook (online) version of this book at https://livebook.manning.com/book/postgresql-mistakes-and-how-to-avoid -them. The complete code for the examples in the book is available for download from the Manning website at www.manning.com, and from GitHub at https://github .com/vyruss/postgresql-mistakes.

liveBook discussion forum

Purchase of *PostgreSQL Mistakes and How to Avoid Them* includes free access to liveBook, Manning's online reading platform. Using liveBook's exclusive discussion features, you can attach comments to the book globally or to specific sections or paragraphs. It's a snap to make notes for yourself, ask and answer technical questions, and receive help from the author and other users. To access the forum, go to https://livebook .manning.com/book/postgresql-mistakes-and-how-to-avoid-them. You can also learn more about Manning's forums and the rules of conduct at https://livebook.manning .com/discussion.

Manning's commitment to our readers is to provide a venue where a meaningful dialogue between individual readers and between readers and the author can take place. It is not a commitment to any specific amount of participation on the part of the author, whose contribution to the forum remains voluntary (and unpaid). We suggest you try asking the author some challenging questions lest his interest stray! The forum and the archives of previous discussions will be accessible from the publisher's website as long as the book is in print.

Author online

Jimmy Angelakos can be found online at the following platforms:

- *YouTube*—https://youtube.com/JimmyAngelakos
- *Mastodon*—https://fosstodon.org/@vyruss
- *Bluesky*—https://bsky.app/profile/vyruss.org
- *LinkedIn*—https://linkedin.com/in/vyruss
- *GitHub*—https://github.com/vyruss
- *Website*—https://vyruss.org/computing
- *Blog*—https://vyruss.org/blog

about the author

JIMMY ANGELAKOS is a systems and database architect and a recognized PostgreSQL expert with over 25 years of experience working with and contributing to open source tools. He has a wealth of experience gained from his career in software architecture and key roles at 2ndQuadrant and EDB, where he developed deep PostgreSQL expertise. A passionate member of the community, Jimmy is a Contributor to the PostgreSQL project and an active member of PostgreSQL Europe and PostgreSQL US. He regularly shares his insights as a speaker at conferences and events focused on databases and open source software. Jimmy studied computer science at the University of Aberdeen.

about the cover illustration

The figure on the cover of *PostgreSQL Mistakes and How to Avoid Them,* titled "Le Corse," or "Man from Corsica," is taken from a book by Louis Curmer published in 1841. Each illustration is finely drawn and colored by hand.

In those days, it was easy to identify where people lived and what their trade or station in life was just by their dress. Manning celebrates the inventiveness and initiative of the computer business with book covers based on the rich diversity of regional culture centuries ago, brought back to life by pictures from collections such as this one.

Why PostgreSQL matters—and why talking about mistakes does too

This chapter covers

- Learning about PostgreSQL
- Identifying and talking about PostgreSQL mistakes
- Categorizing PostgreSQL mistakes
- Using this book to learn

Welcome to *PostgreSQL Mistakes and How to Avoid Them*! Presumably, you got your hands on this book to learn more about PostgreSQL, and that is indeed the book's purpose. However, it's not a tutorial book in the traditional sense, nor is it an administration guide—there are good books already on those subjects. This book makes it a point that mistakes do happen, and they are good learning opportunities. In this chapter, we will see why PostgreSQL is important right now, how this book examines PostgreSQL-related mistakes, and why this is a worthwhile endeavor.

1.1 Why learning about PostgreSQL matters

As we mentioned before, PostgreSQL (aka Postgres) is a disruptive technology that has started unseating giant database vendors from their thrones. It is a robust and reliable feature-rich database and very extensible, and it is gaining more enterprise features with each new release. It has found wide acceptance not only in the database community but also in commercial circles, with hundreds of vendors now offering code contributions, professional support, enhanced capabilities versions, and even hosted, cloud, or database-as-a-service (DBaaS) Postgres offerings.

Importantly, the PostgreSQL Project is a prime example of community-led and community-driven free software, as expressed in the PostgreSQL license. This license is particularly significant with most every other database vendor adhering to proprietary software and with both established and emerging database efforts switching to non–open source compliant licenses in an attempt to chase profitability by restricting the ways others can make money with their product. On the other hand, you can freely profit from PostgreSQL by selling support, hosting, training, or services; you may even base your own open source or proprietary product on it with no nasty legal surprises hiding around the corner. The lack of vendor lock-in combined with the ability to base your business entirely on Postgres with no licensing restrictions is a powerful differentiator that makes Postgres shine bright in the database field.

This license won't change. Jonathan Katz of the Core Team pointed out in March 2024: "The PostgreSQL Project began as a collaborative open source effort and is set up to prevent a single entity to take control. This carries through in the project's ethos almost 30 years later, and is even codified throughout the project policies" (http://jkatz05.com/post/postgres/postgres-license-2024/).

PostgreSQL's power and extensibility have helped it find use cases in a very wide array of industries and applications. Notably, huge banking, credit, and retail systems are putting it to use in Online Transaction Processing (OLTP) scenarios and taking advantage of its advanced querying and reporting capabilities to perform large-scale business analytics, including Online Analytical Processing (OLAP). Extensions such as PostGIS for Geographic Information Systems (GIS), Citus columnar stores, TimescaleDB for time-series data, and pgvector for vector search added a lot of specialized functionality to further expand its user base. Hotel chains, film studios, shipping firms, insurance companies, state organizations, health institutions, and space agencies are using one form of Postgres or another, and the list goes on. For these uses, robustness, scalability, and reliability are of paramount importance. Of course, this ecosystem is completed by several large and small vendors, consultants, and contractors who enable all these applications with their expertise.

1.2 Why talking about PostgreSQL mistakes matters

In line with PostgreSQL becoming more popular with use cases increasing every day, we see a multitude of users either trying to apply practices they've learned from using other database management systems (DBMSs) or misunderstanding Postgres features. These practices can be in the form of repeating something that works on another database system or using a feature without a full understanding of its documentation. For example, PostgreSQL supports complex data types like arrays, whereas you would have to insert multiple rows with repeated data in other databases. Sometimes it's just a case of using the wrong tool for the job—for example, the wrong function or data type. It can even be the case that a choice that you have made works right now but will stop working in the future for various reasons, such as a table becoming much larger.

These factors and more often lead to costly mistakes if they happen on a production system. It's better to be aware and catch them early, as these mistakes can also be time-consuming to rectify and may involve a high degree of difficulty or risk, such as changing something on a live system.

It is important to spread the awareness of potential mistakes and pitfalls to

- Save person-hours spent dealing with their consequences.
- Protect the stored data.
- Future-proof database designs.
- Eliminate antipatterns detrimental to design and performance.
- Embrace standard solutions instead of reinventing the wheel.
- Build awareness of database best practices elsewhere in your team or organization.
- Get the most out of PostgreSQL.

It's also important to protect the reputation of your favorite database! Too often have we seen blog posts or articles decrying PostgreSQL because the author didn't understand the technology. They try to do something in an unorthodox way, fail, and come to the mistaken conclusion that Postgres is an inadequate platform.

1.3   *What you will learn*

PostgreSQL Mistakes and How to Avoid Them will hopefully help you

- Educate yourself about potential PostgreSQL pitfalls relevant to various aspects of PostgreSQL configuration, administration, and operation.
- Learn how to avoid aforementioned pitfalls before their consequences manifest themselves or employ workarounds to correct them.
- Gain a wider understanding of fundamental database operating principles and best practices to be applied.
- Better understand the differences and nuances that distinguish PostgreSQL from other databases.
- Understand the effect of enforcing best practices on PostgreSQL usage and performance

What it will help you do—or do better—in your everyday life on the job is

- Save time and effort by recognizing best practices and associated usage patterns.
- Be proactive in addressing potential problems before they become damaging.
- Shield yourself against accidental or intentional misuse of the database by others by taking preventive measures.
- Educate your peers by sharing this knowledge and make everyone's experience with PostgreSQL more productive and enjoyable.

1.4   Typical kinds of PostgreSQL mistakes

Let's examine some of the different ways that you can inadvertently find yourself doing something in PostgreSQL that turns out to be a mistake.

1.4.1   Coming with expectations from other databases

Many newcomers to Postgres find themselves confused and frustrated when taking their first steps with the database. One possible reason is that other databases frequently require a lengthy and complicated installation wizard where you have to make important (and often irreversible) decisions before you can start using the database. With Postgres, many users are stunned by the unexpected realization that, in most cases, once you've installed it, you're able to use the database server straight away. No frills—connect your database client to the server, and you can get busy exploring the possibilities. However, doing so comes with a risk: out of the box, Postgres is configured with some "sensible defaults." How sensible this default configuration is really depends on what you intend to use the database for. The default configuration is almost certainly not suitable for most production usage scenarios.

Another possible source of confusion is that most DBMSs have their own way of doing things, often diverging from the SQL Standard (the international standard for Structured Query Language; currently ISO/IEC 9075:2023) for historical, business, or implementation reasons. PostgreSQL has its way of doing things as well, and it is generally recognized as the most SQL Standard–compliant database currently available. Consequently, sometimes people come to expect what they're used to from their previous exposure to other database systems. For example, users may expect that creating a database USER will create a SCHEMA with the same name, with implied ownership of its objects by the same user. Also, although some databases will silently autoconvert between types, such as being able to insert 1s and 0s into a BOOLEAN column, PostgreSQL will tell you that this is an error. It makes sense that users would be surprised to find that none of these things work in Postgres.

1.4.2   Misunderstanding PostgreSQL

Postgres is a general-purpose database. Regardless, that doesn't mean it's suitable for every single use imaginable. I have witnessed people attempting to use it

- As an embedded database
- As a distributed database with homebrew replication
- As a log server
- As bulk video storage for films
- For in-memory use cases better suited to Redis
- As a graph database (guilty!)

Yes, it can do all these things to an extent. But you should always be aware of available solutions for the particular niche you are trying to inhabit and weigh the pros and cons of using a generic database solution versus something specialized.

1.4.3   *Misunderstanding the documentation*

PostgreSQL is very richly documented, which is enforced in the governance of the project. It is well established that no patch gets accepted without the submission of accompanying documentation: if you build or change something, you must document it. All documentation material is available at https://postgresql.org/docs/.

Often, this official documentation is presented in a very technical or academic way (in line with the PostgreSQL Project's origins). For laypersons used to tutorial-style walkthroughs or notes including more practical applications, the documentation may be hard to follow. As a result, it is possible to misunderstand the nature of a feature or the correct way to utilize it.

It may also be possible to miss important side notes or lack the context that more advanced users may have gained through experience. Sometimes, parts of the documentation feel incomplete because insights, terms, or details that are essential for understanding have to be located elsewhere in the documentation. Finally, you need to make sure you are reading the specific documentation for the version of PostgreSQL you are using to avoid confusion and misunderstandings.

1.4.4   *Using relics from the SQL Standard*

Just because it's in the official SQL Standard doesn't mean you have to use it. Many holdovers exist in the standard that either are relevant to an older era, seemed like a good idea at the time, or are forgotten by nearly everyone. Some are poorly defined implementation-wise and work differently in every database system. Some SQL features have been retained for backward compatibility purposes, and the reasons why they are not to be preferred or used at all are broadly understood. A good example of this is the TIME WITH TIME ZONE type, explained in chapter 3.

1.4.5   *Not following best practices*

Best practices for the design, development, administration, and maintenance of IT systems have been established through decades of observation and industry experience. Many systems have commonalities that lend themselves to similar best practices, and it makes sense to apply these to database systems as well. Databases are complex systems that have numerous correctness, performance, and security considerations, and Postgres is no exception to the rule.

Failing to follow best practices when you are designing your application's database schema, planning for usage patterns or concurrency, implementing high availability and disaster recovery solutions, and establishing security policies can lead to serious problems. It is a surefire way to trip yourself up somewhere down the road.

1.5   *How this book works*

As I already mentioned, most, if not all, of the mistakes and ideas in this book have come from observation of PostgreSQL installations and their users' behavior in the field, either first-hand or through documented stories shared by others in the industry or community who were kind enough to do so.

A story, or narrative, is key to comprehending the setting and context of a theoretical or practical problem. It sets the stage for understanding the mindset of whoever is attempting to solve it and sheds light on their decision-making process. From there, we can get into the general use case and the specific problem at hand. We will see the formation of the resolution attempt and the chain of events that led to the mistake. We will then dive deeper into why it is a mistake, its causes, and its potential consequences down the line. Finally, we will discuss the correct solution and how to implement it. All of this discussion is supplemented, where needed, with actual samples of database schema and data, as well as SQL or PL/pgSQL code, for both erroneous solutions and the right way to do things. The expected output for each case is also provided.

> **TIP** PL/pgSQL is an easy procedural language for PostgreSQL that can be used to create functions, procedures, and triggers. It adds control structures to the SQL language; can use all user-defined types, functions, and operators; and can perform complex computations.

At the time of writing, the current release is PostgreSQL 17, so that's the version we are going to use in this book. Of course, the vast majority of the book's content will be applicable to older recent versions of Postgres as well. Where there are differences, they will be pointed out.

1.5.1   Mental models

Something useful to always keep in mind is that PostgreSQL is a client-server and multiprocess database management system. Consequently, any client application connects to the database server (or Postgres server) running inside a single host to run queries and retrieve data. This connection is handled by one or more Postgres backend processes running inside the server. Postgres includes other internal processes that may not directly interact with the client. The multiprocess design allows parallelization and utilization of all available CPUs but behaves in some ways that are different from multithreaded database systems. Figure 1.1 shows what this model looks like.

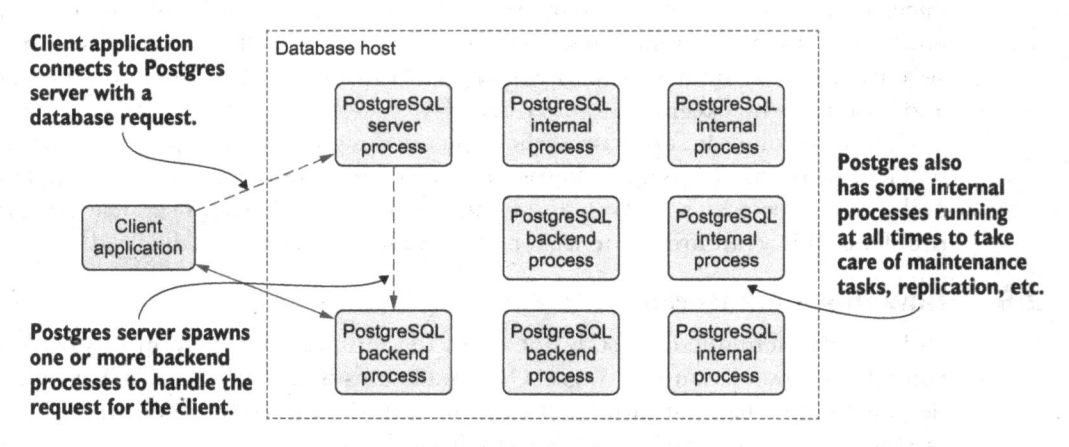

Figure 1.1   How the PostgreSQL client-server architecture works

This book works as follows. We start with a narrative that provides context for our use case. We examine the problem and the resolution attempt that leads to a mistake. Then we determine why this attempt is wrong, its consequences, and potential workarounds. Finally, we come to the correct solution and look at how to implement it. Figure 1.2 shows the process.

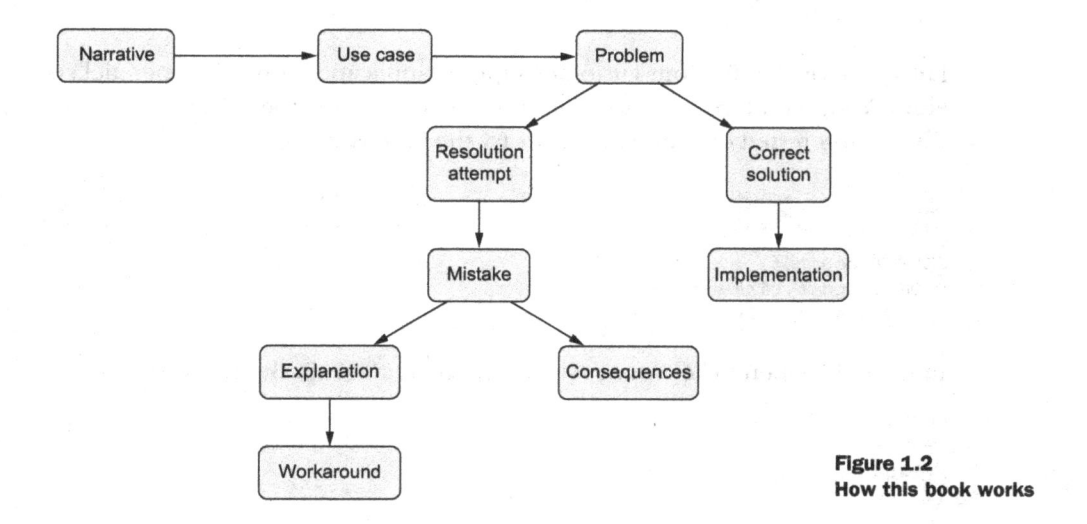

Figure 1.2
How this book works

1.5.2 Example mistake

Let's now look at a possible mistake to help illustrate briefly how this book walks through the narrative, problem, and resolution steps. Assume that you have a table with hundreds of thousands of customer support tickets, such as the one in this (overly simple) model:

```
CREATE TABLE support.tickets (id int, content text, status smallint);
```

> **NOTE** This example isn't particularly thrilling and may not even apply exclusively to Postgres, but it shows how this book treats problems according to the mental model presented in figure 1.2.

For our sample data, we will assume that a ticket's status = 10 means "open", and status = 20 means "closed". Let's insert a few hundred thousand rows of closed tickets:

```
INSERT INTO support.tickets
SELECT id, 'case description text', 20
FROM generate_series(1, 499750) AS id;
```

And now let's insert a few hundred rows of recent, still-open tickets:

```
INSERT INTO support.tickets
SELECT id, 'case description text', 10
FROM generate_series(499751, 500000) AS id;
```

For the sake of simplicity, we will assume that parallelization is not possible, so let's disable it via

```
SET max_parallel_workers_per_gather = 0;
```

We will be tracking query duration by enabling timing in `psql`:

```
\timing
Timing is on.
```

Let's now say that for your customer support application, only the open tickets are relevant. You, therefore, want to count how many of those open tickets you have because you are interested only in them. Let's try the following.

Listing 1.1   Trying to solve the problem

```
SELECT count(*)
FROM support.tickets
WHERE status = 10;
```

Indeed, this open ticket count returns the correct result. But it is slow:

```
count
-------
   250
(1 row)

Time: 110.036 ms
```

Let's see why it is slow by running `EXPLAIN`, which shows us how PostgreSQL will execute the query (the *query plan*):

```
EXPLAIN SELECT count(*)
FROM support.tickets
WHERE status = 10;
                           QUERY PLAN
-------------------------------------------------------------------
 Aggregate  (cost=9927.28..9927.29 rows=1 width=8)
   -> Seq Scan on tickets  (cost=0.00..9927.28 rows=1 width=0)
         Filter: (status = 10)
(3 rows)
```

This tells us that to run the `Aggregatecount()`, PostgreSQL is planning to use a `Seq Scan` on the table `tickets` and then `Filter` the results by `status = 10`. Sequential scans (also known as full table scans) are slow. So, you think, I'll create an index. Indexes make everything faster, right?

```
CREATE INDEX ON support.tickets(status);
CREATE INDEX
Time: 732.403 ms
```

Now that the index has been created, we try again:

```
SELECT count(*)
FROM support.tickets
WHERE status = 10;
 count
-------
   250
(1 row)

Time: 3.715 ms
```

That's much better. EXPLAIN will confirm why it is much faster now: an Index Only Scan is being used:

```
                              QUERY PLAN
--------------------------------------------------------------------------------
 Aggregate  (cost=4.44..4.45 rows=1 width=8)
   ->  Index Only Scan using tickets_status_idx on tickets
     (cost=0.42..4.44 rows=1 width=0)
         Index Cond: (status = 10)
(3 rows)
```

However, this index is quite big.

Listing 1.2 Why doesn't this work?

```
\x
\di+ support.tickets*
List of relations
-[ RECORD 1 ]-+-------------------
Schema        | support
Name          | tickets_status_idx
Type          | index
Owner         | frogge
Table         | tickets
Persistence   | permanent
Access method | btree
Size          | 3408 kB
Description   |
```

Imagine hundreds of millions of tickets in your customer support history, but only around the latest 250 are ever open at the same time. Large indexes, of course, take up more disk space. But they are also slower because there's more data to traverse, and they slow down write operations because they need to get updated with every INSERT or UPDATE.

In our case, we only care about the comparatively few open tickets. So we can save on the index size by using what's known as a *partial index* and add only the rows that we are interested in: WHERE status = 10.

We now drop the previous index and create a new partial index.

```
DROP INDEX support.tickets_status_idx;
CREATE INDEX ON support.tickets(status)
WHERE status = 10;
```

Look at how much smaller this index is! It makes sense because we're only indexing around 0.05% of the total rows, right?

```
\di+ support.tickets*
List of relations
-[ RECORD 1 ]-+--------------------
Schema        | support
Name          | tickets_status_idx
Type          | index
Owner         | frogge
Table         | tickets
Persistence   | permanent
Access method | btree
Size          | 16 kB
Description   |
```

This shows what the execution time looks like now, after having reduced the index size by a factor of more than 200:

```
SELECT count(*)
FROM support.tickets
WHERE status = 10;
 count
-------
   250
(1 row)

Time: 0.762 ms
```

And EXPLAIN now shows the following:

```
                              QUERY PLAN
-----------------------------------------------------------------------------
 Aggregate  (cost=4.16..4.17 rows=1 width=8)
   ->  Index Only Scan using tickets_status_idx on tickets
       (cost=0.14..4.16 rows=1 width=0)
(2 rows)
```

The operation is still an Index Only Scan but of a much smaller index, so it takes far less time to execute.

So, we have seen that just plopping an index on a column technically works, but it is not the optimal solution when you consider things such as large data volumes and performance requirements.

1.6   *Sample database: Frogge Emporium*

Every database book needs a sample database schema, and why go with something that's been floating around the web for decades? Here's Frogge Emporium, which, as a self-respecting retail chain, will certainly have processes, files, records, archives, and datasets relevant to its business. These can, of course, be represented as relational tables. Some of the tables that its database will have include, among others,

- `branches` with
- `stock`,
- `customers`,
- `suppliers`,
- `products`, lots and lots of
- `orders`,
- `payments` with
- `payment_types`

and more.

See appendix A for the full database schema.

> **NOTE**   The test data generation script in appendix A creates data using the current date and works its way back one year. As a result, your generated test data will reflect the date when you run the script, which means it won't exactly match the output shown in the examples in this book. This feature is by design to ensure that the script remains dynamic and useful for testing in any time period.

Summary

- PostgreSQL is a powerful, free, and standards-compliant database that is disrupting the industry and gaining in popularity every day.
- It's important to learn about and from Postgres mistakes to save time and effort and safeguard your data.
- Raising awareness of potential problems benefits everyone.
- Understanding how Postgres works and in what ways it is different from other DBMSs allows you to avoid making mistakes, especially if you are coming from another system; not all databases are created equal.
- Understanding PostgreSQL's client-server multi-process architecture is important context for the rest of this book.
- Following best practices and examining the documentation carefully will guide you to the correct technical solution to your problem.
- This book uses a use-case narrative, accompanied by code, to demonstrate how you can prevent a mistake or recover from one that you've made.

Bad SQL usage

This chapter covers
- Avoiding SQL pitfalls
- Exercising due care with your query results
- Improving performance of complex queries
- Checking your queries for correctness

Let's begin our journey into the land of PostgreSQL mistakes with what most relational database users are familiar with: Structured Query Language (SQL). In this chapter, we examine some bad SQL habits that can lead to bad query performance or, even worse, wrong query results. Postgres is very particular about the way it wants queries to be written and, in most cases, follows a strict interpretation of the SQL Standard. As a result, you need to be careful about the way you construct those queries and always check that you are actually getting exactly the results you want.

2.1 Using NOT IN to exclude

It's often that we need to specify a condition with a negative expression. No, that doesn't mean that we are trying to be unpleasant! It's simply that, sometimes, to define a query, instead of specifying what we want in our results, we specify what we don't want in our results—the inverse of the desired condition.

Lingo: Predicate

A predicate is simply a conditional expression that resolves to a boolean value: either TRUE or FALSE. A good example of a predicate is the content of our WHERE clause.

Negative predicates are expressed with the NOT keyword, and they can be used to invert any SQL expression, including those based around IN.

Listing 2.1 Example queries with IN/NOT IN

```
SELECT * FROM (VALUES ('Harper', 'salesperson'),
                      ('Parker', 'driver'),
                      ('Riley', 'electrician'),
                      ('Skyler', 'manager'))
            AS t(first_name, job_title)
WHERE job_title IN ('salesperson', 'driver', 'electrician');
 first_name |  job_title
------------+-------------
 Harper     | salesperson
 Parker     | driver
 Riley      | electrician
(3 rows)


SELECT * FROM (VALUES ('Harper', 'salesperson'),
                      ('Parker', 'driver'),
                      ('Riley', 'electrician'),
                      ('Skyler', 'manager'))
            AS t(first_name, job_title)
WHERE job_title NOT IN ('manager');
 first_name |  job_title
------------+-------------
 Harper     | salesperson
 Parker     | driver
 Riley      | electrician
(3 rows)
```

We see that specifying NOT IN can save a bit of typing and make queries simpler to read, especially if you are only looking to exclude a small number of values.

Now let's assume the folks at Frogge Emporium want to do exactly that. Their problem is that they want to run a promotion, and they need to find all the email addresses of customers from states where they do not have a supplier so that they can send promotional items from the central warehouse. The customer_contact_details table looks like table 2.1.

Table 2.1 Sample row from `customer_contact_details`

id	email	street_address	city	state	country	phone_no
100	jordan.barber@example.com		Albany	NY	United States of America	

The `suppliers` table looks like table 2.2.

Table 2.2 Sample row from `suppliers`

id	company_name	state	country	phone_no	email
1	Omni Consumer Products	MI	United States of America		ocp@example.com

Therefore, someone at Frogge Emporium comes up with the following query:

```
SELECT email
FROM erp.customer_contact_details
WHERE state NOT IN (SELECT state
                    FROM erp.suppliers);
```

They select all emails from `customer_contact_details` where the customer's state is not contained in the list of states from all suppliers. However, when it runs, the following happens:

```
 email
-------
(0 rows)
```

Why does it get zero results when there are certainly customers in states that do not have suppliers?

Let's say the Frogge Emporium folks know that they don't have suppliers in Kansas. Here's an SQL query that checks for at least one customer in a state without suppliers:

```
SELECT email
FROM erp.customer_contact_details
WHERE state = 'KS'
LIMIT 1;
         email
------------------------
 river.smith@example.com
(1 row)
```

This result is a consequence of how SQL treats NULL in predicates. In our example, not all suppliers are in a US state, so we have some suppliers with NULL in the `state` field. Let's check for at least one supplier that is not in a US state:

```
SELECT *
FROM erp.suppliers
WHERE state IS NULL;
 id | company_name | state | country | phone_no |        email
----+--------------+-------+---------+----------+---------------------
  2 | Yoyodyne     |       | Japan   |          | yoyodyne@example.com
(1 row)
```

The state column for this supplier is NULL. This causes the subquery SELECT state FROM erp.suppliers to return at least one NULL value.

What is probably unexpected is that the predicate state NOT IN (SELECT state FROM erp.suppliers) can never return TRUE if even one NULL is present. The expression evaluates to "unknown" if the subquery returns any null values, effectively negating the predicate and leading to an empty result set.

Why is that? Let's look at the logic queries using NOT IN, considering both cases—with and without NULL values.

Without Nulls:

```
SELECT email, state
FROM erp.customer_contact_details
WHERE state NOT IN ('Fake state')
LIMIT 1;
          email            | state
---------------------------+-------
 jordan.barber@example.com | NY
(1 row)
```

With NULLs:

```
SELECT email, state
FROM erp.customer_contact_details
WHERE state NOT IN ('Fake state', null)
LIMIT 1;
 email | state
-------+-------
(0 rows)
```

This is the same as writing NOT (state IN ('Fake state')), so basically, NOT (FALSE); therefore, TRUE. Adding a NULL makes the predicate unknown because NOT (state IN ('Fake state', null)) evaluates to NOT (NULL), which is the same as NULL, and so it cannot be TRUE. We must remember that SQL is a query language and not a high-level programming language like Python where the equivalent 1 not in [2, None] is True.

2.1.1 *Performance Implications*

Queries using NOT IN (SELECT …) can't be optimized well by Postgres. Specifically, it can't automatically convert such expressions into an anti-join in the query plan and chooses a hashed or plain subplan. This produces an inferior execution strategy as the hashed subplan works fast but is only chosen for small result sets, while the plain subplan is very slow. Consequently, this query execution plan may offer decent performance on a small scale but can slow down by whole orders of magnitude if you cross a size threshold. The

PostgreSQL documentation on using EXPLAIN has some more information on query plans (https://www.postgresql.org/docs/current/using-explain.html).

> **Lingo: Anti-join**
>
> Assuming we have tables a and b, an anti-join is a query for only the rows from a that result in no rows being returned from a correlated subquery on b. It comes from relational algebra, and the operation is usually expressed with the predicate NOT EXISTS in PostgreSQL (https://www.postgresql.org/docs/current/functions-subquery.html #FUNCTIONS-SUBQUERY-EXISTS).

2.1.2 *Alternative*

It is obvious that in most cases NOT IN (SELECT …), which can counterintuitively end up being NULL, would not be what you want. A way of writing this query that can yield more predictable results would be the following alternative, which uses NOT EXISTS:

```
SELECT ccd.email
FROM erp.customer_contact_details ccd
WHERE NOT EXISTS (SELECT FROM erp.suppliers s
                  WHERE ccd.state = s.state)
AND ccd.state IS NOT NULL;
          email
--------------------------
 river.smith@example.com
 drew.anderson@example.com
(2 rows)
```

This query finally gives the correct results. It should also be faster to execute, as the query planner this time chooses an anti-join. The NOT EXISTS query plan looks like the following:

```
EXPLAIN SELECT ccd.email
FROM erp.customer_contact_details ccd
WHERE NOT EXISTS (SELECT FROM erp.suppliers s
                  WHERE ccd.state = s.state)
AND ccd.state IS NOT NULL;
                          QUERY PLAN
--------------------------------------------------------------------------------
 Hash Anti Join  (cost=19.45..319.48 rows=2 width=25)
   Hash Cond: (ccd.state = s.state)
   -> Seq Scan on customer_contact_details ccd  (cost=0.00..300.00 rows=2
    width=28)
         Filter: (state IS NOT NULL)
   -> Hash  (cost=14.20..14.20 rows=420 width=32)
         -> Seq Scan on suppliers s  (cost=0.00..14.20 rows=420 width=32)
(6 rows)
```

The following alternative query explicitly demonstrates the anti-join mechanism and allows you to better visualize how rows are getting excluded based on the lack of matches:

```
SELECT ccd.email
FROM erp.customer_contact_details ccd
LEFT JOIN erp.suppliers s USING (state)
WHERE s.state IS NULL;
```

We can see that there are compelling reasons to not use the NOT IN syntax. However, if you are positive that your subquery cannot return any nulls or if you are providing a list of constant values (such as in Listing 2.1), it should be safe to use. Negative predicates can be an efficient way to exclude data, but their usage requires careful consideration of NULL values.

2.2 Selecting ranges with BETWEEN

BETWEEN is a convenient SQL feature that allows you to specify a range of values in relative shorthand, such as the following example that selects customers with id from 1 to 100.

> Listing 2.2 Example query with BETWEEN

```
SELECT *
FROM erp.customers
WHERE id BETWEEN 1 AND 100;
 id  | first_name | middle_name | last_name | marketing_consent
-----+------------+-------------+-----------+-------------------
   1 | River      | J           | Smith     | t
   2 | Drew       |             | Anderson  | t
                        ...
 100 | Jordan     | A           | Barber    | t
(100 rows)
```

Team members at Frogge Emporium have decided they need a query that runs early every morning to calculate the total amount of payments that the company received during the previous day. They write this query as follows:

```
WITH t(today) AS (SELECT CURRENT_DATE::timestamptz)
SELECT sum(amount)
FROM erp.payments, t
WHERE tstamp BETWEEN t.today - INTERVAL '1 day' AND t.today;
```

This query retrieves the current date and casts it to a timestamp, which gives us the start of the current day at midnight. Then we sum up all payment amounts from payments that happened between midnight yesterday and midnight today. Running the query yields

```
    sum
-----------
 5179739.95
(1 row)
```

So, everything's fine, right? Well, not exactly. We've forgotten that BETWEEN is inclusive of both ends of the range, the upper and lower bounds. That's easy to spot because, if you remember from Listing 2.2, we got both 1 and 100 in what was returned; this is also called a *closed interval*. What does that mean for our results? Let's select yesterday's last payment:

```
WITH t(today) AS (SELECT CURRENT_DATE::timestamptz)
SELECT max(tstamp)
FROM erp.payments, t
WHERE tstamp BETWEEN t.today - INTERVAL '1 day' AND t.today;
         max
------------------------
 2024-05-27 00:00:00+01
(1 row)
```

And now, let's select today's first payment:

```
WITH t(today) AS (SELECT CURRENT_DATE::timestamptz)
SELECT min(tstamp)
FROM erp.payments, t
WHERE tstamp BETWEEN t.today AND t.today + interval '1 day';
         min
------------------------
 2024-05-27 00:00:00+01
(1 row)
```

Notice something? It's the same timestamp. So, if payments occur exactly at midnight, you'll count them twice, which is bad when you're dealing with money. Essentially, this query is the same as

```
WITH t(today) AS (SELECT CURRENT_DATE::timestamptz)
SELECT sum(amount)
FROM erp.payments, t
WHERE tstamp >= t.today - INTERVAL '1 day'
AND tstamp <= t.today;
```

Whenever we want to select rows for specific consecutive ranges, we need to make sure that we don't include overlapping data at the ends of the range. A safer way to write this query is to exclude the upper bound with an explicit range definition like the following (note the lack of an equals sign in the expression AND tstamp < t.today):

```
WITH t(today) AS (SELECT CURRENT_DATE::timestamptz)
SELECT sum(amount), count(amount)
FROM erp.payments, t
WHERE tstamp >= t.today - INTERVAL '1 day'
AND tstamp < t.today;
    sum     | count
------------+-------
 5179680.00 | 86400
(1 row)
```

Let's verify the difference by examining the total payment amounts and number of rows:

```
WITH t(today) AS (SELECT CURRENT_DATE::timestamptz)
SELECT sum(amount), count(amount)
```

```
FROM erp.payments, t
WHERE tstamp BETWEEN t.today - INTERVAL '1 day' AND t.today;
    sum     | count
------------+-------
 5179739.95 | 86401
(1 row)
```

It may cost you a few more keystrokes, but defining ranges explicitly is cleaner and easier to read at a glance. The more complicated your queries become, the more you'll appreciate clarity and understandability. So remember, BETWEEN is shorthand for "greater than or equals AND less than or equals" (figure 2.1).

Figure 2.1 BETWEEN is inclusive.

2.3 Not using CTEs

Common Table Expressions (CTEs), or WITH syntax, are useful bits of syntactic sugar that allow you to tidy up your query. If you have complex queries, CTEs can make them more readable by breaking the SQL into smaller, more digestible pieces. Compared to subqueries, CTEs can save you some repetition because you can reference them multiple times within the same query.

Let's look at an example of a complicated query that is not very readable. Frogge Emporium needs to compile a list of email addresses of customers who have already been notified that they have an unpaid invoice for purchased services (i.e., not purchased items). The query initially looks like the following.

Listing 2.3 Non-CTE query example

```
SELECT DISTINCT email
FROM erp.customer_contact_details ccd
JOIN erp.invoices i ON i.customer = ccd.id
JOIN erp.order_groups og ON i.order_group = og.id
JOIN erp.sent_emails se ON se.invoice = i.id
JOIN erp.orders o ON o.order_group = og.id
WHERE ccd.id IN (
    SELECT customer
    FROM erp.invoices
    WHERE paid = false
)
AND i.order_group IN (
    SELECT order_group
    FROM erp.invoices
    WHERE paid = false
)
```

```
AND se.email_type = 'Invoice reminder'
AND o.item IS NULL;
```

It's functional but not great to read because of its convoluted structure with multiple joins, filters, and subqueries. Running it with EXPLAIN ANALYZE to see how it fares when it comes to efficiency, we get the following long output shown in figure 2.2.

```
                                                                    QUERY PLAN
-----------------------------------------------------------------------------------------------------------------------------------------
Unique  (cost=17472.51..17472.66 rows=1 width=25) (actual time=42.934..49.193 rows=8 loops=1)
   -> Nested Loop  (cost=17472.51..17472.66 rows=1 width=25) (actual time=42.953..49.190 rows=8 loops=1)
      -> Gather Merge  (cost=17472.09..17472.21 rows=1 width=49) (actual time=42.925..49.168 rows=8 loops=1)
         Workers Planned: 1
         Workers Launched: 1
      -> Sort  (cost=16472.08..16472.09 rows=1 width=49) (actual time=40.868..40.872 rows=4 loops=2)
            Sort Key: ccd.email
            Sort Method: quicksort  Memory: 25kB
            Worker 0: Sort Method: quicksort  Memory: 25kB
            -> Parallel Hash Semi Join  (cost=12648.82..16472.07 rows=1 width=49) (actual time=40.736..40.844 rows=4 loops=2)
               Hash Cond: (i.customer = invoices.customer)
               -> Nested Loop  (cost=8576.55..12399.79 rows=1 width=65) (actual time=32.546..32.653 rows=4 loops=2)
                  -> Parallel Hash Join  (cost=8576.26..12399.49 rows=1 width=32) (actual time=32.527..32.623 rows=4 loops=2)
                     Hash Cond: (o.order_group = i.order_group)
                     -> Parallel Seq Scan on orders o  (cost=0.00..5820.59 rows=701 width=8) (actual time=6.956..7.012 rows=675 loops=2)
                        Filter: (item IS NULL)
                        Rows Removed by Filter: 124325
                     -> Parallel Hash  (cost=8576.21..8576.21 rows=4 width=24) (actual time=25.525..25.527 rows=675 loops=2)
                        Buckets: 2048 (originally 1024)  Batches: 1 (originally 1)  Memory Usage: 152kB
                        -> Hash Join  (cost=4116.03..8576.21 rows=4 width=24) (actual time=25.018..25.299 rows=675 loops=2)
                           Hash Cond: (i.id = se.invoice)
                           -> Parallel Hash Semi Join  (cost=4072.28..8529.52 rows=775 width=32) (actual time=24.725..24.872 rows=675 loops=2)
                              Hash Cond: (i.order_group = invoices_1.order_group)
                              -> Parallel Seq Scan on invoices i  (cost=0.00..4062.59 rows=147059 width=24) (actual time=0.005..6.724 rows=125000 loops=2)
                              -> Parallel Hash  (cost=4062.59..4062.59 rows=775 width=8) (actual time=7.198..7.198 rows=675 loops=2)
                                 Buckets: 2048  Batches: 1  Memory Usage: 80kB
                                 -> Parallel Seq Scan on invoices invoices_1  (cost=0.00..4062.59 rows=775 width=8) (actual time=6.983..7.055 rows=675 loops=2)
                                    Filter: (NOT paid)
                                    Rows Removed by Filter: 124325
                           -> Hash  (cost=26.00..26.00 rows=1350 width=8) (actual time=0.281..0.281 rows=1350 loops=2)
                              Buckets: 2048  Batches: 1  Memory Usage: 69kB
                              -> Seq Scan on sent_emails se  (cost=0.00..26.00 rows=1350 width=8) (actual time=0.008..0.147 rows=1350 loops=2)
                                 Filter: (type = 'Invoice reminder'::email_type)
                  -> Index Scan using customer_contact_details_pkey on customer_contact_details ccd  (cost=0.29..0.51 rows=1 width=33) (actual time=0.006..0.006 rows=1 loops=8)
                     Index Cond: (id = i.customer)
               -> Parallel Hash  (cost=4062.59..4062.59 rows=775 width=8) (actual time=7.940..7.941 rows=675 loops=2)
                  Buckets: 2048  Batches: 1  Memory Usage: 80kB
                  -> Parallel Seq Scan on invoices  (cost=0.00..4062.59 rows=775 width=8) (actual time=7.729..7.795 rows=675 loops=2)
                     Filter: (NOT paid)
                     Rows Removed by Filter: 124325
   -> Index Only Scan using order_groups_pkey on order_groups og  (cost=0.42..0.45 rows=1 width=8) (actual time=0.002..0.002 rows=1 loops=8)
      Index Cond: (id = i.order_group)
      Heap Fetches: 0
Planning Time: 2.229 ms
Execution Time: 49.244 ms
(45 rows)
```

Figure 2.2   Non-CTE query plan

The planning and execution times are not that good because that's the nature of complicated queries. They're not only harder for us to understand but also harder for Postgres's query planner to optimize.

Let's rewrite the query to return the same result, but we will use CTEs to see how they can help. Here, we use CTE unp to get the unpaid invoices and CTE ni to get service orders ("no items").

Listing 2.4   CTE query example

```
WITH
unp AS (
    SELECT id, customer c, order_group AS og
    FROM erp.invoices
    WHERE paid = false
),
```

```
ni AS (
    SELECT og.id
    FROM erp.order_groups og
    JOIN erp.orders o ON o.order_group = og.id
    WHERE o.item IS NULL
)
SELECT DISTINCT email
FROM erp.customer_contact_details ccd
JOIN unp ON unp.c = ccd.id
JOIN ni ON ni.id = unp.og
JOIN erp.sent_emails se ON se.invoice = unp.id
AND se.email_type = 'Invoice reminder';
```

Hopefully, the new query makes it clearer that the table `invoices` provides `customer` and `order_group` data only for unpaid invoices, while the table `order_groups` isolates service orders by selecting rows with `NULL` item values. We then join our CTEs with a table `sent_emails` and filter on invoice reminder emails. `EXPLAIN ANALYZE` of the new query yields the plan shown in figure 2.3. This plan is much simpler, and the planning and execution of the query were faster, too.

```
                                                                       QUERY PLAN
---------------------------------------------------------------------------------------------------------------------------------------------
Unique  (cost=8933.91..8936.18 rows=1 width=25) (actual time=18.037..23.136 rows=8 loops=1)
  -> Nested Loop  (cost=8933.91..8936.18 rows=1 width=25) (actual time=18.036..23.133 rows=8 loops=1)
       Join Filter: (og.id = o.order_group)
       -> Gather Merge  (cost=8933.49..8933.68 rows=1 width=41) (actual time=18.029..23.111 rows=8 loops=1)
            Workers Planned: 1
            Workers Launched: 1
            -> Sort  (cost=7933.48..7933.48 rows=1 width=41) (actual time=16.100..16.102 rows=4 loops=2)
                 Sort Key: ccd.email
                 Sort Method: quicksort  Memory: 25kB
                 Worker 0: Sort Method: quicksort  Memory: 25kB
                 -> Nested Loop  (cost=4109.62..7933.47 rows=1 width=41) (actual time=15.967..16.078 rows=4 loops=2)
                      -> Parallel Hash Join  (cost=4109.53..7932.56 rows=1 width=24) (actual time=15.949..16.051 rows=4 loops=2)
                           Hash Cond: (o.order_group = invoices.order_group)
                           -> Parallel Seq Scan on orders o  (cost=0.00..3820.59 rows=701 width=8) (actual time=7.729..7.787 rows=675 loops=2)
                                Filter: (item IS NULL)
                                Rows Removed by Filter: 124325
                           -> Parallel Hash  (cost=4109.28..4109.28 rows=4 width=16) (actual time=7.960..7.961 rows=675 loops=2)
                                Buckets: 1024  Batches: 1  Memory Usage: 184kB
                                -> Hash Join  (cost=43.75..4109.28 rows=4 width=16) (actual time=7.655..7.813 rows=675 loops=2)
                                     Hash Cond: (invoices.id = se.invoice)
                                     -> Parallel Seq Scan on invoices  (cost=0.00..4062.59 rows=775 width=24) (actual time=7.366..7.428 rows=675 loops=2)
                                          Filter: (NOT paid)
                                          Rows Removed by Filter: 124325
                                     -> Hash  (cost=26.88..26.88 rows=1350 width=8) (actual time=0.281..0.281 rows=1350 loops=2)
                                          Buckets: 2048  Batches: 1  Memory Usage: 69kB
                                          -> Seq Scan on sent_emails se  (cost=0.00..26.88 rows=1350 width=8) (actual time=0.007..0.146 rows=1350 loops=2)
                                               Filter: (type = 'Invoice reminder'::email_type)
                      -> Index Scan using customer_contact_details_pkey on customer_contact_details ccd  (cost=0.29..0.90 rows=1 width=33) (actual time=0.006..0.006 rows=1 loops=8)
                           Index Cond: (id = invoices.customer)
       -> Index Only Scan using order_groups_pkey on order_groups og  (cost=0.42..2.48 rows=1 width=8) (actual time=0.002..0.002 rows=1 loops=8)
            Index Cond: (id = invoices.order_group)
            Heap Fetches: 0
Planning Time: 0.471 ms
Execution Time: 23.168 ms
(34 rows)
```

Figure 2.3 CTE query plan

Lingo: Selectivity

Selectivity is the measure of how many rows we expect our query to retrieve for the given predicate. So, low selectivity would be a relatively small number of rows to scan and filter. In this context, high selectivity probably has the opposite meaning of what being highly selective means in daily usage.

What has happened here is that the optimizer has determined that there is a faster way to retrieve this data by reordering things. By applying filters with low selectivity early on, we weed out most of the data that we don't need to carry over.

The fact that we have now placed the CTEs first doesn't mean they will get executed first. PostgreSQL has effectively *inlined* the CTEs, or merged them into the main query's execution plan, to find an optimal order of execution based on the statistics of table contents that it keeps. Also, we are replacing IN operations with more optimized JOINs.

> **NOTE** Another benefit of CTEs is that they will get evaluated just once, regardless of how many times they are referenced in the larger query or other CTEs.

Sometimes, when we know very well what our tables contain and the selectivity of each (sub)query, we can craft targeted CTEs. For example, if we know that a really expensive query or function returns a few things that are reused many times and are important for determining the selectivity of the rest of the query, we can specify that the CTE be MATERIALIZED so that we can force its evaluation early. Finally, CTEs are generally easier to run standalone than a correlated subquery, which can aid in optimization and troubleshooting, and they also allow us to run recursive SQL queries.

> **NOTE** Do not choose names for your CTEs that clash with the names of your existing objects, such as tables or views, because inside the query, your CTE name will override the object name and be used instead. This can lead to wrong results and confusion. You should also avoid choosing names already in use by SQL functions, etc.

2.4   *Using uppercase identifiers*

By default, PostgreSQL ignores case and always turns every identifier you input into lowercase. So, if you're coming from a certain database background that likes to put everything IN_UPPERCASE, it may make sense for you to carry this habit over into your daily Postgres usage.

However, using uppercase can end up causing problems and broken code. Postgres preserves case only when you double quote it, and double-quoted identifiers, also known as *delimited identifiers*, are case sensitive. So, inconsistency with your quoting can lead to errors. A very plausible way this can happen is if you sometimes forget to double quote identifiers when creating queries by hand, but the ORM you're using double quotes everything.

Let's look at an example. Say the DBA creates some tables:

```
SET search_path = erp, "$user", public;
CREATE TABLE Customers (
    id bigint PRIMARY KEY GENERATED ALWAYS AS IDENTITY,
    first_name text,
    middle_name text,
    last_name text,
```

```
    marketing_consent boolean DEFAULT false
);


CREATE TABLE "Invoices" (
    "Invoice ID" bigint PRIMARY KEY GENERATED ALWAYS AS IDENTITY,
    "Amount" numeric NOT NULL,
    "Customer" bigint NOT NULL REFERENCES Customers(id),
    "Paid" boolean NOT NULL DEFAULT false
);
```

This results in the creation of two tables: one is called customers (case-insensitive), and the other is called "Invoices" (case-sensitive). If we attempt to use the customers table, the following will happen:

```
TABLE Customers;
 id | first_name | middle_name | last_name | marketing_consent
----+------------+-------------+-----------+-------------------
(0 rows)
```

This works fine. The table name has effectively been turned to lowercase, the same as every other Postgres identifier:

```
\d customers
                    Table "erp.customers"
      Column       |  Type   | Collation | Nullable |       Default
-------------------+---------+-----------+----------+---------------------
 id                | bigint  |           | not null | generated always as
                   |         |           |          |  identity
 first_name        | text    |           |          |
 middle_name       | text    |           |          |
 last_name         | text    |           |          |
 marketing_consent | boolean |           |          | false
Indexes:
    "customers_pkey" PRIMARY KEY, btree (id)
```

Let's look at the other table:

```
TABLE Invoices;
ERROR:  relation "invoices" does not exist
LINE 1: TABLE Invoices;
              ^
```

This doesn't work fine.

> **NOTE** The SQL command TABLE table_name can be used as shorthand for SELECT * FROM table_name.

The same is also true for column names:

```
CREATE TABLE "Invoices" (
    "Invoice ID" bigint PRIMARY KEY GENERATED ALWAYS AS IDENTITY,
    "Amount" numeric NOT NULL,
```

```
"Customer" bigint NOT NULL REFERENCES Customers(id),
"Paid" boolean NOT NULL DEFAULT false
);
```

Here, we created all mixed-case column names, which become case-sensitive because they are quoted:

```
SELECT count(Customer)
FROM "Invoices";
ERROR:  column "customer" does not exist
LINE 1: SELECT count(Customer)
                     ^
HINT:  Perhaps you meant to reference the column "Invoices.Customer".
```

Forgetting to use the column identifier with double quotes results in an error.

We can see that using case in identifiers creates a usability problem in the sense that once you've done it, you have to always use the quoted names from that point onward:

```
SELECT count("Customer")
FROM "Invoices";
 count
-------
     1
(1 row)
```

It is best practice if you don't quote identifiers. However, if the reason you're using quoted identifiers is for better alignment with your coworkers—for instance, if they want reports where the columns are named like "Entry Date" or "Reconciliation Amount"—you can satisfy them by simply using column aliases in your queries used to generate their reports. You don't have to put their fancy reporting names in your database, and they'll be none the wiser

```
SELECT reconc_amt AS "Reconciliation Amount", entry_date AS "Entry Date"
FROM financials
WHERE entry_date = '2023-02-02';
```

yields

```
 Reconciliation Amount | Entry Date
-----------------------+------------
                235.11 | 2023-02-02
(1 row)
```

2.5   *Dividing INTEGERs*

Say we decide that we want to find out how many orders we have received that are for physical stock items versus orders for services. Therefore, we write the following query to select from table orders:

```
WITH
i AS (
    SELECT count(*) c
    FROM erp.orders
    WHERE item IS NOT NULL
),
s AS (
    SELECT count(*) c
    FROM erp.orders
    WHERE service IS NOT NULL
)
SELECT
    i.c AS "Item orders",
    s.c AS "Service orders",
    i.c + s.c AS "Total",
    i.c / (i.c + s.c) * 100 AS "Item order %",
    s.c / (i.c + s.c) * 100 AS "Service order %"
    FROM i, s;
```

The result is

```
Item orders | Service orders | Total  | Item order % | Service order %
------------+----------------+--------+--------------+-----------------
     248650 |           1350 | 250000 |            0 |               0
(1 row)
```

Wait, that can't be right. Look at the last two columns: the math doesn't check out. We do have orders. What has happened here is that we divided two integers, an operation that could give a fractional result if performed by hand but works out differently in SQL.

The PostgreSQL documentation tells us the following about the division operator /: "For integral types (int and bigint), division truncates the result towards zero" (https://www.postgresql.org/docs/current/functions-math.html#FUNCTIONS -MATH-OP-TABLE). This can give you wildly inaccurate numeric results where you least expect them.

What we need to do is cast to a type that can be divided without this consequence, such as a float or a double precision floating-point number:

```
SELECT
    10 / 4 AS "int division",
    pg_typeof(10 / 4) AS "-> output type",
    10::double precision / 4 AS "double division",
    pg_typeof(10::double precision / 4) AS "-> output type";

int division | -> output type | double division |  -> output type
-------------+----------------+-----------------+-----------------
           2 | integer        |             2.5 | double precision
(1 row)
```

But, you say, we only converted one of the integers into double, and it worked. Here, Postgres silently and automatically casts the integer into a compatible type to divide it with a double precision number.

NOTE   In PostgreSQL, you can CAST between types with the :: shorthand. pg_typeof() is the function that we can use to find out the Postgres data type of the value that is passed to it.

Armed with this knowledge, we now write our query as

```
WITH
i AS (
    SELECT count(*)::float c
    FROM erp.orders
    WHERE item IS NOT NULL
),
s AS (
    SELECT count(*)::float c
    FROM erp.orders
    WHERE service IS NOT NULL
)
SELECT
    i.c AS "Item orders",
    s.c AS "Service orders",
    i.c + s.c AS "Total",
    round((i.c / (i.c + s.c) * 100)::numeric, 1) AS "Item order %",
    round((s.c / (i.c + s.c) * 100)::numeric, 1) AS "Service order %"
FROM i, s;
```

We get the correct result, with some casts and rounding applied as well:

```
 Item orders | Service orders | Total  | Item order % | Service order %
-------------+----------------+--------+--------------+----------------
      248650 |           1350 | 250000 |         99.5 |             0.5
(1 row)
```

Another somewhat related and potentially painful mistake is when you allow division by zero to happen—something mathematics frowns upon and computers definitely don't like. You should generally never have application code that allows this type of input to reach the database query, but if you do, the following is what is going to happen:

```
WITH zero AS (SELECT count(*) FROM erp.customers WHERE 1=2)
SELECT 10 / zero.count
FROM zero;
ERROR:  division by zero
```

NOTE   Here, WHERE 1=2 is an impossible condition that cannot be met, so the subquery's count() of zero rows returns 0.

What you can do now is make the result undefined (in other words, NULL) if you encounter a zero, as in our first column here, or you may decide to replace the 0 with another value known to be safe, such as 1 in our second column:

```
WITH zero AS (SELECT count(*) FROM erp.customers WHERE 1=2)
SELECT
    10 / NULLIF(zero.count, 0) AS nullified,
    10 / COALESCE(NULLIF(zero.count, 0), 1) AS replaced
```

```
FROM zero;
 nullified | replaced
-----------+----------
           |        10
(1 row)
```

> **NOTE** `NULLIF` returns null if the first argument equals the second, and `COALESCE` returns the first non-null argument.

2.6   *COUNTing NULL values*

Something you need to be aware of when you're trying to count values or rows is whether the column you're using for the `count()` aggregate is nullable or not. Frogge Emporium is trying to count the number of orders placed since the beginning of the year. Its query is

```
SELECT count(item)
FROM erp.orders
WHERE placed_at > date_trunc('year', CURRENT_DATE);
```

When the people at Frogge Emporium run it, they get the following result:

```
 count
--------
 198908
(1 row)
```

However, some orders were not for physical items but for services. Those orders don't have an item attached, so their column `item` is NULL:

```
SELECT id, status, placed_at, item, service
FROM erp.orders
WHERE service IS NOT NULL
LIMIT 1;
   id   | status |       placed_at        | item | service
--------+--------+------------------------+------+---------
 168521 | Placed | 2024-05-26 08:55:21+01 |      |      21
(1 row)
```

Let's check how many orders it really has in total by counting rows instead of items:

```
SELECT count(*)
FROM erp.orders
WHERE placed_at > date_trunc('year', CURRENT_DATE);
 count
--------
 200000
(1 row)
```

The result is because `count()` ignores NULL values (you can't count something that isn't there), and we were counting using the nullable `item` column. In this case, you need to count the entire row to get the correct result.

This also has an interesting side effect: you can use it to your advantage to count what your percentage of orders for services are (knowing that item orders will have a NULL service), like this:

```
SELECT round(count(service)::numeric
    / count(*)::numeric * 100, 1) AS "Service orders %"
FROM erp.orders
WHERE placed_at > date_trunc('year', CURRENT_DATE);
 Service orders %
-----------------
             0.5
(1 row)
```

2.7   *Querying indexed columns with expressions*

When you have an index on a column, it makes certain types of queries extremely fast. However, when you query the same indexed column using an expression, such as passing it through a function or casting it so that the data type doesn't match the index's data type, it can cause Postgres to not use the index at all.

This situation is a serious performance problem. You are effectively paying the price for having an index (such as more disk space usage, slower writes to the table, etc.) without benefiting from the index.

Let's see an example with our payments table, which holds Frogge Emporium's timestamped payment data. If we select payments from a specific timestamp, we get an efficient and pretty much instant response:

```
EXPLAIN (ANALYZE, FORMAT YAML)
SELECT * FROM erp.payments
WHERE tstamp = '2023-10-18 03:40:34.000';
                                QUERY PLAN
-----------------------------------------------------------------------------
 - Plan:                                                                    +
    Node Type: "Index Scan"                                                 +
    Parallel Aware: false                                                   +
    Async Capable: false                                                    +
    Scan Direction: "Forward"                                               +
    Index Name: "payments_tstamp_idx"                                       +
    Relation Name: "payments"                                               +
    Alias: "payments"                                                       +
    Startup Cost: 0.42                                                      +
    Total Cost: 8.46                                                        +
    Plan Rows: 2                                                            +
    Plan Width: 31                                                          +
    Actual Startup Time: 0.010                                              +
    Actual Total Time: 0.011                                                +
    Actual Rows: 0                                                          +
    Actual Loops: 1                                                         +
    Index Cond: "(tstamp = '2023-10-18 03:40:34+01'::timestamp with time
    zone)"                                                                  +
    Rows Removed by Index Recheck: 0                                        +
 Planning Time: 0.051                                                       +
 Triggers:                                                                  +
```

```
Execution Time: 0.022
(1 row)
```

This caused an `Index Scan`, which was very fast.

Now let's assume the Frogge folks wants to make the query such that they don't have to specify the timestamp in millisecond accuracy. They decide to use the function `date_trunc()` to reduce the accuracy down to the level of seconds. This query will return payments that took place during a specific second:

```
EXPLAIN (ANALYZE, FORMAT YAML)
SELECT * FROM erp.payments
WHERE date_trunc('s', tstamp) = '2023-10-18 03:40:34';
                            QUERY PLAN
-------------------------------------------------------------------------------
 - Plan:                                                                      +
     Node Type: "Seq Scan"                                                    +
     Parallel Aware: false                                                    +
     Async Capable: false                                                     +
     Relation Name: "payments"                                               +
     Alias: "payments"                                                        +
     Startup Cost: 0.00                                                       +
     Total Cost: 5589.00                                                      +
     Plan Rows: 1250                                                          +
     Plan Width: 31                                                           +
     Actual Startup Time: 1.900                                               +
     Actual Total Time: 35.880                                                +
     Actual Rows: 1                                                           +
     Actual Loops: 1                                                          +
     Filter: "(date_trunc('s'::text, tstamp) = '2023-10-18 03:40:34+01'
       ::timestamp with time zone)"                                           +
     Rows Removed by Filter: 249999                                           +
   Planning Time: 0.038                                                       +
   Triggers:                                                                  +
   Execution Time: 35.892
(1 row)
```

What happened here? We can see that this query did not use the index and instead performed a full table scan, which was orders of magnitude slower.

The reason behind this slowness is that the column is indexed against direct queries for the timestamp values stored. Changing the predicate causes it to no longer match the index, and so that is not used.

One possible workaround is to move the transformation to the other side of the predicate comparison operator, like this:

```
EXPLAIN (ANALYZE, FORMAT YAML)
SELECT * FROM erp.payments
WHERE tstamp >= '2023-10-18 03:40:34'::timestamptz
AND tstamp < '2023-10-18 03:40:34'::timestamptz + INTERVAL '1 s';
                            QUERY PLAN
-------------------------------------------------------------------------------
 - Plan:                                                                      +
     Node Type: "Index Scan"                                                  +
```

```
      Parallel Aware: false                                                    +
      Async Capable: false                                                     +
      Scan Direction: "Forward"                                               +
      Index Name: "payments_tstamp_idx"                                       +
      Relation Name: "payments"                                               +
      Alias: "payments"                                                        +
      Startup Cost: 0.42                                                       +
      Total Cost: 8.44                                                         +
      Plan Rows: 1                                                             +
      Plan Width: 31                                                           +
      Actual Startup Time: 0.014                                              +
      Actual Total Time: 0.015                                                +
      Actual Rows: 1                                                           +
      Actual Loops: 1                                                          +
      Index Cond: "((tstamp >= '2023-10-18 03:40:34+01'::timestamp with time  +
   zone) AND (tstamp < ('2023-10-18 03:40:34+01'::timestamp with time zone
   + '00:00:01'::interval)))"                                                  +
      Rows Removed by Index Recheck: 0                                        +
 Planning Time: 0.058                                                          +
 Triggers:                                                                     +
 Execution Time: 0.023
(1 row)
```

We now see that this query uses the index and benefits from full performance again because we have moved the function from the column to the value to be compared.

Also, remember one of PostgreSQL's awesome features: indexes on expressions. If we know that we will always be querying this column using date_trunc, for example, to find all payments that took place during that minute, we can use an expression index to include the function and speed up those queries

```
CREATE INDEX ON erp.payments(date_trunc('m', tstamp AT TIME ZONE 'UTC+1'));
```

which can then be queried as follows

```
SELECT * FROM erp.payments
WHERE date_trunc('m', tstamp AT TIME ZONE 'UTC+1')
    = '2023-10-18 03:40' AT TIME ZONE 'UTC+1';
```

Beware, though: this will create a *lossy* index, which will not apply to queries that do not use the same functions and casts that it was created with!

When a query applies a function or transformation to an indexed column, the database has to evaluate the function for each row individually. This prevents it from using the index to locate matching values, as the transformed data does not align with the indexed data. Consequently, the database must do extra work to process more rows.

2.8 *Upserting NULLs in a composite unique key*

UPSERT, short for UPDATE and INSERT, is the operation of entering data into a table where you want to ensure that it's either updated if it already exists or inserted if it doesn't. To apply this logic, you need to use a UNIQUE constraint or index. In PostgreSQL, upserts can be performed using INSERT… ON CONFLICT… or with the newer MERGE syntax.

To go hand in hand with a revamp of the inventory management frontend, Frogge Emporium tasks a developer with developing an upsert query for the following proposed `inventory` table to keep the company's stock levels accurate:

```
CREATE TABLE erp.inventory (
    product_id int NOT NULL,
    warehouse_id int,
    area text,
    quantity int NOT NULL,
    updated_at timestamptz NOT NULL DEFAULT now()
);
CREATE UNIQUE INDEX ON erp.inventory (product_id, warehouse_id, area);
```

The unique index created for stock tracking is the combination of product, warehouse, and area. The idea is that each product can exist in multiple warehouses and be in different areas within that warehouse. We can see that the table allows null in the area column because some products may just be in the common stock area instead of a specific location like in the freezer.

The upsert query the developer came up with to test the concept used the ON CONFLICT DO syntax and looked like

```
INSERT INTO erp.inventory (product_id, warehouse_id, area, quantity)
VALUES (99999, 1, 'freezer', 10)
ON CONFLICT (product_id, warehouse_id, area) DO UPDATE
    SET quantity = EXCLUDED.quantity;
```

which returned

```
INSERT 0 1
```

So far, so good. Now, let's try updating the quantity of `product_id` 99999 in `warehouse_id` 1 to 20 with this upsert:

```
INSERT INTO erp.inventory (product_id, warehouse_id, area, quantity,
    updated_at)
VALUES (99999, 1, 'freezer', 20, now())
ON CONFLICT (product_id, warehouse_id, area) DO UPDATE
    SET quantity = EXCLUDED.quantity;
```

This returns

```
INSERT 0 1
```

Let's check the inventory:

```
TABLE erp.inventory;
 product_id | warehouse_id |  area    | quantity |        updated_at
------------+--------------+----------+----------+---------------------------
      99999 |            1 | freezer  |       20 | 2024-10-28 21:04:26.04033.
            |              |          |          | .8+00
```

Okay, that seems to have updated the value, marking a successful upsert.

Let's put a quantity of this product in the common stock area of that warehouse with

```
INSERT INTO erp.inventory (product_id, warehouse_id, area, quantity)
VALUES (99999, 1, null, 5)
ON CONFLICT (product_id, warehouse_id, area) DO UPDATE
    SET quantity = EXCLUDED.quantity;
```

which produces

```
TABLE erp.inventory;
 product_id | warehouse_id | area  | quantity |          updated_at
------------+--------------+-------+----------+-----------------------------
      99999 |            1 | free. |       20 | 2024-10-28 21:04:26.040338+0.
            |              | .zer  |          | .0
      99999 |            1 |       |        5 | 2024-10-28 21:05:14.020143+0.
            |              |       |          | .0
```

Let's update this quantity to 7 now:

```
INSERT INTO erp.inventory (product_id, warehouse_id, area, quantity,
    updated_at)
VALUES (99999, 1, null, 7, now())
ON CONFLICT (product_id, warehouse_id, area) DO UPDATE
    SET quantity = EXCLUDED.quantity;
```

Let's check:

```
TABLE erp.inventory;
 product_id | warehouse_id | area  | quantity |          updated_at
------------+--------------+-------+----------+-----------------------------
      99999 |            1 | free. |       20 | 2024-10-28 21:04:26.040338+0.
            |              | .zer  |          | .0
      99999 |            1 |       |        5 | 2024-10-28 21:05:14.020143+0.
            |              |       |          | .0
      99999 |            1 |       |        7 | 2024-10-28 21:07:57.067498+0.
            |              |       |          | .0
```

Oops. What's happening here? If a product with the same `product id`, `warehouse_id`, and `area` already exists, its quantity is updated; otherwise, a new row is inserted. However, we stumbled upon a critical problem that arises when NULL values are involved.

The problem stems from how PostgreSQL handles NULL values in a composite unique key. In SQL, a NULL value signifies the lack of a value or "unknown". Consequently, PostgreSQL (or any database, for that matter) cannot compare NULL values for equality. Therefore, the two rows with NULL in the area column are treated as distinct, even though they look like they should represent the same record in the database. This leads to the unexpected creation of multiple rows with NULL in the area field instead of updating the existing tuple.

Up until PostgreSQL 14, this problem created a real conundrum because the behavior of ON CONFLICT when NULL values were involved was unpredictable. In some cases, it would insert new rows, and in others, it wouldn't. This could lead to application bugs and data integrity issues.

From version 15 onward, PostgreSQL allows you to address this issue by explicitly defining the conflict resolution behavior of ON CONFLICT with unique constraints containing NULL fields. All you have to do is add the NULLS NOT DISTINCT clause when creating the index. This changes the legacy default behavior of treating NULL values as distinct and enables proper upserts in this scenario.

Let's illustrate by deleting the bad row and re-creating the index with the new option:

```
DELETE FROM erp.inventory WHERE quantity = 7;
DROP INDEX erp.inventory_product_id_warehouse_id_area_idx;
CREATE UNIQUE INDEX ON erp.inventory (product_id, warehouse_id, area)
NULLS NOT DISTINCT;
```

Upserting now works:

```
INSERT INTO erp.inventory (product_id, warehouse_id, area, quantity,
    updated_at)
VALUES (99999, 1, null, 7, now())
ON CONFLICT (product_id, warehouse_id, area) DO UPDATE
    SET quantity = EXCLUDED.quantity;
TABLE inventory;
 product_id | warehouse_id | area | quantity |         updated_at
------------+--------------+------+----------+----------------------------
      99999 |            1 | free.|       20 | 2024-10-28 21:04:26.040338+0.
            |              | .zer |          | .0
      99999 |            1 |      |        7 | 2024-10-28 21:22:07.914464+0.
            |              |      |          | .0
```

With this index, the upsert behavior now ensures that rows with NULL in the area column are considered duplicates if they match all other columns in the unique constraint. The database will then properly update existing rows instead of inserting new ones.

Although newer PostgreSQL releases offer this workaround, relying on NULL in composite unique constraints is probably not a good practice. You may be better off switching NULL with a meaningful value (e.g., 'common_area') or restructuring the table's schema.

2.9 *Selecting and fetching all the data*

In general, you should not SELECT more columns than you need to perform your query. Moreover, you should not fetch large amounts of data from the database to the client side, and then perform operations such as sorting and filtering outside of the database. Try to minimize the amount of data selected and fetched at every level, and that will have a positive impact on the performance of your queries.

Our developer wants to get the primary key of all tickets with status = 10, but proceeds to SELECT * instead of SELECT id because they know that they can just discard the columns they don't need in the application code. Let's write some sample code to see if fetching all the results can really make a difference in performance.

Let's do some prep work to get a clean Python environment running:

```
virtualenv ve
. ve/bin/activate
pip install psycopg
```

Now let's code both use cases, SELECT every column from the table versus just the one we want.

Listing 2.5 fetch.py: Fetch all the columns

```
import psycopg, datetime

with psycopg.connect("dbname=frogge user=frogge") as conn:
    with conn.cursor(row_factory=psycopg.rows.dict_row) as cur:
        t1 = datetime.datetime.now()
        cur.execute('''SELECT *
                        FROM support.tickets
                        WHERE status = 10''')
        res = cur.fetchall()
        tkts = []
        for row in res:
            tkts += row['id'],
        t2 = datetime.datetime.now()
        print(f'"SELECT *"  took {t2-t1} seconds.')
    with conn.cursor(row_factory=psycopg.rows.dict_row) as cur:
        t3 = datetime.datetime.now()
        cur.execute('''SELECT id
                        FROM support.tickets
                        WHERE status = 10''')
        res = cur.fetchall()
        tkts = []
        for row in res:
            tkts += row['id'],
        t4 = datetime.datetime.now()
        print(f'"SELECT id" took {t4-t3} seconds.')
```

Running this produces

```
$ python3 fetch.py
"SELECT *"  took 0:00:00.244571 seconds.
"SELECT id" took 0:00:00.093342 seconds.
```

From this, we can learn that selecting and fetching data that we then discard incurs a performance penalty because of the overhead, both on the database side and on the application side, because more data gets transferred, marshaled into memory, etc. Also, remember that this is just on our development machine; over slower network connections, it may make for an even bigger difference in performance.

Even worse, our developer can make the mistake of fetching the entire table "to avoid the hassle of writing SQL queries" because they're a good developer and they know how to filter data efficiently on the application side. Believe me, this is something that has actually been seen "in the wild."

Listing 2.6 fetch2.py: Fetch all the rows

```python
import psycopg, datetime

with psycopg.connect("dbname=frogge user=frogge") as conn:
    with conn.cursor(row_factory=psycopg.rows.dict_row) as cur:
        t1 = datetime.datetime.now()
        cur.execute('''SELECT *
                        FROM support.tickets''')
        res = cur.fetchmany(10000)
        while (res):
            tkts = []
            for row in res:
                if row['status'] == 10:
                    tkts += row['id'],
            res = cur.fetchmany(10000)
        t2 = datetime.datetime.now()
        print(f'"SELECT *" with no predicate took {t2-t1} seconds.')
```

Let's run it:

```
$ python3 fetch2.py
"SELECT *" with no predicate took 0:06:41.919264 seconds.
```

This run time is disastrous. Granted, this is an egregious example with a very large table and the developer forgoing index use. In real life, this usually results in the developer or end user complaining to the IT manager that "PostgreSQL is slow," and leads to orders of unnecessary top-tier hardware needed to speed up the bad query.

Use the database for what it's good at: data retrieval! PostgreSQL has had almost 30 years of query optimizations to benefit from.

> **Causing Index Scans vs. Index-Only Scans**
>
> If you are only selecting a column that is indexed, the operation will result in a fast Index-Only scan. Adding more columns to the selection will cause the database to perform an Index Scan, which will also read from the table and not just the index, and this can be much slower. Keeping this in mind can be especially useful when writing subqueries or CTEs that need to select the minimum amount of data and be as optimized as possible.

2.10 Not taking advantage of checkers/linters or large language models

Modern tools like checkers, linters, and AI assistance can catch many common mistakes before they cause problems. They can significantly improve code quality, enforce best practices, and prevent errors. However, they are not a replacement for understanding PostgreSQL's nuances and making informed decisions.

2.10.1 Code checkers/linters

Every developer worth their salt knows that having a second pair of eyes (or more) on your code is valuable because you can get additional insights or identify errors that escaped your scrutiny. Unfortunately, it's not always easy or feasible to find one or more people and show them your SQL query for feedback.

However, you can get second opinions for free because there's software that can look at your code and comment. Even if you think mechanical eyes aren't as good as human eyes, at the very least, you lose nothing by passing your code through a checker or linter.

SQLFLUFF

SQLFluff is an SQL linter and code formatter that also supports Postgres. The following is an example of how it can be used to catch syntax and formatting errors, retrieved from the SQLFluff repository:

```
$ pip install sqlfluff
```

This installed our tool. Next, we'll create a query and save it to a file:

```
$ echo "  SELECT a  +  b FROM tbl;  " > test.sql
```

Now let's lint that query:

```
$ sqlfluff lint test.sql --dialect ansi
== [test.sql] FAIL
L:   1 | P:   1 | LT01 | Expected only single space before 'SELECT' keyword.
                      | Found ' '. [layout.spacing]
L:   1 | P:   1 | LT02 | First line should not be indented.
                      | [layout.indent]
L:   1 | P:   1 | LT13 | Files must not begin with newlines or whitespace.
                      | [layout.start_of_file]
L:   1 | P:  11 | LT01 | Expected only single space before binary operator
                      | '+'.
                      | Found ' '. [layout.spacing]
L:   1 | P:  14 | LT01 | Expected only single space before naked identifier.
                      | Found ' '. [layout.spacing]
L:   1 | P:  27 | LT01 | Unnecessary trailing whitespace at end of file.
                      | [layout.spacing]
L:   1 | P:  27 | LT12 | Files must end with a single trailing newline.
                      | [layout.end_of_file]
All Finished ? ?!
```

The linter has detected problems with our query's formatting and reported where exactly in the file it found the problem.

SQLFluff can be found at https://github.com/sqlfluff/sqlfluff.

PLPGSQL_CHECK

plpgsql_check is a linter for PL/pgSQL code implemented as a PostgreSQL extension. Because it uses Postgres's own parser and expression evaluator, it can expose errors that would occur if you actually ran your code on the server. Among its other features, it has an active check mode you can use by calling function plpgsql_check_function_tb() to directly check the function and return the result in tabular form. Its repository's example demonstrates how it can catch errors:

```
postgres=# CREATE EXTENSION plpgsql_check;
LOAD
```

Now the extension is enabled. Let's create a table and function:

```
postgres=# CREATE TABLE t1(a int, b int);
CREATE TABLE

postgres=#
CREATE OR REPLACE FUNCTION public.f1()
RETURNS void
LANGUAGE plpgsql
AS $function$
DECLARE r record;
BEGIN
  FOR r IN SELECT * FROM t1
  LOOP
    RAISE NOTICE '%', r.c; -- there is bug - table t1 missing "c" column
  END LOOP;
END;
$function$;

CREATE FUNCTION
postgres=# \sf+ f1
    CREATE OR REPLACE FUNCTION public.f1()
     RETURNS void
     LANGUAGE plpgsql
1    AS $function$
2    DECLARE r record;
3    BEGIN
4      FOR r IN SELECT * FROM t1
5      LOOP
6        RAISE NOTICE '%', r.c; -- there is bug - table t1 missing "c" column
7      END LOOP;
8    END;
9    $function$
```

As we can see, the function is faulty. Let's run it:

```
postgres=# select f1(); -- execution doesn't find a bug due to empty table t1
  f1
 ----

(1 row)
```

It can perform a check on the function:

```
postgres=# \x
Expanded display is on.
postgres=# select * from plpgsql_check_function_tb('f1()');
-[ RECORD 1 ]-------------------------------------
functionid | f1
lineno     | 6
statement  | RAISE
sqlstate   | 42703
message    | record "r" has no field "c"
detail     | [null]
hint       | [null]
level      | error
position   | 0
query      | [null]
```

As we can see, it detected the problematic condition on line 6 of the function's code listing. It also offers a passive mode, where a module loaded in the Postgres server scans all code before it gets executed at run time; obviously, this is only for debugging in testing and should be avoided on production systems.

You can find the `plpgsql_check` tool for PL/pgSQL linting at https://github .com/okbob/plpgsql_check.

SQUAWK

squawk is a tool that can scan the database migration (i.e., schema change) code that you are planning to run and warn you about potential problems your series of DDL commands can cause if executed on a database that is in use.

Let's look at some examples of how it can catch potential problems before they occur, from its own documentation:

```
> squawk example.sql
example.sql:2:1: warning: prefer-text-field

   2 | --
   3 | -- Create model Bar
   4 | --
   5 | CREATE TABLE "core_bar" (
   6 |     "id" serial NOT NULL PRIMARY KEY,
   7 |     "alpha" varchar(100) NOT NULL
   8 | );

note: Changing the size of a varchar field requires an ACCESS EXCLUSIVE lock.
help: Use a text field with a check constraint.

example.sql:9:2: warning: require-concurrent-index-creation

   9 |
  10 | CREATE INDEX "field_name_idx" ON "table_name" ("field_name");

  note: Creating an index blocks writes.
  note: Create the index CONCURRENTLY.
```

```
example.sql:11:2: warning: disallowed-unique-constraint

11 |
12 | ALTER TABLE table_name ADD CONSTRAINT field_name_constraint
   UNIQUE (field_name);

note: Adding a UNIQUE constraint requires an ACCESS EXCLUSIVE lock
   which blocks reads.
help: Create an index CONCURRENTLY and create the constraint using
   the index.
```

You can find the Squawk migration checker at https://github.com/sbdchd/squawk.

2.10.2 Large language models

It's impressive how generative AI, specifically large language models (LLMs) trained on a corpus of whatever their creators found on the Internet, can process natural language queries and produce a coherent result. PostgreSQL code is no exception, and already, we can see how you can give an LLM some information and then ask it to write SQL queries to complete your task.

LLMs can certainly be a useful tool to bounce off of and check your thought process or, if you're stuck, get some SQL inspiration. For fun, let's give ChatGPT some schema snippets, tell it what we want our query to achieve, and have it produce the SQL for it.

 I have the following PostgreSQL schema:

```
CREATE TABLE Customers (
    id bigint PRIMARY KEY
        GENERATED ALWAYS AS IDENTITY,
    first_name text,
    middle_name text,
    last_name text,
    marketing_consent boolean DEFAULT false
);
CREATE TABLE "Invoices" (
    "Invoice ID" bigint PRIMARY KEY
        GENERATED ALWAYS AS IDENTITY,
    "Amount" numeric NOT NULL,
    "Customer" bigint NOT NULL,
    "Paid" boolean NOT NULL DEFAULT false
);
```

I want to find how many customers have unpaid invoices.

After a couple of iterations, it settles around this output:

 To find how many customers have unpaid invoices, you can use an SQL query that joins the "Customers" and "Invoices" tables and counts the number of unique customers with unpaid invoices. Here's a query to achieve this:

```
SELECT COUNT(DISTINCT c.id) AS number_of_customers_with_unpaid_invoices
FROM Customers c
```

```
JOIN "Invoices" i ON c.id = i."Customer"
WHERE i."Paid" = false;
```

This query performs the following steps:

1 It selects all columns from the "Customers" table and aliases it as "c".

2 It joins the "Customers" table with the "Invoices" table on the "Customer" column, which relates customers to their invoices.

3 It filters the results to only include rows where the "Paid" column in the "Invoices" table is false, indicating unpaid invoices.

4 Finally, it counts the distinct customer IDs in the filtered results and gives you the number of customers with unpaid invoices.

The result of this query will be a count of unique customers who have unpaid invoices.

At first glance, this looks impressive, straightforward, and polished. However, closer scrutiny reveals some flaws:

1 Our query most certainly does not select all columns from the Customers table.

2 It's inconsistent with the quoting of table names in the textual explanation of the query, which is a problem in PostgreSQL.

3 It assumes that a foreign key relationship exists between Customers and "Invoices" where none is evident.

4 It presumes the order of execution in Postgres, which, as we know, you can't do without asking for an EXPLAIN plan.

There is certainly potential here, and no doubt these models will be refined. However, at the end of the day, you have to remember that this is a text generator that keeps appending to the end of its output whatever *seems* most likely to follow next, according to the model. It has no concept of correctness and will write whatever it thinks sounds plausible enough with no attempt to verify if it's correct. Sometimes, it makes up things that are patently wrong in SQL or PostgreSQL that don't even run.

Be aware of the implications

When you are pasting your schema or code into an online analysis tool or a chatbot/LLM, you are effectively uploading it onto someone else's server—with the implications that may have for any security rules it is subject to—and the LLM's terms of use probably mention that they are now allowed to use your input for further training of their product, etc.!

Remember the difference between running software you chose on your computer and trusting an online service to do something for you, as shown in figure 2.4.

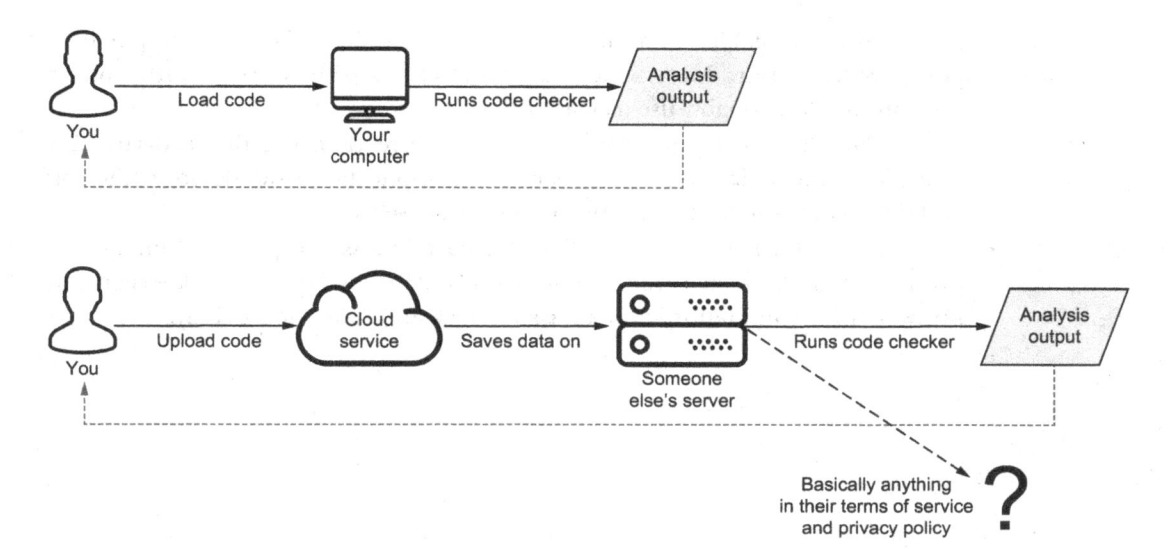

Figure 2.4 Your computer vs. an online service

Finally, also be aware that this may all very well stop working at some point in the future. If everyone starts using generative AI and the Internet gets filled with generated text, it will poison the LLMs' corpus of training data ("poisoning the well"). Remember, in most cases, if you feed AI output to AI training input, you get rubbish as the end result.

Summary

- Don't use NOT IN to exclude a list of values that can include even one null because that will return an empty result set. Consider the use of NOT EXISTS.
- Filtering with BETWEEN—for example, between two timestamps—can return overlapping results in subsequent queries because its ranges are inclusive.
- CTEs can not only improve readability of queries but also improve performance by letting the optimizer decide to merge and reorder parts of the query.
- Quoting identifiers makes them case-sensitive, while the Postgres convention is for all identifiers to be case-insensitive, and this can lead to reduced usability and errors.
- Performing division between integers will yield an often unexpected, truncated integer result.
- count() ignores NULL values so if you count a nullable column, you won't get the number of rows returned but the number of rows that didn't have NULL in that field.
- When you query indexed data that has had a data transformation applied to it, Postgres may not use the index at all.

- Avoid using nullable columns in composite unique keys when possible. PostgreSQL 15 introduces NULLS NOT DISTINCT to address issues with upserts but you should probably use a cleaner design.
- Don't slow down your queries by selecting more than strictly necessary and don't fetch more data than you need to the application side; do your filtering and data management operations on the database side.
- Use tools to check and lint your SQL for correctness and potential impacts to production and take advantage of generative AI to make your work easier, but be aware of the limitations and always recheck and have the final say.

Improper data type usage

PostgreSQL is very rich in data types and probably supports more than most databases. It even goes a step further and allows you to define your own data types with their own indexes, functions, and operations! We will now take a look at some popular data types and how their use or misuse can lead to consequential mistakes.

3.1 TIMESTAMP (WITHOUT TIME ZONE)

Let's begin with data types used for storing date and time. Timestamps are a really popular type that is used to store both at the same time. If you type TIMESTAMP, PostgreSQL will, by default, assume that you want TIMESTAMP WITHOUT TIME ZONE because that is a behavior required by the SQL Standard.

Our friends at Frogge Emporium have decided to use TIMESTAMP to hold when a customer service ticket was opened and when it was closed. Because of the way Frogge Emporium's customer service system works, it stores the time a ticket was opened at the local time of the customer's location.

Let's take, for example, this ticket, opened by a customer on the US West Coast on October 28, 2023 at 16:00 Pacific Daylight Time (8 hours behind Universal Time Coordinate or UTC-8) and closed by a customer service agent (who was in the UK) on October 29, 2023 at 09:00 Greenwich Mean Time (GMT or UTC+0):

```
-[ RECORD 1 ]------------------------------------------------------------
id        | 132591
content   | Kindly close our account, as we don't need it anymore. Thank you
status    | 20
opened_at | 2023-10-28 16:00:00
closed_at | 2023-10-29 09:00:00
```

If we try to calculate the duration of how long it took to close the ticket (e.g., for quality assurance purposes), we will get the following:

```
SELECT pg_typeof(closed_at - opened_at), closed_at - opened_at
FROM support.tickets
WHERE id = 132591;
```

The result is

```
 pg_typeof | ?column?
-----------+----------
 interval  | 17:00:00
(1 row)
```

Seventeen hours? This is obviously wrong. From the perspective of the customer, the ticket would have been closed on October 29, 2023, at 02:00 Pacific Daylight Time (UTC-8), which is only 10 hours.

Why did we get this result? TIMESTAMP WITHOUT TIME ZONE, also known as a *naive* timestamp, does not store time zone information. As a result, performing arithmetic (such as our subtraction here) between timestamps entered at different time zones is meaningless because it will give the wrong results.

Let's now assume that this behavior has been taken into account and the application developers have agreed with the database administrator to only store times in the Europe/London time zone regardless of the application user's location. This way, calculations can be performed because everything is in the same time zone. Our entry would become

```
-[ RECORD 1 ]------------------------------------------------------------
id        | 132591
content   | Kindly close our account, as we don't need it anymore. Thank you
status    | 20
opened_at | 2023-10-29 00:00:00
closed_at | 2023-10-29 09:00:00
```

The time the ticket was open was

```
 pg_typeof | ?column?
-----------+----------
 interval  | 09:00:00
(1 row)
```

Oops! What happened here is that in London, daylight savings time (DST) or summer time ended at 2:00 a.m. on October 29, and the clocks were turned back by 1 hour. So, on the 29th, we effectively had 1:00 a.m. British summer time (BST, UTC+1) followed by 1:00 a.m. GMT (UTC+0).

Even if we get around the daylight savings problem by using UTC everywhere, it's still wrong to use TIMESTAMP to store it. The database doesn't know it's storing UTC, and it will be unable to convert between time zones to produce the correct calculations.

The simplest way to solve this problem is to use TIMESTAMPTZ or TIMESTAMP WITH TIME ZONE as the data type. This way, we can enter timestamps at any time zone, and the database takes care of all conversions when time calculations are needed. Now our table and data would look as follows when we insert the data properly:

```
INSERT INTO support.tickets (content, status, opened_at, closed_at) VALUES
('Kindly close our account, as we don't need it anymore. Thank you',
 '10',
 '2023-10-28 16:00 PDT',
 '2023-10-29 09:00 GMT');
```

> **NOTE** Notice that in the previous query above, we can insert an apostrophe without conflict with the single quotes delimiting the string by doubling it: `''`.

Seen from a database client in the Europe/London time zone, the record is

```
-[ RECORD 1 ]------------------------------------------------------------
id        | 1
content   | Kindly close our account, as we don't need it anymore. Thank you
status    | 10
opened_at | 2023-10-29 00:00:00+01
closed_at | 2023-10-29 09:00:00+00
```

The duration calculation yields the correct result:

```
 pg_typeof | ?column?
-----------+----------
 interval  | 10:00:00
(1 row)
```

TIMESTAMP WITH TIME ZONE stores a moment in time, which makes time arithmetic meaningful because you can know how much time elapses between two moments. By contrast, TIMESTAMP WITHOUT TIME ZONE is more like taking a photo of a calendar and a watch, capturing the time and date with no additional context.

TIMESTAMPTZ is also great because while it displays in the client's time zone, you can ask PostgreSQL to display it for a specific time zone according to your needs:

```
SELECT opened_at AT TIME ZONE 'PDT' AS "Ticket opened",
       closed_at AT TIME ZONE 'PDT' AS "Ticket closed"
FROM support.tickets;
```

The output is

```
   Ticket opened    |   Ticket closed
--------------------+--------------------
 2023-10-28 16:00:00 | 2023-10-29 02:00:00
```

Also, you're not using any extra storage space; both TIMESTAMP types are 8 bytes in length. With its compact storage, you can use TIMESTAMPTZ as a natural primary key for time-series data. Do you really need a *surrogate* (artificial) key when it can be used to identify tickets uniquely? As an added bonus, it partitions and indexes wonderfully, so you can use it as a practical partition key and then use the key to craft really efficient queries.

To summarize, TIMESTAMPTZ is the preferred data type for recording a specific moment in time. The naive TIMESTAMP is of no use for time math and has no performance or storage advantage over the time zone–aware type.

3.2   TIME WITH TIME ZONE

For some data, it is sufficient to capture only the time without the date. So it's easy to assume that TIME WITH TIME ZONE or TIMETZ is a good choice for the data field; after all, we saw previously that omitting the time zone can cause problems sometimes.

Let's assume that Frogge Emporium has a table storing the energy usage of each of its branches, measured by a smart meter. The smart meter marks the time of each reading, and the data ingested from it is stored in a TIMETZ column. For branch 41, we have the following consecutive readings:

```
branch_id |     reading_time      | reading | unit
----------+-----------------------+---------+------
       41 | 01:17:27.612383+01    | 54921.8 | kWh
       41 | 01:17:21.356247+00    | 54988.0 | kWh
```

The first and second times we recorded sit across the DST boundary. We know that they are about 1 hour apart, but let's see what happens when we try to subtract them to find the interval between them:

```
SELECT '01:17:27.612383+01'::timetz - '01:17:21.356247+00'::timetz;
```

This results in

```
ERROR:  operator does not exist: time with time zone - time with time zone
LINE 1: select '01:17:27.612383+01'::timetz - '01:17:21.356247+00'::...
                                             ^
HINT:  No operator matches the given name and argument types. You might
need to add explicit type casts.
```

Okay, so we notice that the offset stored can vary with DST and that we cannot perform time math with this type. From this, we can understand that TIMETZ has questionable usefulness. If we use the (naive) TIME data type instead, we will run into the same problems performing calculations across DST boundaries as we have just seen with naive TIMESTAMP. The fact of the matter is, in the real world, time zones have little meaning without dates to provide the necessary context.

In short, TIMETZ is included in PostgreSQL just for SQL Standard compliance. As it also takes up 8 bytes of storage space, there's really no reason to ever use it, and using TIMESTAMPTZ instead is recommended.

3.3   *CURRENT_TIME*

All right, CURRENT_TIME is not exactly a data type, but it all ties nicely together with the previous section about TIME WITH TIME ZONE. current_time is a time function that returns the current time of day as the data type TIME WITH TIME ZONE:

```
SELECT CURRENT_TIME, pg_typeof(CURRENT_TIME);
```

This returns

```
   current_time     |       pg_typeof
--------------------+---------------------
 20:46:27.094953+00 | time with time zone
```

If you decide to use CURRENT_TIME, you will face the same problems that you encounter using TIMETZ. It's a cleaner solution to use a timestamp that represents that specific moment in time. If you don't need the date part afterward, you can just discard it either with EXTRACT() or date_part() or programmatically on your application's side. The space used for storage of the field will be the same anyway.

To use the correct date/time construct, you need to be aware of what each function returns (table 3.1).

Table 3.1   **PostgreSQL time functions and return types**

Function	Return Type	Sample output
CURRENT_TIMESTAMP or now()	timestamp with time zone	2023-11-20 21:03:34.349275+00
CURRENT_DATE	date	2023-11-20
CURRENT_TIME	time with time zone	21:03:34.349275+00
LOCALTIMESTAMP	timestamp without time zone	2023-11-20 21:03:34.349275
LOCALTIME	time without time zone	21:03:34.349275

CURRENT_TIME and the data type it returns, TIMETZ, are just not very useful, and you should probably use something else that will better match your use case from the previous table.

You can find more information on date/time functions in the PostgreSQL documentation at https://www.postgresql.org/docs/current/functions-datetime.html.

3.4   *CHAR(n)*

Let's now discuss PostgreSQL character types, or what you use to store strings of text inside the database, beginning with CHAR(*n*) or CHARACTER(*n*). This is a fixed-length, blank-padded textual type; it is always of length *n* as declared, and if the string is less than *n* characters long, the rest of the field is padded with blank characters. You should generally avoid using CHARACTER(*n*), and it will become apparent why in the next few paragraphs.

> **NOTE**   Because it's a **bl**ank **p**added **char**acter type of length *n*, it is also known as type BPCHAR(*n*). It was previously only used as an internal type designation, but it is now documented, starting with PostgreSQL 16.

The string `'postgres'` inside a CHAR of length 10 looks like

```
SELECT 'postgres'::CHAR(10);
   bpchar
------------
 postgres
(1 row)
```

Figure 3.1 makes what we're looking at a bit clearer (where blanks are represented by ⎵).

Figure 3.1   String padding with CHAR(10)

Because `'postgres'` is 8 characters long, 2 blank characters are added at the end to pad out the field to length 10. These padding spaces are ignored, or treated as *semantically not significant*, when comparing strings like so:

```
SELECT 'postgres'::CHAR(10) = 'postgres'::CHAR(20);
 ?column?
----------
 t
(1 row)
```

But beware: padding is not ignored when performing pattern matching with LIKE and regular expressions (regex)!

```
SELECT 'postgres'::CHAR(10) LIKE '%ostgres';
 ?column?
----------
 f
(1 row)
```

LIKE does not match a string ending in `ostgres` because our CHAR(10) value ends in two blank characters.

Similarly, regular expression matching a string ending in `ostgres` will fail:

```
SELECT 'postgres'::CHAR(10) ~ '.*ostgres$';
 ?column?
----------
 f
(1 row)
```

We see that the same is true for POSIX regular expressions using the ~ regex match operator.

Another annoyance is that if you cast a string that is longer than n to a CHAR(n), it will be truncated with no warning or error raised, as this behavior is required by the SQL Standard!

```
SELECT 'I heart PostgreSQL'::CHAR(10);
   bpchar
------------
 I heart Po
(1 row)
```

Even if you need to enforce the length of a string in a column as exactly n characters, using CHAR(n) is not the proper way to do that, as it will happily accept shorter strings.

What's even worse with this data type is that it's not even stored as a fixed-width field internally in PostgreSQL. As characters may need more than 1 byte to store (depending on the character encoding), the stored string is represented as a variable-length value on disk. So, you can end up wasting disk space storing irrelevant blank spaces because these are explicitly stored. The performance implication is that when you use CHAR(n), your server spends extra computation time stripping spaces in order to perform string operations and comparisons.

Finally, indexes created for CHAR(n) columns may not work for queries with a TEXT parameter passed to the database from a PostgreSQL connector or driver (similarly to what we saw in chapter 2, section 2.7).

The bottom line here is, for almost every use case, you should just go ahead and use TEXT, the variable unlimited length textual data type (confusingly, also known as VARCHAR with no limit specification). TEXT gives you more flexibility by not restricting you further down the line and can give a performance advantage over fixed-length CHAR types.

3.5 *VARCHAR(n)*

CHARACTER VARYING(n) or VARCHAR(n) is a variable-length field for textual data with a length limit, so you can store any string up to that length. Consequently, inserting longer strings will result in an error:

```
CREATE TEMP TABLE test1 (col VARCHAR(5));
CREATE TABLE

INSERT INTO test1 VALUES ('12345678');
ERROR:  value too long for type character varying(5)
```

Weirdly, if the extra characters beyond n are spaces, the string will be truncated silently to length n with no error reported, as dictated by the SQL Standard:

```
INSERT INTO test1 VALUES ('1234    ');
INSERT 0 1
```

```
TABLE test1;
  col
-------
 1234
```

We see that the string inserted was '1234 '—five characters, ending in a space. These behaviors are shared with CHAR(n). Similarly, if a longer value is cast to VARCHAR(n), it's truncated without warning or error:

```
SELECT 'Just use TEXT'::VARCHAR(10);
  varchar
------------
 Just use T
(1 row)
```

In contrast, VARCHAR(n) doesn't store any blank padding at the end of the string, so the problems of wasting storage space and string comparisons that we saw with CHAR(n) are avoided.

However, you are again getting absolutely no benefit by enforcing a length limit, as the storage on disk is identical to TEXT. Even worse, just when you think you have everything sorted out with your table suppliers and its column company_name VARCHAR(50), along comes this supplier, and they're annoyed that they don't see their full company name when they log into your portal:

```
SELECT length('Peterson''s and Sons and Friends Bits & Parts Limited');
 length
--------
     52
(1 row)
```

Instead of having to resize your column with ALTER TABLE and deal with all the locking needed by the DDL—never mind the fact that shrinking down to a smaller limit is impossible—using VARCHAR(n) is more trouble than it's worth.

If you positively want to restrict the length of the field, let's say for compliance reasons, just enforce a CHECK constraint, which you can then change easily. CHECK integrity constraints specify requirements for the value that can be stored in a column, like so:

```
DROP TABLE test1;
DROP TABLE

CREATE TEMP TABLE test1 (col TEXT CHECK(length(col)<=5));
CREATE TABLE

INSERT INTO test1 VALUES ('12345678');
ERROR:  new row for relation "test1" violates check constraint
 "test1_col_check"
DETAIL:  Failing row contains (12345678).
```

Alternately, you can use CREATE DOMAIN over the TEXT data type to enforce constraints. Domains are data types with constraints already specified that are useful for not repeating your CHECK definitions.

Again, the bottom line here is don't use the VARCHAR(n) type: it can end up restricting you in a way that is difficult or tedious to circumvent, and it has no performance advantage over the unrestricted kind. So, you should just use TEXT.

NOTE For more information on character types in PostgreSQL, be sure to check the tip about performance in the documentation (https://www.post gresql.org/docs/current/datatype-character.html#DATATYPE-CHARACTER).

Type BPCHAR

Also documented since PostgreSQL 16, the type BPCHAR with no length specification is for storing blank-trimmed strings with unlimited variable length. Like VARCHAR, BPCHAR also accepts strings of any length, but trailing spaces are semantically not significant. Beware that this means it has significantly different behavior from VARCHAR.

Let's illustrate the difference between BPCHAR and VARCHAR in how they treat trailing whitespace:

```
CREATE TEMP TABLE trailing_ws (v VARCHAR, b BPCHAR);
CREATE TABLE

INSERT INTO trailing_ws VALUES ('vvv   ', 'bbb   ');
INSERT 0 1

SELECT v, ('vvv' = v), b, ('bbb' = b) FROM trailing_ws;
   v   | ?column? |   b   | ?column?
-------+----------+-------+----------
 vvv   | f        | bbb   | t
(1 row)
```

From this, we can see that BPCHAR ignores the trailing spaces and treats 'bbb   ' with three trailing spaces the same as 'bbb', whereas VARCHAR thinks the strings 'vvv   ' and 'vvv' differ.

3.6 *MONEY*

Our friends at Frogge Emporium want to store payment amounts for the payments it receives. Naturally, they are considering using the data type MONEY. It can store a currency amount with some specific fractional precision set by the database. Frogge Emporium creates the following table:

```
CREATE TABLE erp.payments (
    id bigint PRIMARY KEY GENERATED ALWAYS AS IDENTITY,
    tstamp timestamp with time zone NOT NULL,
    amount money NOT NULL,
    invoice bigint NOT NULL
);
```

Inserting a sample payment, we get

```
INSERT INTO erp.payments (tstamp, amount, invoice)
VALUES (now(), 99.99, 0);
INSERT 0 1
```

```
TABLE erp.payments;
 id |           tstamp            | amount | invoice
----+----------------------------+--------+---------
  1 | 2023-11-20 21:25:12.501561+00 | £99.99 |       0
(1 row)
```

Let's unpack what happened here. In the writer's sample database, PostgreSQL's locale setting LC_MONETARY has inherited the system default of en_GB, which selects the British pound (GBP). So the database has assumed we inserted £99.99 in that currency. This is a bad initial sign: MONEY doesn't actually store the currency type but goes with whatever is configured on your server.

Notwithstanding that, what happens if we want to retroactively apply a 25% discount on all of the customer's payments as a token of appreciation? Calculating that should be simple. After all, we know that the discount equals

```
SELECT 99.99 * 0.25;
 ?column?
----------
  24.9975
(1 row)
```

So, let's apply this to the value stored in our table:

```
SELECT amount * 0.25
FROM erp.payments
WHERE id = 1;
 ?column?
----------
   £25.00
(1 row)
```

Er, oops. MONEY cannot handle fractions of a penny or a cent, or any other denomination, so you will end up losing money, which is unacceptable for most intents and purposes. From this, it is clear that MONEY will not have the required accuracy for currency conversions either, where rounding is not an option.

It turns out that MONEY is, counterintuitively, a rubbish type for storing monetary data. Suitably, the MONEY data type is happy to accept garbage input:

```
SELECT ',123,456,,7,8.1,0,9'::MONEY;
      money
----------------
 £12,345,678.11
(1 row)
```

Accepting invalid input into a monetary data type is astoundingly bad. Is this really a data type you want to utilize inside your database? The reality is that, for these reasons, the PostgreSQL core developers have tried to deprecate MONEY multiple times. Every time it's been attempted, there have been persistent requests to bring back the type because some people had existing databases using it and did not want to change them to migrate to a more sensible type.

NOTE Beware that you should not use any floating-point number types, such as real or double precision for handling money because they have the potential for rounding errors. By definition, these are inexact numeric types, and the approximations of numbers that they offer are not suitable for storing exact amounts, such as currency.

The proposed solution is to use NUMERIC instead of MONEY, and it's also a very good idea to store the currency associated with the monetary value in another adjacent column on the table.

TIP There is no difference between NUMERIC and DECIMAL in PostgreSQL.

3.7   *SERIAL data type*

SERIAL is a PostgreSQL extension, that is, a non–SQL Standard way to ask the database to create an autoincrementing integer field. The same applies to its bigger brother BIGSERIAL, which autoincrements a BIGINT. It used to be a useful shorthand, but today, it is actually more trouble than it's worth. To elaborate, let's see how it works by creating a table with a SERIAL primary key:

```
CREATE TEMP TABLE transactions (
    id SERIAL PRIMARY KEY,
    amount numeric NOT NULL);
CREATE TABLE

\d transactions
                         Table "pg_temp_4.transactions"
 Column | Type    | Collation | Nullable |            Default
--------+---------+-----------+----------+--------------------------------
 id     | integer |           | not null | nextval('transactions_id_seq'::
        |         |           |          | regclass)
 amount | numeric |           | not null |
Indexes:
    "transactions_pkey" PRIMARY KEY, btree (id)
```

As expected, it automatically creates a sequence transactions_id_seq to generate values for the id column.

Now, let's give permission to another user to use this table:

```
CREATE USER jimmy;
CREATE ROLE

GRANT ALL ON TABLE transactions TO jimmy;
GRANT
```

Let's see whether jimmy can insert into this table by switching roles:

```
SET ROLE jimmy;
SET

INSERT INTO transactions (amount) VALUES (10.00);
ERROR:  permission denied for sequence transactions_id_seq
```

Other users cannot insert into the table even if we have granted them this privilege because they don't have permission to use the automatically created sequence. This is a major shortcoming: permissions for sequences created via the use of SERIAL need to be managed separately from the actual table.

More worryingly, if you use CREATE TABLE … LIKE to create a similar table, the new table will use the same sequence!

```
CREATE TEMP TABLE new_tx (LIKE transactions INCLUDING ALL);
CREATE TABLE

\d new_tx
                        Table "pg_temp_4.new_tx"
 Column |   Type    | Collation | Nullable |              Default
--------+-----------+-----------+----------+-----------------------------------
 id     | integer   |           | not null | nextval('transactions_id_seq'::r.
        |           |           |          | .egclass)
 amount | numeric   |           | not null |
Indexes:
    "new_tx_pkey" PRIMARY KEY, btree (id)
```

This result is unexpected and is probably not what you want. It also has the consequence that you can't drop the original table because the sequence the new table uses depends on it. To avoid these problems, you can use identity columns instead of the serial types, like this:

```
DROP TABLE new_tx;
DROP TABLE

CREATE TEMP TABLE new_tx (
    id int GENERATED BY DEFAULT AS IDENTITY PRIMARY KEY,
    amount numeric not null
);
CREATE TABLE

\d new_tx
                        Table "pg_temp_4.new_tx"
 Column |   Type    | Collation | Nullable |              Default
--------+-----------+-----------+----------+-----------------------------------
 id     | integer   |           | not null | generated by default as identity
 amount | numeric   |           | not null |
Indexes:
    "new_tx_pkey" PRIMARY KEY, btree (id)
```

With an identity column, you don't need to know the name of the sequence to manipulate it:

```
ALTER TABLE new_tx ALTER COLUMN id RESTART WITH 1000;
ALTER TABLE

INSERT INTO new_tx (amount) VALUES (10.00);
INSERT 0 1
```

```
TABLE new_tx;
  id  | amount
------+--------
 1000 |  10.00
(1 row)
```

If you use the CREATE TABLE ... LIKE construct with a table that has identity columns, the new table will get its own new sequences, so you won't encounter any problems.

As a final word, if your application needs to generate a serial sequence of identifiers with no gaps (e.g., for receipt numbers), as required in some localities, it is better to generate the sequence on the application side to guarantee correctness. After all, PostgreSQL sequences will generate new numbers even for transactions that are not committed and then rolled back. Consequently, you'll then have to find the actual last identifier in the table and reset the sequence to serve the next number.

3.8 XML

Let's begin by acknowledging that PostgreSQL does offer the option of using the data type XML, however ill-advised that may be, and many of the same arguments against using XML outside of the database also apply here. Starting with the problems independent of the database, XML as a document format offers the worst of both worlds: it is basically as, or less, efficient than a flat text file and can sometimes be just barely human readable—just a cut above a binary data file.

Some more practical reasons to avoid using XML include the following:

- It mandates having a single root element, which means that things like concatenation of XML content require specific parsing and become much harder.
- It uses the concept of namespaces and introduces the additional problem of namespace collision handling.
- As a text-based format, it can allow inconsistencies in the textual representation of numeric data. One good example is including numbers that were entered at different locales, where there's a good chance that things like the decimal divider rules and separator will be different.
- It simultaneously supports multiple different ways of escaping characters, and the rules on escaping differ whether you're inside text, an attribute, a comment, CDATA, etc.
- The likelihood is that you will receive badly formed XML and be forced to parse it anyway. The probability of someone editing XML by hand may be higher than someone editing JSON data, which is usually used for serializing/deserializing application objects through conversion library functions.

All of the previous reasons don't even get into why XML is a bad choice for your application because of the memory allocation nightmares that are involved in parsing it, which mean you need to examine the advantages and disadvantages of DOM versus SAX/streaming parsers, etc.

There are additional concerns on the database side, specifically in PostgreSQL:

- The DOCTYPE Document Type Declaration (DTD) is problematic as it requires an external or inline DTD definition (which will be entirely irrelevant to your database). PostgreSQL does not validate input values against it and has no support for other XML schema languages such as XML Schema.
- Character encoding, as specified in the XML declaration, may actually be different from the character set that the XML text was saved in. Complicating matters even more, you may have different character encodings on the client and server side, as well as on the XML data side. By default, PostgreSQL converts all character data passed between client and server in both directions, which includes the string representations of values in your XML, and it may render the XML encoding declaration invalid. This makes it your responsibility to ensure that all three encodings and the XML declaration are aligned.
- The same goes for the language identification attribute `xml:lang`; it is simply irrelevant inside a PostgreSQL database.
- There are no applicable comparison operators for the XML type, as a well-known and trusted comparison algorithm for XML data does not exist, even outside of Postgres. As a result, you cannot retrieve rows by comparing an XML column against a search value. So, the main option you're left with is converting everything to TEXT and comparing strings, which is less than ideal.
- XML is queryable using XPath 1.0, but this is a moot point, as the type is not indexable. Compare this to JSONB, which is very well indexable using the GIN and GiST index types.
- It is very verbose, which makes for a lot of redundant bytes and, consequently, a waste of storage space.
- In PostgreSQL, it offers no advantages over the much more compact notation of the same data as JSON. Consider this fragment, which doesn't even include the basic overhead and declarations needed to be considered an XML document:

```
SELECT
'<property>
    <key>color</key>
    <value>00000</value>
</property>'::XML,
pg_column_size(
'<property>
    <key>color</key>
    <value>00000</value>
</property>'::XML
);

            xml             | pg_column_size
----------------------------+----------------
 <property>                +|             72
     <key>color</key>      +|
     <value>00000</value>+|
 </property>                |
(1 row)
```

Compare this to a more stripped down way to represent essentially the same data:

```
SELECT
'{"color":0}'::JSON,
pg_column_size(
'{"color":0}'::JSON
);

    json     | pg_column_size
-------------+----------------
 {"color":0} |             15
(1 row)
```

> **NOTE** pg_column_size() is the function we use to measure the space in bytes used to store any individual data value.

In conclusion, XML is error-prone, inefficient, and slow. Don't use XML for any heavy lifting, especially inside your Postgres database. You will be much better off using JSON or, even better, JSONB for your structured data needs. You can find out more about JSONB inside the PostgreSQL documentation (https://www.postgresql.org/docs/current/datatype-json.html).

Summary

- There is no benefit to using TIMESTAMP (WITHOUT TIME ZONE), as it can lead to time calculation errors due to lack of time zone and DST context. TIMESTAMP WITH TIME ZONE is the proper data type for recording timestamps as specific moments in time.
- TIMETZ and CURRENT_TIME have questionable usefulness because time zones have no meaning without the context of dates. Again, it is preferable to use TIMESTAMPTZ even if we don't need to display the date part of the timestamp.
- MONEY doesn't store which currency and suffers from a limited and flawed implementation. It should be avoided in favor of using NUMERIC or other number formats that can accurately store exact values, potentially in conjunction with storing the currency as a separate column.
- The two serial types SERIAL and BIGSERIAL have been effectively superseded by identity columns, which have more predictable behavior when it comes to role ownership and use of sequences, and clarity regarding which table the sequence belongs to.
- You don't save storage space by using the limited character types CHAR(n) and VARCHAR(n), and the whitespace stored with CHAR(n) can be detrimental to performance. Additionally, you run the risk of running into SQL quirks and painting yourself into a corner with maximum lengths. TEXT is the better choice.
- XML is a terrible choice for document storage unless you're just copying immutable XML data inside the database. If you intend to query/manipulate the data, you should use JSON(B).

Table and index mistakes

This chapter covers

- Table inheritance, an unusual feature
- Why partitioning is important and how to get it right
- Using the right type of key and index for your tables

Some PostgreSQL particularities give it additional flexibility compared to other Relational Database Management Systems (RDBMSs) and can enable powerful and expressive database designs. However, these same features also have the potential to become pitfalls when coming to Postgres with preconceptions from other systems or if the documentation is misunderstood.

4.1 Table Inheritance

At the time of writing, PostgreSQL describes itself as a "powerful, open source object-relational database system." This wording may throw some people off, as it seems to be a description from another era in computing. It may well be an outdated reference to object-oriented programming (OOP), which, as some of you may remember, used to be all the rage in past years. The PostgreSQL project was very keen on showing support for OOP, and one of the advanced features that was particularly relevant to OOP was table inheritance.

Simply put, table inheritance lets you create tables that inherit columns from other tables—the same way that object classes might inherit variables and methods from their parent classes. Using it is as simple as CREATE TABLE (...) INHERITS .... For example, if we think of a meeting as a kind of event, we can create a table `meetings` that includes the attributes of table `events`.

> **Listing 4.1 Table inheritance**

```
CREATE SCHEMA calendar;
SET search_path = calendar, "$user", public;

CREATE TABLE events (
    id int PRIMARY KEY,
    scheduled_time timestamptz,
    status smallint
);
CREATE TABLE

CREATE TABLE meetings (
    invited_emails text[],
    confirmed_emails text[],
    location text
) INHERITS (events);
CREATE TABLE

\d events
                        Table "calendar.events"
     Column     |            Type             | Collation | Nullable | Default
----------------+-----------------------------+-----------+----------+---------
 id             | integer                     |           |          |
 scheduled_time | timestamp with time zone    |           |          |
 status         | smallint                    |           |          |
Number of child tables: 1 (Use \d+ to list them.)

\d meetings
                        Table "calendar.meetings"
     Column     |            Type             | Collation | Nullable | Default
----------------+-----------------------------+-----------+----------+---------
 id             | integer                     |           |          |
 scheduled_time | timestamp with time zo.     |           |          |
                | .ne                         |           |          |
 status         | smallint                    |           |          |
 invited_emails | text[]                      |           |          |
 confirmed_emails | text[]                    |           |          |
 location       | text                        |           |          |
Inherits: events
```

So, we see that the relationship between the tables has been established and is being reported by PostgreSQL. Let's see what we can do now. What happens when we insert a meeting?

```
INSERT INTO meetings (id, scheduled_time, status, invited_emails,
    location)
VALUES (1981, '2024-02-01 09:00', 10,
    ARRAY['kerry.moss@example.com', 'morgan.avenal@example.com'],
    'https://webmeetings.example.com/pas/ok/1981');
INSERT 0 1

TABLE meetings;
-[ RECORD 1 ]----+---------------------------------------------------
id               | 1981
scheduled_time   | 2024-02-01 09:00:00+00
status           | 10
invited_emails   | {kerry.moss@example.com,morgan.avenal@example.com}
confirmed_emails |
location         | https://webmeetings.example.com/pas/ok/1981

TABLE events;
-[ RECORD 1 ]--+----------------------
id             | 1981
scheduled_time | 2024-02-01 09:00:00+00
status         | 10
```

We see that inserting a meeting also generates a row in events with the corresponding inherited fields filled in. That's pretty neat, and it must have seemed like a good idea before object-relational mapping tools (ORMs) started appearing.

Before PostgreSQL 10, table inheritance was also used to implement partitioning by defining the relationships between the parent table and the (child) partition tables. However, since PostgreSQL 10, when declarative table partitioning was introduced, there has been practically no reason to use the much more complicated inheritance path for partitioning tables.

Let's see what happens when we decide that this table will grow to be too large, so we try to create a partitioned version and attach the current table as the first partition:

```
CREATE TABLE events_partitioned (
    id int,
    scheduled_time timestamptz,
    status smallint
) PARTITION BY RANGE (scheduled_time);
CREATE TABLE

ALTER TABLE events_partitioned ATTACH PARTITION events
FOR VALUES FROM ('2000-01-01') TO ('2025-01-01');
ERROR:  cannot attach inheritance parent as partition
```

Whoopsie! Inheritance is fundamentally incompatible with declarative partitioning. You cannot inherit from a partitioned table, and you cannot add inheritance to a partitioned table. So what can you do now that you're stuck with table inheritance? You would need to find some way to undo it.

Fortunately, it isn't all that complicated: you can simply replace the relationship defined by table inheritance with foreign key relationships. You shouldn't really have second thoughts about this because, by forfeiting table inheritance, you won't be missing out on any important functionality anyway. All you need to do is to create a new table to hold the data, and add the foreign key column. Let's do this for the meetings table:

```
CREATE TABLE new_meetings (LIKE meetings);
CREATE TABLE

ALTER TABLE new_meetings ADD event_id int;
ALTER TABLE
```

Then, you copy the data from the old table into the new one (which may take a long time):

```
INSERT INTO new_meetings
SELECT *, id FROM meetings;
INSERT 0 520628
```

Following that, you can create all required constraints, indexes, triggers, etc., for new_meetings.

There is a dirty hack you can resort to if your table is huge and you are performing this on a live system. It involves creating the foreign key constraint but not validating it immediately. This would, of course, presuppose that you trust the data that's inside your tables—namely, that the data in the foreign key column is valid (which it probably will be, being an exact copy of the original table). However, actions such as this are generally not recommended as they involve touching the PostgreSQL catalog.

NOTE Modifying the PostgreSQL catalog is something that should be avoided because unless you know exactly what you're doing, you can make a change that causes data corruption or the database to become unusable.

Having stated the risk, here is what you can do:

```
ALTER TABLE new_meetings ADD
CONSTRAINT event_id_fk FOREIGN KEY (event_id)
REFERENCES events (id) NOT VALID;
UPDATE pg_constraint SET convalidated = true WHERE conname = 'event_id_fk';
```

If this is a live system, you should also probably create triggers to replicate the changes that are coming into meetings to new_meetings too. Also, you'd need triggers to replicate changes to events as meetings changes are easy now that we have the foreign key.

Finally, you perform all the DDL at once inside a single code block:

```
DO $$
BEGIN
    ALTER TABLE meetings RENAME TO old_meetings;
    ALTER TABLE new_meetings RENAME TO meetings;
    DROP TABLE old_meetings;
    COMMIT;
END $$ LANGUAGE plpgsql;
```

That's it; you're now free of table inheritance and can do things such as experimenting with partitioning (which, fortuitously, is discussed in the next section).

4.2   *Neglecting table partitioning*

We previously discussed table partitioning, but what is it all about? In a relational database context, it's simply the division of a table into distinct independent tables. Also known as *horizontal partitioning*, it makes it so that rows that are different in some particular respect end up in different tables. Having heard a decade of complaints by users of databases made by other vendors that PostgreSQL didn't support partitioning, I have always been stunned to discover how few people are aware of partitioning in Postgres.

PostgreSQL 10 introduced *declarative partitioning* (the ability to do it via CREATE TABLE) in 2017, and less elegant ways of implementing partitioning had been available since at least PostgreSQL 8.1, released way back in 2005! PostgreSQL has continued to improve partitioning features in later versions, such as adding foreign key support in version 12 and enhancing performance for partitioned tables.

Now we come to the question of when leaving your tables unpartitioned turns out to be a mistake. Frogge Emporium has a large payments table. Let's assume it doesn't make sense to index it because it is receiving a very large volume of data, and Frogge doesn't want to slow down insert performance. Searching for a payment looks like the following:

```
SELECT count(*) FROM erp.payments;
   count
-----------
 150001000
(1 row)

SET jit=off; SET max_parallel_workers_per_gather=0;
SET
SET

EXPLAIN (ANALYZE, BUFFERS)
    SELECT * FROM erp.payments WHERE tstamp='2022-03-09 22:58:20.431946+00';

                             QUERY PLAN
--------------------------------------------------------------------------------
 Seq Scan on payments  (cost=0.00..3026445.20 rows=1 width=31) (actual
 time=38723.267..62110.334 rows=1 loops=1)
   Filter: (tstamp = '2022-03-09 22:58:20.431946+00'::timestamp with time
 zone)
   Rows Removed by Filter: 150000999
   Buffers: shared hit=812 read=1151157
 Planning Time: 0.115 ms
 Execution Time: 62110.373 ms
(6 rows)
```

Wow! It takes a full minute to find a row in this table. What's even worse is that we appear to have read 1,151,157 buffers or 9 whole GB of data from the disk. Similarly, if we want to delete the oldest month of data, which happens to be September 2021, we must write

```
\timing
Timing is on.

DELETE FROM erp.payments WHERE tstamp < '2021-10-01';
DELETE 1209894
Time: 65914.030 ms (01:05.914)
```

That's quite bad for an OLTP database that has performance requirements. Partitioning the table can help with this workload because it can split it into smaller tables that perform better in our use case and are easier to maintain.

PostgreSQL declarative partitioning is, simply put, specifying for your table

- A partitioning method
- A partition key, which can be one or more columns or expressions
- Partition boundaries

And it's done simply with DDL. Let's create an empty partitioned version of the payments table, like this:

```
CREATE TABLE erp.payments_p (
    id bigint GENERATED ALWAYS AS IDENTITY,
    tstamp timestamp with time zone NOT NULL,
    amount numeric NOT NULL,
    invoice bigint NOT NULL
) PARTITION BY RANGE (tstamp);
CREATE TABLE
```

An additional reason to partition your tables is that PostgreSQL has some hard size limits when it comes to tables. Admittedly, they are hard to reach, but it's not impossible given the ever-increasing amounts of data people are handling today.

Postgres supports an unlimited data size, which is great news. It also supports having 1.4 billion tables per database, regardless of how bad an idea that would be. However, a very real limitation is the maximum table size, which for the default block size of 8,192 bytes is 32 terabytes. The maximum number of rows per table limitation is less clear: it's as many rows as can fit in 4.2 billion blocks.

Here's where dimensioning comes in. It's important to plan ahead so that you don't get stuck with an unmanageably large table a few months or years down the line. You should get your calculator out and take into account your system's data ingestion rate, both in terms of the number of rows getting created and the data size in bytes. Something else to factor in are projected increases, which may even be outside of the IT system, such as Frogge Emporium having 25 retail locations, which are projected to grow to 200 over the next four years. Finally, you need to take into account your data retention requirements, such as, for example, the law mandating you keep 10 years' worth of records around.

The capacity planning exercise you perform will inform your choice of partitioning method and key. For instance, let's say you determine that from each device from a sensor network of 1,000, you receive 1,440 measurements per day. You can then extrapolate this number to see how many measurements you ingest per year. Obviously, you need to keep checking that this estimate remains valid and be prepared to revise accordingly.

Frogge Emporium has determined that the most meaningful partition size is one month. It can use `tstamp` as the partition key and divide the table by RANGE partitioning, which is suitable for ranges of time, identifiers, etc. Therefore, the Frogge Emporium team writes a script to create monthly partitions for the table we just created:

```
DO $$
BEGIN
  FOR i IN 0..28
  LOOP
    EXECUTE format('CREATE TABLE erp.%s PARTITION OF erp.payments_p
        FOR VALUES FROM (''%s'') TO (''%s'')',
        'payments_p_' ||
        extract('year' FROM date_trunc('month', now()) -
            (i * INTERVAL '1 month')) || '_' ||
        extract('month' FROM date_trunc('month', now()) -
            (i * INTERVAL '1 month')),
        date_trunc('month', now()) - (i * INTERVAL '1 month'),
        date_trunc('month', now()) + ((1 - i) * INTERVAL '1 month'));
  END LOOP;
END;
$$;
DO
```

The script's loop starts 28 months before the current month and creates each month's partition like so:

```
CREATE TABLE erp.payments_p_<year>_<month>
PARTITION OF erp.payments_p
FOR VALUES FROM (<first day of month>) TO (<last day of month>);
```

The resulting partition structure looks like this:

```
payments_p
├── payments_p_2021_1
├── payments_p_2021_2
├── payments_p_2021_3
├── ...
├── payments_p_2022_1
├── payments_p_2022_2
└── ...
```

We copy the data from the unpartitioned table into our new tables (this takes a long time):

```
INSERT INTO erp.payments_p (tstamp, amount, invoice)
    SELECT tstamp, amount, invoice FROM erp.payments;
INSERT 0 150001000
```

Now let's see how long it takes to find the same row in the partitioned table:

```
EXPLAIN (ANALYZE, BUFFERS)
    SELECT * FROM erp.payments_p
    WHERE tstamp='2022-03-09 22:58:20.431946+00';

                              QUERY PLAN
-------------------------------------------------------------------------------
 Seq Scan on payments_p_2022_3 payments_p  (cost=0.00..111450.00 rows=1
 width=32) (actual time=1780.649..2535.625 rows=1 loops=1)
   Filter: (tstamp = '2022-03-09 22:58:20.431946+00'::timestamp with time
   zone)
   Rows Removed by Filter: 5349599
   Buffers: shared read=44580
 Planning:
   Buffers: shared hit=20 dirtied=2
 Planning Time: 0.406 ms
 Execution Time: 2535.658 ms
(8 rows)
```

At only 2.5 seconds, it is 24.5 times faster than the unpartitioned table. Because PostgreSQL does what is known as *partition pruning*, or not searching in partitions that cannot possibly contain the row we're looking for, it only needed to check partition `payments_p_2022_3` and to read just 44,580 buffers or 348 MB from the disk. Partition pruning is enabled by our inclusion of the partition key as a predicate to our query, therefore letting the internal query planner know which rows we are *not* looking for.

Let's see how much faster it is to drop a month's partition than to delete that month's data:

```
\timing
Timing is on.

DROP TABLE erp.payments_p_2021_9;
DROP TABLE
Time: 43.113 ms
```

This performance is simply stunning and makes data management and maintenance a lot easier.

> **NOTE** You can find more details on selecting a partitioning method and key in the official PostgreSQL documentation (https://www.postgresql.org/docs/current/ddl-partitioning.html).

Partitioning can help with

- *Performance*—You have sequential and index scans of smaller amounts of data due to partition pruning.
- *Maintenance*—You can DROP TABLE to delete old data, and VACUUM of multiple smaller tables can parallelize and complete quicker than one very long-running operation for one huge table.
- *Disk size limitations*—You can put partitions on different *tablespaces* (which in PostgreSQL can live on different filesystems or disks). Consequently, you can

put different partitions on slower and cheaper disks, and you can decide whether to create indexes on some of them and not others.

- *Circumventing a pitfall of extremely large tables*—Tables are split into 1 GB files, and PostgreSQL loops through some code that's the same for each 1 GB segment, so it would execute that 32,000 times for a 32 TB table.

You need to be aware that choosing the wrong partitioning method, partition key, or partition sizing may actually lead to performance degradation. For example, you should favor keys with sufficient cardinality to distribute the data evenly across your partitions. Additionally, if your queries don't include the partition key in the WHERE clause, they will not use partition pruning, which can lead to worse execution plans.

Using a poorly selected partitioning strategy and key may lead to having too many partitions with just a few rows in each. If the partitioning key doesn't group the data effectively, you may incur higher overheads with excessive partition scans, which will lead to increased I/O and, consequently, slower queries.

To summarize, partitioning with due diligence can make your tables easier to manage, help you get around PostgreSQL limitations when you're dealing with big data, and give you a significant performance boost for your queries.

4.3 *Partitioning by multiple keys*

In the PostgreSQL documentation's CREATE TABLE partitioning section, you can easily find the syntax for partitioning by multiple keys. Sometimes it makes sense to partition a table by multiple columns to have better granularity or a larger number of partitions more finely tuned to the data.

Frogge Emporium wants to partition its energy usage table both by month and branch so that the data in each table will be more specific. Let's try partitioning by multiple keys:

```
CREATE TABLE erp.energy_usage (
    branch_id integer NOT NULL,
    reading_time timestamptz DEFAULT CURRENT_TIMESTAMP,
    reading numeric NOT NULL,
    unit varchar DEFAULT 'kWh' NOT NULL
)
PARTITION BY RANGE (reading_time, branch_id);
CREATE TABLE
```

Now that the base table is created, let's create a partition for January 2024 and branch IDs 1–10:

```
CREATE TABLE erp.energy_usage_2024_01_01to10
PARTITION OF erp.energy_usage
FOR VALUES FROM ('2024-01-01', 1) TO ('2024-02-01', 10);
CREATE TABLE
```

That went well. Now let's create the next partition for the same month for data from branches 11–20:

```
CREATE TABLE erp.energy_usage_2024_01_11to20
PARTITION OF erp.energy_usage
FOR VALUES FROM ('2024-01-01', 11) TO ('2024-02-01', 20);
ERROR:  partition "energy_usage_2024_01_11to20" would overlap partition
"energy_usage_2024_01_01to10"
LINE 3: FOR VALUES FROM ('2024-01-01', 11) TO ('2024-02-01', 20);
```

We got an error! We can see that PostgreSQL states that, effectively, a `reading_time` value such as `'2024-02-01 10:00:00'` can only exist inside the first partition, regardless of `branch_id`!

Why is this? Taking a closer look at what we were trying to do reveals that what we did was define partition boundaries on two keys. This choice simply restricts the values for each key that can go into each partition. Be careful! This is not partitioning on multiple levels.

What we actually need for our use case (having one partition per month for a specific set of branches) is called *sub-partitioning*. Sub-partitioning is, simply put, partitioning the partitions. Since each partition is a separate table, it can be a partitioned table itself.

WARNING Partitioning by multiple keys is not the same as multi-level partitioning.

Let's see the right way to do this. We create the base table with `reading_time` as the partition key:

```
CREATE TABLE erp.energy_usage (
    branch_id integer NOT NULL,
    reading_time timestamptz DEFAULT CURRENT_TIMESTAMP,
    reading numeric NOT NULL,
    unit varchar DEFAULT 'kWh' NOT NULL
)
PARTITION BY RANGE (reading_time);
CREATE TABLE
```

Then we create partitions for each month, and afterward, we partition those monthly partitions by `branch_id`:

```
CREATE TABLE erp.energy_usage_2024_01
PARTITION OF erp.energy_usage
FOR VALUES FROM ('2024-01-01') TO ('2024-02-01')
PARTITION BY RANGE (branch_id);
CREATE TABLE

CREATE TABLE erp.energy_usage_2024_01_01to10
PARTITION OF erp.energy_usage_2024_01
FOR VALUES FROM (1) TO (10);
CREATE TABLE

CREATE TABLE erp.energy_usage_2024_01_11to20
PARTITION OF erp.energy_usage_2024_01
FOR VALUES FROM (11) TO (20);
CREATE TABLE
```

And so on. Our schema now looks lovely!

```
\dt erp*
                        List of relations
    Schema |            Name            |       Type        | Owner
  ---------+---------------------------+-------------------+--------
    erp    | energy_usage              | partitioned table | frogge
    erp    | energy_usage_2024_01      | partitioned table | frogge
    erp    | energy_usage_2024_01_01to10 | table           | frogge
    erp    | energy_usage_2024_01_11to20 | table           | frogge
  (4 rows)
```

`\d+  erp.energy_usage_2024_01` for January 2024's partitioned table reports the following:

```
Partition of: erp.energy_usage FOR VALUES FROM ('2024-01-01 00:00:00+00') TO
  ('2024-02-01 00:00:00+00')
Partition constraint: ((reading_time IS NOT NULL) AND (reading_time >=
  '2024-01-01 00:00:00+00'::timestamp with time zone) AND (reading_time <
  '2024-02-01 00:00:00+00'::timestamp with time zone))
Partition key: RANGE (branch_id)
Partitions: erp.energy_usage_2024_01_01to10 FOR VALUES FROM (1) TO (10),
            erp.energy_usage_2024_01_11to20 FOR VALUES FROM (11) TO (20)
```

If we continue down this path, our partitioning will start looking like this:

```
energy_usage
├── energy_usage_2024_01
│    ├── energy_usage_2024_01_01to10
│    └── energy_usage_2024_01_11to20
├── energy_usage_2024_02
│    ├── energy_usage_2024_02_01to10
│    └── energy_usage_2024_02_11to20
├── energy_usage_2024_03
│    └── ...
└── ...
```

Partitioning by multiple columns certainly has its usefulness—for example, keeping scientific data separate and allowing rapid access via partition pruning (provided WHERE clauses for both columns are specified in the query). What's easy to miss in the documentation is this part: "For example, given PARTITION BY RANGE (x,y), a partition bound FROM (1, 2) TO (3, 4) allows x=1 with any y>=2, x=2 with any non-null y, and x=3 with any y<4."

In most cases, sub-partitioning may be more practically useful to you than this syntax, so it's good to be aware.

4.4   *Using the wrong index type*

PostgreSQL offers a wide variety of indexes alongside the incredibly powerful capability to write your own index types. Each built-in index type uses its own algorithm that is suitable for specific uses—namely, improving query performance for specific types of queries on certain types of data.

The default index type is the B-Tree Index, and again, it's surprising to find out how many people think it's the only index type in PostgreSQL. B-Tree Indexes can speed up queries with equality or ordering comparisons. They can also offer some querying capabilities with the LIKE operator for pattern matching and the ~ operator for regular expressions.

Let's see what we can do with the default index type for a dataset such as ArXiv's Open Access research metadata, which has entries for 2.4 million articles, complete with titles, authors, categories, abstracts, etc.

NOTE You can create a Kaggle account to download the dataset at https://www.kaggle.com/datasets/Cornell-University/arxiv/

After unzipping the 4.2 GB JSON dataset, we run the following to escape backslashes and make Postgres happier with our JSON file:

```
sed -i 's/\\/\\\\/g' 'arxiv-metadata-oai-snapshot.json'
```

We then copy it into our database table called `arxiv`, with everything inside a `jsonb` column called `data`:

```
CREATE TABLE test.arxiv (data jsonb);
CREATE TABLE

\copy test.arxiv FROM 'arxiv-metadata-oai-snapshot.json'
COPY 2417693
```

We can access the elements of each entry, such as the title, like this:

```
SELECT data ->> 'title' FROM test.arxiv TABLESAMPLE BERNOULLI (0.1) LIMIT 1;
                                ?column?
-----------------------------------------------------------------
 Modeling of hydrogen and hydroxyl group migration on graphene
(1 row)
```

We can now create an index to speed up searching through those titles by indexing only the title element from the entire JSON document. We'd rather use case-insensitive search, so let's turn everything into lowercase and specify that we need the index for `text_pattern_ops`:

```
CREATE INDEX ON test.arxiv (lower(data->>'title') text_pattern_ops);
CREATE INDEX

ANALYZE test.arxiv;
ANALYZE
```

Now that the index is created, we can search for articles with titles beginning, for example, with "Modeling of hydrogen." Remember to always use the expression that was previously used in the index creation in the WHERE clause for querying:

```
EXPLAIN ANALYZE
    SELECT data->'doi'
    FROM test.arxiv
    WHERE lower(data->>'title') LIKE 'modeling of hydrogen%';
                            QUERY PLAN
----------------------------------------------------------------------------
 Index Scan using arxiv_lower_idx on arxiv  (cost=0.56..9.19 rows=242
 width=32) (actual time=0.085..0.085 rows=1 loops=1)
   Index Cond: ((lower((data ->> 'title'::text)) ~>=~
 'modeling of hydrogen'::text) AND (lower((data ->> 'title'::text)) ~<~
 'modeling of hydrogeo'::text))
   Filter: (lower((data ->> 'title'::text)) ~~ 'modeling of
 hydrogen%'::text)
 Planning Time: 0.755 ms
 Execution Time: 0.134 ms
(5 rows)
```

That wasn't too bad. Let's try filtering by titles *containing* "modeling of hydrogen" (notice the query pattern change to `'%modeling of hydrogen%'`):

```
SET jit=off; SET max_parallel_workers_per_gather=0;
SET
SET

EXPLAIN ANALYZE
    SELECT data->'doi'
    FROM test.arxiv
    WHERE lower(data->>'title') LIKE '%modeling of hydrogen%';
                            QUERY PLAN
----------------------------------------------------------------------------
 Seq Scan on arxiv  (cost=0.00..488032.26 rows=242 width=32) (actual
 time=539.217..8624.051 rows=5 loops=1)
   Filter: (lower((data ->> 'title'::text)) ~~ '%modeling of
 hydrogen%'::text)
   Rows Removed by Filter: 2417688
 Planning Time: 0.084 ms
 Execution Time: 8624.065 ms
(5 rows)
```

That was much, much worse. The index wasn't used at all because B-Tree Indexes are only good for equality and sorting searches, even with the `text_pattern_ops` specifier. (Did you notice that PostgreSQL was looking for index keys in between `'modeling of hydrogen%'` and `'modeling of hydrogeo%'` in the previous query's plan?)

So, the default index type is no good for searching for substrings that are not at the beginning (or end) of the value, and that makes it pretty much unsuitable for full-text search. But even if it magically was capable of that, we'd run into this issue if we tried, for example, to index the abstract instead of the title:

```
CREATE INDEX ON test.arxiv (lower(data->>'abstract') text_pattern_ops);
ERROR:  index row size 2728 exceeds btree version 4 maximum 2704 for index
 "arxiv_lower_idx1"
DETAIL:  Index row references tuple (213838,4) in relation "arxiv".
HINT:  Values larger than 1/3 of a buffer page cannot be indexed.
```

```
Consider a function index of an MD5 hash of the value, or use full text
indexing.
```

You can't really index values that long, which makes a B-Tree Index unsuitable for indexing documents in most cases. But it's actually quite cool of Postgres to tell us what we're probably doing wrong here!

Let's also notice the size of the B-Tree Index:

```
\di+ test.arxiv*
List of relations
-[ RECORD 1 ]-+----------------
Schema        | test
Name          | arxiv_lower_idx
Type          | index
Owner         | frogge
Table         | arxiv
Persistence   | permanent
Access method | btree
Size          | 239 MB
Description   |
```

The proper index to use here is PostgreSQL's Generalized Inverted Index (GIN), which works very well for full-text search with the tsvector data type. Creating the index on titles looks like this:

```
DROP INDEX test.arxiv_lower_idx;
DROP INDEX

CREATE INDEX ON test.arxiv
    USING gin (to_tsvector('english', data->>'title'));
CREATE INDEX
```

Querying reveals how much better the GIN index is for this sort of thing:

```
EXPLAIN ANALYZE
    SELECT data->'doi'
    FROM test.arxiv
    WHERE to_tsvector('english', data->>'title')
    @@ plainto_tsquery('english', 'modeling of hydrogen');
                            QUERY PLAN
-------------------------------------------------------------------------
 Bitmap Heap Scan on arxiv  (cost=38.89..292.85 rows=60 width=32) (actual
 time=1.829..4.949 rows=236 loops=1)
   Recheck Cond: (to_tsvector('english'::regconfig, (data ->>
   'title'::text)) @@ '''model'' & ''hydrogen'''::tsquery)
   Heap Blocks: exact=236
   -> Bitmap Index Scan on arxiv_to_tsvector_idx  (cost=0.00..38.87
   rows=60 width=0) (actual time=1.783..1.783 rows=236 loops=1)
         Index Cond: (to_tsvector('english'::regconfig, (data ->>
         'title'::text)) @@ '''model'' & ''hydrogen'''::tsquery)
 Planning Time: 3.455 ms
 Execution Time: 4.989 ms
(7 rows)
```

That's awesome performance for millions of documents. We should expect performance to be comparable for the abstracts, or we could concatenate both elements and index them together.

What's even better is the index size, which is smaller than a B-Tree Index:

```
\di+ test.arxiv*
List of relations
-[ RECORD 1 ]-+--------------------
Schema        | test
Name          | arxiv_to_tsvector_idx
Type          | index
Owner         | frogge
Table         | arxiv
Persistence   | permanent
Access method | gin
Size          | 100 MB
Description   |
```

However, GIN can be used improperly, too. Separate from full-text search, you can use GIN to index entire JSON documents to speed up access to the elements contained within. It's easy to assume that this one big index covers every use case:

```
DROP INDEX test.arxiv_to_tsvector_idx ;
DROP INDEX

CREATE INDEX ON test.arxiv USING gin (data);
CREATE INDEX

\di+ test.arxiv*
List of relations
-[ RECORD 1 ]-+---------------
Schema        | test
Name          | arxiv_data_idx
Type          | index
Owner         | frogge
Table         | arxiv
Persistence   | permanent
Access method | gin
Size          | 1680 MB
Description   |
```

Let's use the index to search for specific article Digital Object Identifiers (DOIs):

```
EXPLAIN ANALYZE
    SELECT *
    FROM test.arxiv
    WHERE data @> '{"doi": "10.1039/c0cp01009j"}';
                            QUERY PLAN
----------------------------------------------------------------------------
 Bitmap Heap Scan on arxiv  (cost=56.90..1011.01 rows=242 width=1345)
   (actual time=0.127..0.127 rows=1 loops=1)
   Recheck Cond: (data @> '{"doi": "10.1039/c0cp01009j"}'::jsonb)
   Heap Blocks: exact=1
```

```
 -> Bitmap Index Scan on arxiv_data_idx  (cost=0.00..56.84 rows=242
   width=0) (actual time=0.116..0.116 rows=1 loops=1)
      Index Cond: (data @> '{"doi": "10.1039/c0cp01009j"}'::jsonb)
Planning Time: 2.345 ms
Execution Time: 0.159 ms
(7 rows)
```

That's great performance. But if we're only ever looking for DOIs, is it really the right choice? Let's compare:

```
DROP INDEX test.arxiv_data_idx ;
DROP INDEX

CREATE INDEX ON test.arxiv((data->>'doi'));
CREATE INDEX

\di+ test.arxiv*
List of relations
-[ RECORD 1 ]-+---------------
Schema        | test
Name          | arxiv_expr_idx
Type          | index
Owner         | frogge
Table         | arxiv
Persistence   | permanent
Access method | btree
Size          | 61 MB
Description   |
```

That's tiny! Let's find our DOI:

```
EXPLAIN ANALYZE
    SELECT * FROM test.arxiv
    WHERE data->>'doi' = '10.1039/c0cp01009j';
                            QUERY PLAN
--------------------------------------------------------------------------
 Bitmap Heap Scan on arxiv  (cost=254.11..42289.79 rows=12088 width=1345)
   (actual time=0.043..0.044 rows=1 loops=1)
   Recheck Cond: ((data ->> 'doi'::text) = '10.1039/c0cp01009j'::text)
   Heap Blocks: exact=1
   -> Bitmap Index Scan on arxiv_expr_idx  (cost=0.00..251.09 rows=12088
     width=0) (actual time=0.034..0.034 rows=1 loops=1)
      Index Cond: ((data ->> 'doi'::text) = '10.1039/c0cp01009j'::text)
Planning Time: 0.554 ms
Execution Time: 0.076 ms
(7 rows)
```

Look at that speed! B-trees are awesome when it comes to comparing identifiers. Remember to use the right index for the right queries, depending on each index type's strengths.

You can also look up in the PostgreSQL documentation when using a *lossy* index, such as a Generalized Search Tree (GiST), would be beneficial in place of GIN—for instance, when you have a huge dataset but query times aren't critical. GiST indexes come in handy for Postgres range types, such as `daterange`. Along the same lines, you can use a lossy Block Range Index (BRIN), which is orders of magnitudes smaller than a B-Tree Index, for searching in ranges of values such as timestamps, if it is sufficient for what you are planning to query. As updating indexes is slow, especially for complicated index types such as GIN, remember to only index what you need and for whatever level of performance you deem to be acceptable.

More information on these index types and their usage can be found here:

- https://www.postgresql.org/docs/current/textsearch-indexes.html
- https://www.postgresql.org/docs/current/brin.html

Summary

- If you discover table inheritance and think you need it, you're probably wrong. Implement the parent–child relationships with foreign keys and triggers if needed.
- You can use table partitioning to make the management and maintenance of large tables easier and speed up the queries hitting those tables.
- Take care when sub-partitioning because partitioning by multiple keys is not the same thing. Unfortunately, it is not obvious from the documentation what the multiple key partitioning syntax does, when best to use it, and what its implications are.
- Each index type offered in PostgreSQL has its strengths and weaknesses. By adapting your indexing plan to the type of data you have and the type of queries you need to run, you can optimize performance and storage space. When you get it right, your queries can run orders of magnitude faster.

Improper feature usage

This chapter covers

- What choosing the `SQL_ASCII` encoding entails
- Creating rules and the associated pitfalls
- Misusing NoSQL features for SQL queries
- How improvising distributed/multi-master systems can lead to problems

The rich feature set of PostgreSQL is what makes it such a powerful tool for data processing. Far from being a traditional relational database management system (RDBMS), additional features such as NoSQL capabilities, logical replication, foreign data wrappers, and rules give you the flexibility to design a wide variety of database-oriented systems (and to make mistakes with those designs)!

5.1 Selecting SQL_ASCII as the encoding

Since the dawn of computing, character encoding, or the numeric representation of text characters, has used various encoding schemes for mapping characters to numeric values for storage. With the use of computers expanding around the globe, the need to create more (and almost always incompatible) *code pages* or *character sets* for use with different languages' written characters became a hot topic.

> **Encoding/code page/character set**
>
> A *character set* is simply a grouping of characters and symbols, such as the ones necessary to properly represent a language and locale combination. It is also known as a *code page* in some legacy environments. The term *encoding* refers to how this character set is represented internally as 1 or more bytes per character. So, for instance, we have the very large Unicode character set, also known as the Universal Coded Character Set (UCS), which can be represented in a binary form by the UTF-8 encoding.

PostgreSQL supports lots of character sets or text encodings, mostly for reasons of compatibility with legacy data already using those encodings. These are also known as server-side encodings, and you can have a global default selected for the entire PostgreSQL server, which is set at initialization time, and, at the same time, individual databases each having their own encoding. Depending on the encoding, 1 or multiple bytes per character can be used.

If the locale is not set, as can sometimes be the case on badly configured cloud compute instances, Postgres will default to SQL_ASCII. Your databases will then look something like this:

```
\l
List of databases
-[ RECORD 1 ]-----+----------------------
Name              | frogge
Owner             | frogge
Encoding          | SQL_ASCII
Locale Provider   | libc
Collate           | C
Ctype             | C
ICU Locale        |
ICU Rules         |
Access privileges |
-[ RECORD 2 ]-----+----------------------
Name              | postgres
Owner             | postgres
Encoding          | SQL_ASCII
Locale Provider   | libc
Collate           | C
Ctype             | C
ICU Locale        |
ICU Rules         |
Access privileges |
...
```

Our friends at Frogge Emporium want to store ticket content text in the tickets table, but their customer base can use multiple languages. So, they decide to stay with database encoding SQL_ASCII, which seems to accept characters from any character set that the customer may use without complaining.

In the PostgreSQL documentation, we can see under section 24.3.1 (PostgreSQL Character Sets) the PostgreSQL character sets (table 5.1).

Table 5.1 PostgreSQL character sets

Name	Description	Language	Server?	ICU?	Bytes/Char	Aliases
SQL_ASCII	unspecified (see text)	*any*	Yes	No	1	

And under section 24.3.4 (Available Character Set Conversions), we find the character set conversions (table 5.2).

Table 5.2 Available character set conversions

Server Character Set	Available Client Character Sets
SQL_ASCII	*any (no conversion will be performed)*

Let's see what happens when we accept writes from any client encoding into our SQL_ASCII database. In the following snippet, we'll generate text input in three different encodings application-side and then insert it straight into our database.

Listing 5.1 sql_ascii_in.py: Inserting multi-language text

```python
import psycopg

english_text = ("Good evening, I would like to return my last order "
                + "please.").encode('iso-8859-1')
greek_text = ("Καλησπέρα, θα ήθελα να επιστρέψω την τελευταία μου παραγγελία "
              + "παρακαλώ.").encode('windows-1253')
japanese_text = ("こんばんは、前回の注文を返品したいのですがお願いします。"
                 ).encode('shift_jis')

with psycopg.connect("dbname=frogge user=frogge") as conn:
    with conn.cursor() as cur:
        cur.execute('''INSERT INTO support.tickets (content, status)
                    VALUES (%s, 20), (%s, 20), (%s, 20)''',
                    (english_text, greek_text, japanese_text))
```

Okay, that seemed to work. Let's see what we put inside our database now:

```
SELECT id, content FROM support.tickets;
 id |                              content
----+------------------------------------------------------------------
  1 | \x476f6f64206576656e696e672c204920776f756c64206c696b6520746f207265747.
    |.5726e206d79206c617374206f7264657220706c656173652e
  2 | \xcae1ebe7f3f0ddf1e12c20e8e120dee8e5ebe120ede120e5f0e9f3f4f1ddf8f920f.
    |.4e7ed20f4e5ebe5f5f4e1dfe120eceff520f0e1f1e1e3e3e5ebdfe120f0e1f1e1eae1.
    |.ebfe2e
  3 | \x82b182f182ce82f182cd8141914f89f182cc928d95b682f095d4956982b582bd82a.
    |.282cc82c582b782aa82a88ae882a282b582dc82b78142
(3 rows)
```

Wait, this is slightly confusing. What are all these crazy hexadecimal values? Ah! I did mention that text encoding is all about the numeric representation of textual characters, so it makes sense. These must be our strings' numeric representations in the encodings that we specified.

Let's read them from the application now! As these are now sequences of bytes representing text, let's retrieve them as such and cast to `bytea` and then print them as UTF-8 text.

Listing 5.2   sql_ascii_out.py: Reading multi-language text

```
import psycopg

with psycopg.connect("dbname=frogge user=frogge") as conn:
    with conn.cursor(row_factory=psycopg.rows.dict_row) as cur:
        cur.execute('''SELECT id, content::bytea FROM support.tickets''')
        res = cur.fetchall()
        for row in res:
            print(row['id'], row['content'].decode('UTF-8'))
```

Running this produces

```
1 Good evening, I would like to return my last order please.
Traceback (most recent call last):
  File "/home/myuser/sql_ascii_out.py", line 8, in <module>
    print(row['id'], row['content'].decode('UTF-8'))
                     ^^^^^^^^^^^^^^^^^^^^^^^^^^^^^^^^
UnicodeDecodeError: 'utf-8' codec can't decode byte 0xca in position 0:
invalid continuation byte
```

Whoops! What happened here? We can see that the first row decoded to UTF-8 fine, but the next one failed. Well, actually, they would all have failed if it wasn't for the happy accident that the first 128 characters in UTF-8 are the same as those in ASCII. Let's rewind and understand what happened here.

When we choose the SQL_ASCII "encoding" in PostgreSQL, the database interprets byte values 0–127 as ASCII and simply ignores byte values 128–255, not interpreting them as anything. These are the values that were inventively used by the erstwhile creators of the early computer character sets that we mentioned previously (for single-byte sets—multi-byte code pages, like those for Asian alphabets, are a whole other mess). The fact that these bytes are uninterpreted characters means that no conversion to other encodings will be performed, as stated in the official documentation (remember what's in parentheses in table 5.2).

This means that in Postgres, SQL_ASCII is not so much an encoding, but rather a lack thereof, and it behaves significantly differently from all other supported encodings. Input data is not validated, and encoding conversion is not possible. Using the SQL_ASCII setting with non-ASCII data from other languages means that it allowed us to "mix and match" encoded data with no way to decode it and has now left us with the conundrum of needing to figure out which encoding each value is in, which is practically impossible unless you manually examine the table data row by row.

TIP In case it's not clear yet, just use UTF-8 for everything.

The UTF-8 encoding of the Unicode standard has practically eclipsed everything else in the modern world, and with good reason. In most cases, it has allowed us to finally stop worrying about text encodings for multilingual data. There are still many legacy applications out there using traditional code pages, but for anything new, there is really no reason to use anything besides UTF-8. And for the application side, you need to make sure that your application input is UTF-8 or, at the very least, for legacy applications, that UTF-8 data is sent to the database.

It is unfortunate that, in the absence of a locale configuration, PostgreSQL defaults to using SQL_ASCII, and if you happen to be using the Latin alphabet for your text, that will appear to work mostly fine—until you try to do any conversions. However, if your system's locale settings are configured properly, PostgreSQL will use UTF8 for your locale.

So what happens if you do have a legacy database and you're stuck with SQL_ASCII? If you know the most likely encoding for your data, you can probably migrate it to UTF8. Extracting the data and converting it to UTF-8 is not so hard:

```
SELECT id,
    convert_from(convert(content::bytea, 'ISO-8859-1', 'UTF8'), 'UTF8')
FROM support.tickets
WHERE id = 1;
 id |                        convert_from
----+------------------------------------------------------------
  1 | Good evening, I would like to return my last order please.
```

This is good; it means you can now obtain UTF-8 strings for your text, which you can export. The encoding of a database cannot be changed, so you will need to create a new one for the migration. Even in a misconfigured system, you can still create a UTF8 database:

```
CREATE DATABASE frogge_new ENCODING UTF8 LC_COLLATE 'en_US.UTF-8'
LC_CTYPE 'en_US.UTF-8' TEMPLATE template0;
CREATE DATABASE
\x\l frogge*
Expanded display is on.
List of databases
-[ RECORD 1 ]-----+------------
Name              | frogge
Owner             | frogge
Encoding          | SQL_ASCII
Locale Provider   | libc
Collate           | C
Ctype             | C
ICU Locale        |
ICU Rules         |
Access privileges |
-[ RECORD 2 ]-----+------------
Name              | frogge_new
Owner             | frogge
Encoding          | UTF8
```

```
Locale Provider   | libc
Collate           | en_US.UTF-8
Ctype             | en_US.UTF-8
ICU Locale        |
ICU Rules         |
Access privileges |
```

When we create our schema in the new database, Unicode strings work as expected:

```
INSERT INTO support.tickets (content, status) VALUES
('Good evening, I would like to return my last order please.', 20),
('Καλησπέρα, θα ήθελα να επιστρέψω την τελευταία μου παραγγελία παρακαλώ.',20),
('こんばんは、前回の注文を返品したいのですがお願いします。', 20);
INSERT 0 3
SELECT id, content FROM support.tickets;
 id |                          content
----+------------------------------------------------------------------------
  1 | Good evening, I would like to return my last order please.
  2 | Καλησπέρα, θα ήθελα να επιστρέψω την τελευταία μου παραγγελία παρακαλ.
    | .ώ.
  3 | こんばんは、前回の注文を返品したいのですがお願いします。
(3 rows)
```

> **Client encoding**
>
> I mentioned that these are server-side encodings. PostgreSQL also lets you select a client encoding (e.g., with SET client_encoding), and it performs any character set conversion between server and client automatically for you (if the combination of encodings is supported; see the documentation at https://www.postgresql.org/docs/current/multibyte.html#MULTIBYTE-CONVERSIONS-SUPPORTED). By implication, this allows you to use Postgres with legacy applications that use specific encodings or don't speak Unicode.
>
> However, you need to make sure that you write to the server using the proper encoding. For example, our script in listing 5.1 will not work with a UTF-8 database without first encoding the strings to be inserted in UTF-8.

To recap, SQL_ASCII is not a database encoding, and it behaves differently from other PostgreSQL character sets. It doesn't do encoding conversion or validation, and you can end up storing a mixture of encodings with no way to recover the original strings. Unless you are interfacing with a legacy system, and you know exactly which character set that system uses, your safest bet is to always use UTF8. Make sure you are always aware of the selected character encoding when creating a database. If you're migrating your database, convert your strings to UTF8. Finally, pay close attention to your collations, which can affect character classification and sort order.

NOTE You can find a lot of information on collation support in PostgreSQL here: https://www.postgresql.org/docs/current/collation.html

5.2   *CREATE RULE*

PostgreSQL offers a powerful *rule* system that allows you to rewrite and modify the execution of queries. This is a Postgres extension of the SQL Standard for defining actions such as "when we UPDATE table *a*, also INSERT into table *b*" or "when we SELECT from table *x*, instead SELECT from table *y*."

> **NOTE**   The rules system is exclusive to PostgreSQL. It is not related to CREATE RULE in other databases.

Frogge Emporium has a problem with people manually inserting orders instead of using the sales administration user interface because no stock check is made. It has decided to address this by putting in place a rule that logs manual insertions and records who did it, which row was affected, and when:

```
CREATE OR REPLACE RULE log_order_insertions AS
    ON INSERT TO erp.order_groups
    DO ALSO
        INSERT INTO audit.audit_log (what, who, id, tstamp)
        VALUES ('Manual order insertion',
            CURRENT_ROLE::text, NEW.id, clock_timestamp());
```

Let's test the rule by inserting a row into order_groups and selecting that row immediately:

```
\x
Expanded display is on.
INSERT INTO erp.order_groups (status, placed_at, updated_at, customer)
    VALUES ('Placed', clock_timestamp(), clock_timestamp(), 135);
SELECT * FROM erp.order_groups ORDER BY placed_at DESC FETCH FIRST ROW ONLY;
INSERT 0 1
-[ RECORD 1 ]----------------------------
id         | 500001
status     | Placed
placed_at  | 2024-06-04 21:21:57.542003+01
updated_at | 2024-06-04 21:21:57.542003+01
customer   | 135
```

We see that we've inserted the row with id 500001. Let's see what we logged in the audit_log table:

```
TABLE audit.audit_log;
-[ RECORD 1 ]----------------------
what   | Manual order insertion
who    | frogge
id     | 500002
tstamp | 2024-06-04 21:21:57.52818+01
```

What?! We've logged that id 500002 was inserted, and that is incorrect, as we know we inserted the row with id 500001.

What happened here is that, under the covers, when we ran the INSERT query, which automatically selected nextval() from the sequence order_groups_id_seq giving values to id, the rule rewrote it, and it effectively became two queries:

```
INSERT INTO erp.order_groups (id, status, placed_at, updated_at, customer)
    VALUES (nextval('erp.order_groups_id_seq'), 'Placed', clock_timestamp(),
        clock_timestamp(), 135);
INSERT INTO audit.audit_log (what, who, id, tstamp)
    VALUES ('Manual order insertion',
        CURRENT_ROLE::text, nextval('erp.order_groups_id_seq'),
        clock_timestamp());
```

So we can see that the rule did not work the way we expected because it changed our SQL with an unintended side effect—incrementing the order_groups_id_seq sequence. A hint pointing this out would have been the different timestamp we saw in audit_log's tstamp. We can learn two things from this: how side effects like this could have been destructive if, for instance, subsequent queries in the rule used DELETE and that using VOLATILE functions with rules can be tricky because they may be executed multiple times. What we should have done here is use a TRIGGER because trigger behavior is well-understood and predictable.

> **NOTE** PostgreSQL functions are labeled with the volatility classifications VOLATILE, STABLE, or IMMUTABLE. VOLATILE functions can do anything, including modifying the database, whereas STABLE and IMMUTABLE functions can't modify the database. At the same time, STABLE functions must return the same results for the same arguments for all rows within a single statement. IMMUTABLE ones must always return the same results for the same arguments. Declaring the correct volatility category is crucial for improving performance via the Postgres optimizer.

Let's see another troubling aspect of RULE usage. We assume Frogge wants to prevent orders that are more than one year old from ever being updated again. The following rule is written:

```
CREATE OR REPLACE RULE dont_update_old_orders AS
    ON UPDATE TO erp.order_groups
        WHERE old.updated_at < now() - INTERVAL '1 year'
    DO INSTEAD NOTHING;
```

Let's find one that's older than a year:

```
SELECT *
FROM erp.order_groups
TABLESAMPLE BERNOULLI (10)
WHERE updated_at < now() - INTERVAL '1 year';
-[ RECORD 1 ]----------------------------
id         | 651
status     | Fulfilled
placed_at  | 2023-01-23 15:36:48.270475+00
updated_at | 2023-01-23 15:36:48.270475+00
customer   | 88
```

All right, let's carefully check if the rule will prevent us from running the following:

```
BEGIN;
BEGIN

UPDATE erp.order_groups SET status = 'Cancelled'
WHERE updated_at < '2024-01-01';
UPDATE 24067
```

Oops! Not really what we expected. Let's undo:

```
ROLLBACK;
ROLLBACK
```

It's very important to understand that RULEs don't prevent the query from running. We saw that the query did execute fine and affected all rows older than '2024-01-01' but not older than a year. It *did* execute the query but with the added condition WHERE updated_at < now() - INTERVAL '1 year' coming from the rule:

```
                              QUERY PLAN
-----------------------------------------------------------------------------
Update on order_groups  (cost=0.00..1.05 rows=0 width=0)
   -> Seq Scan on order_groups  (cost=0.00..1.05 rows=1 width=10)
         Filter: ((updated_at < '2024-01-01 00:00:00+00'::timestamp with
            time zone) AND ((updated_at < (now() - '1 year'::interval)) IS NOT
            TRUE))
```

Therefore, it updated the 24,067 rows in the table that were updated before 2024 began but were not updated during the past year.

There are other rule pitfalls as well. For example, nothing prevents you from creating circular rules:

- Rule 1: on insert to *x*, instead insert into *y*
- Rule 2: on insert to *y*, instead insert into *x*

Admittedly, RULEs are necessary in one case: making VIEWs writable. You can create rules that define ON INSERT, ON UPDATE, or ON DELETE actions for views that in actuality get performed on the constituent tables behind the view.

By far the biggest problem with the rule system is that it's complicated to understand and, therefore, ripe for making mistakes. Rules don't apply conditional logic, but they are just an SQL rewriter for modifying queries and adding additional actions.

The bottom line is: don't use rules! In most cases, they won't do what you expect them to, and what you should be using instead are triggers. Rules should be regarded as internal implementation components of the Postgres VIEW system and best left untouched by users.

5.3   Relational JSON

The addition of the json and jsonb document store types to PostgreSQL unlocked a whole range of NoSQL capabilities, with the ability to combine relational and schemaless data.

Nowadays, with Javascript-based languages being ubiquitous, it's only natural for developers to gravitate toward using JSON, as it's the native data format they're intimately familiar with. However, PostgreSQL's strength of being able to combine SQL and NoSQL can turn into a detriment if these are mixed in improper ways.

A famous relational database anti-pattern is known as Entity-Attribute-Value or EAV. Also known as "open schema," it allows efficient storage of datasets with sparse attributes (i.e., not every entity or object having the same attributes, even if they are of the same object type) or sparse values (lots of nulls). It's easy to see the parallels with NoSQL here. However, in the RDBMS world, EAV is considered an anti-pattern because it requires you to write more difficult queries to retrieve the data, and often the complexity of those queries makes it easy to get them wrong or write them in a way that performs badly.

The usefulness of JSON storage for similar purposes, such as the ingestion of large amounts of data where we cannot foresee the attributes or whether they're populated, is undeniable. Nevertheless, it's easy for people to get carried away and start using JSON even for data that fits the relational pattern quite well. A good indicator of that is when you start considering the use of SQL JOINs for retrieval of your JSON stored data—NoSQL/"schemaless" was meant to eliminate the need for joins!

I like to call this anti-pattern *relational JSON*. Let's see some examples. Our user has created the following tables to store customer accounts and sales data, where everything in the row is inside a JSON field to allow maximum flexibility:

```
CREATE TABLE test.accounts (
    json_account jsonb NOT NULL
);

CREATE TABLE test.sales (
    json_sale jsonb NOT NULL
);
```

The data held on customers that goes into accounts.json_account looks like this:

```
{
    "id": 52101,
    "name": "Freddie",
    "balance": 1500.37,
    "migrated_account": {
        "system": "legacy",
        "migrated_on": "2023-12-20"
    }
}


{
    "id": 8101,
    "name": "Emory Trenneman",
    "opened_on": "March 12, 2019",
    "balance": 2530.00
}
```

And the records of sales in `sales.json_sale` look something like this:

```
{
    "id": 133045,
    "account_id": 565,
    "timestamp": "2024-01-30 12:54:10",
    "point_of_sale": 311,
    "amount": 35.99
}

{
    "id": 133046,
    "amount": 2138,
    "account_id": 8101,
    "timestamp": "2024-01-30 12:55:46+0 UTC",
    "point_of_sale": 2
}
```

Some things may be already apparent if you have experience with databases, such as the fact that the database can't enforce referential integrity or even ensure that values are of the correct type or within allowable ranges. All this will now need to be handled by the application.

Our user wants to find out the names of customers, not migrated from the legacy system, who have placed an order exceeding 10,000 and who have an account balance less than 20,000. Therefore, a query is formulated:

```
SELECT a.json_account ->> 'name' AS "Name"
FROM test.accounts a
JOIN test.sales s
    ON (s.json_sale ->> 'account_id')::int = (a.json_account ->> 'id')::int
WHERE (a.json_account ->> 'balance')::numeric < 20000
AND (s.json_sale ->> 'amount')::numeric > 10000
AND (NOT a.json_account['migrated_account'] ->> 'system' = 'legacy'
    OR a.json_account -> 'migrated_account' IS NULL);
```

That is one ugly, barely legible query. Does it run? Yes, it runs. But remember, in the previous section, we saw how choosing the wrong index type may be functional but, at the same time, constitute a waste of disk space or a relative loss of performance. For this use case, we will practically have to index the entire contents of the tables with large GIN or GiST indexes. Even then, the index wouldn't help with this query because it would turn into a `Merge Join` with `Materialize` and `Sorts` of `Seq Scans`.

So, even if you go and create a GIN index and use the proper `jsonb` operators to take advantage of it, as follows, you can speed up the query somewhat, but it will still be a nested loop instead of a proper relational join using the index:

```
SELECT a.json_account ->> 'name' AS "Name"
FROM test.accounts a
JOIN test.sales s
    ON (s.json_sale -> 'account_id') @> (a.json_account -> 'id')
WHERE (a.json_account -> 'balance')::numeric < 20000
AND (s.json_sale ->> 'amount')::numeric > 10000
```

```
AND (NOT a.json_account ->
    'migrated_account' @> '{"system": "legacy"}'::jsonb OR NOT
    a.json_account ? 'migrated_account');
```

Really, your alternative would be to create expression-based indexes on JSON keys that each row may or may not have. If you're going to go to that trouble anyway, why not store everything in relational form and avoid the hassle of writing complex, hard-to-read queries? Use json(b) for what it's good at, such as replacing EAV or as a second storage format for retrieving the whole object, and don't shoehorn relational-type data and queries into it.

5.4 *Putting UUIDs everywhere*

An interesting, and often abused, data type in PostgreSQL is UUID (elsewhere known as GUID), which gives you a sequence of 32 hex digits for use as a 128-bit identifier. The variety of UUID that is supported natively in PostgreSQL is UUIDv4, and it gives you values such as 9b287b2a-276d-4ba0-bcc7-b917246169a0.

Without giving it much thought, the uuid data type looks like it's the ideal type to use for worry-free identifiers. It gives you an infinitesimally small probability of having duplicates, and a huge range of values is available for use. It is also opaque and harder to guess than a sequence of integers, being non-serially generated, so it's popular for security-via-obscurity uses.

For reference, let's examine some PostgreSQL data type sizes, as shown in table 5.3.

Table 5.3 PostgreSQL data type sizes

Data type	Size in bytes
boolean	1
int	4
bigint	8
timestamptz	8
double precision	8
uuid	16
text	1 + string bytes (+4 if > 127 bytes)

Let's create a table with uuid identifiers and then index them as the primary key:

```
\timing
Timing is on.

CREATE TABLE test.tab (id uuid, content text);
CREATE
Time: 11.737 ms
```

```
INSERT INTO test.tab
    SELECT gen_random_uuid(), 'test' FROM generate_series(1,100000000);
INSERT 0 100000000
Time: 387838.234 ms (06:27.838)

ALTER TABLE test.tab ADD PRIMARY KEY (id);
ALTER TABLE
Time: 75875.825 ms (01:15.876)
```

That took as long as it took. Now, let's find out our key and index size:

```
\x
Expanded display is on.

SELECT pg_column_size(id) FROM test.tab LIMIT 1;
-[ RECORD 1 ]--+---
pg_column_size | 16

Time: 2.492 ms

\di+ test.tab_pkey
List of relations
-[ RECORD 1 ]-+----------
Schema        | test
Name          | tab_pkey
Type          | index
Owner         | frogge
Table         | tab
Persistence   | permanent
Access method | btree
Size          | 3008 MB
Description   |
```

All right, now that we have a baseline established, let's drop the table and try again with `bigint` serial identifiers:

```
CREATE TABLE test.tab (id bigint, content text);
CREATE TABLE
Time: 5.902 ms

INSERT INTO test.tab SELECT generate_series(1,100000000), 'test';
INSERT 0 100000000
Time: 83137.075 ms (01:23.137)

ALTER TABLE test.tab ADD PRIMARY KEY (id);
ALTER TABLE
Time: 38123.742 ms (00:38.124)
```

That was noticeably faster. Let's check the key and index sizes:

```
SELECT pg_column_size(id) FROM test.tab LIMIT 1;
-[ RECORD 1 ]--+--
pg_column_size | 8
```

```
Time: 1.195 ms

\di+ test.tab_pkey
List of relations
-[ RECORD 1 ]-+----------
Schema        | test
Name          | tab_pkey
Type          | index
Owner         | frogge
Table         | tab
Persistence   | permanent
Access method | btree
Size          | 2142 MB
Description   |
```

Let's put this up on table 5.4 for an easy comparison.

Table 5.4 Differences between UUIDs and serial big integers

	bigint	uuid	Difference
INSERT	01:23	06:28	367% slower
CREATE INDEX	00:38	01:16	100% slower
Index size	2142 MB	3008 MB	40% bigger

These results were to be expected, of course, as UUIDv4 is at the same time larger than a big integer, and it requires generating the next value randomly (something computers are not very good at). Using lots of UUIDs in your table can also push your other data columns to spill over into the *TOAST* table and make everything somewhat less efficient. If the system you're building requires serious performance optimization, these are certainly some things to consider.

> **Lingo: TOAST**
>
> The Oversized-Attribute Storage Technique (TOAST) is PostgreSQL's solution for storing large values inside columns when the page size is just 8 kB and individual rows cannot spill over into the next pages. It supports in-line compression of the values but also stores them out of line (in a different, associated table). You can read a much more detailed description of TOAST at https://www.postgresql.org/docs/current/storage-toast.html.

Most of the time, you don't even need such a big identifier range, as the number of rows you will store will be many orders of magnitude smaller than the available space of UUIDs. Even a PostgreSQL big integer, with 18 quintillion (and change) available values, might offer too big a range for what you're trying to do.

Don't immediately reach out to UUID as a good identifier choice. There are compromises to be made that may be significant for your application.

What is a good case for UUIDs? Possibly as a conflict-free and fast way to generate identifiers for INSERTs from multiple nodes of a distributed system (because there needs to be no coordination regarding the identifiers among the nodes). But there are still disadvantages to this approach, such as that sorting keys such as sequence numbers, timestamps, and node identifiers are not encoded in the UUID. What would probably be a better solution for this usage is Snowflake ID or UUIDv7 (at the time of writing, coming soon to Postgres).

> **TIP** Snowflake IDs and UUIDv7s encode within them precise timestamps and are sortable by time. Additionally, Snowflakes encode a machine-specific ID and local sequence number, enabling greater collision detection and control for distributed systems.

5.5 *Homemade multi-master replication*

For as long as I can remember, people in IT have been asking me: "Can I write to the same filesystem, but on multiple drives?", "Can I write to the same database, but on multiple servers?", etc., which means that essentially they want shared storage but also high availability for that same storage. When I explain that they can't have both without compromises, they then complain that they don't want to take the performance hit of waiting for locking or consistency. It's a fundamental problem that's sadly not well understood: you can only have two out of the following three: consistency, availability, and partition tolerance and one out of consistency or low latency.

CAP/PACELC theorems

In 1998, Eric Brewer stated that distributed systems can only provide two out of the following three guarantees simultaneously: **C**onsistency (that reads get the most recent data or error out), **A**vailability (every request gets a response without the guarantee that it's the most recent data), and network **P**artition tolerance (continued operation despite messages being dropped or delayed). This was formally proven and is now known as the **CAP** theorem.

By extension, in 2010, Daniel Abadi took things a step further and stated that if you have a network **P**artition, you have to choose either **A**vailability or **C**onsistency; **E**lse, the choice is between **L**atency and loss of **C**onsistency. This is much more relevant for our discussion about databases, and specifically PostgreSQL, as we expect them to be online most of the time. It is known as **PACELC** and, as a theorem, it has also received formal proof.

The understanding that we can gain from these theorems is that there are unavoidable tradeoffs to be made when constructing distributed systems.

PostgreSQL replication is a shared-nothing architecture in keeping with the requirement to provide redundancy and high availability. Therefore, currently, the only sane way to have a multi-master database cluster is to establish replication connections between multiple independent database instances running on different nodes.

PostgreSQL offers a wonderful feature in logical replication, and there is also an extension out there called pglogical that gives you some additional features over native logical replication. So, our friends at Frogge Emporium thought, why not use unidirectional logical replication in both directions to make it bi-directional or multi-master? It's easy enough to set this up going in both directions by reading the manual, and we won't go into too many details here (especially as I don't particularly want you to be using it), but let's look at what happens next.

The first problem has to do with the concept of *replication origins,* or which database or node the transaction that's being replicated originated from. Remember that Postgres replication is just WAL getting streamed from one node to the other. If you don't filter out other nodes when you set up the logical replication publications and subscriptions, you will attempt to replicate your own transactions that the other nodes received and sent back to you. Inevitably, this will cause messages to ping-pong across your cluster with the eventual result of this feedback loop being your disks filling up with extraneous WAL.

NOTE   The Write-Ahead Log (WAL) is PostgreSQL's transaction log, used to ensure data integrity. More information on WAL can be found here: https://www.postgresql.org/docs/current/wal-intro.html

Once that is dealt with via the `origin=NONE` or `forward_origins='{}'` options for native logical replication or pglogical, respectively, we can see that our hack appears to work. Let's set up a bi-directional multi-master replication between hosts `alpha` and `beta`, previously configured to allow connectivity between them, and populate a table with sample data.

To set up logical replication, you need to configure things such as `wal_level=logical`, `listen_addresses`, and Host-Based Authentication (HBA) as per the documentation (https://www.postgresql.org/docs/current/logical-replication.html).

From host `alpha`, we create our publication and table:

```
CREATE PUBLICATION multi_alpha FOR ALL TABLES;
CREATE PUBLICATION

CREATE TABLE support.tickets (
    id integer PRIMARY KEY GENERATED ALWAYS AS IDENTITY,
    content text,
    status smallint,
    opened_at timestamptz DEFAULT CURRENT_TIMESTAMP NOT NULL,
    closed_at timestamptz
);
CREATE TABLE

INSERT INTO support.tickets (content) VALUES ('first'), ('second');
INSERT 0 2

SELECT id, content FROM support.tickets;
 id | content
----+---------
  1 | first
  2 | second
(2 rows)
```

Great, that's what we expect to see (see figure 5.1).

Now let's go to host `beta`, create the same schema, subscribe to `alpha`, and create a publication too:

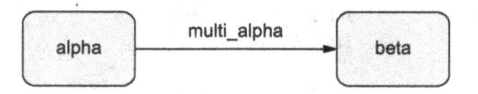

Figure 5.1 Unidirectional logical replication

```
CREATE TABLE support.tickets (
    id integer PRIMARY KEY GENERATED ALWAYS AS IDENTITY,
    content text,
    status smallint,
    opened_at timestamptz DEFAULT CURRENT_TIMESTAMP NOT NULL,
    closed_at timestamptz
);
CREATE TABLE

CREATE SUBSCRIPTION multi_alpha
    CONNECTION 'host=alpha dbname=frogge'
    PUBLICATION multi_alpha
    WITH (origin=NONE);
NOTICE:  created replication slot "multi_alpha" on publisher
CREATE SUBSCRIPTION

SELECT id, content FROM support.tickets;
 id | content
----+---------
  1 | first
  2 | second
(2 rows)

CREATE PUBLICATION multi_beta FOR ALL TABLES;
CREATE PUBLICATION
```

Figure 5.2 shows the arrangement we've set up now.

Nice, so all we need to do now is subscribe `alpha` to `beta`, and we have bidirectional replication. On `alpha`:

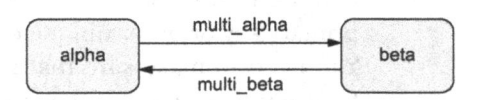

Figure 5.2 Logical replication in both directions

```
CREATE SUBSCRIPTION multi_beta
    CONNECTION 'host=beta dbname=frogge'
    PUBLICATION multi_beta
    WITH (origin=NONE);
WARNING:  subscription "multi_beta" requested copy_data with origin = NONE
  but might copy data that had a different origin
DETAIL:  The subscription being created subscribes to a publication
  ("multi_beta") that contains tables that are written to by other
  subscriptions.
HINT:  Verify that initial data copied from the publisher tables did not
  come from other origins.
NOTICE:  created replication slot "multi_beta" on publisher
CREATE SUBSCRIPTION
```

Err . . . all right? It's warning us that because we set our subscription to ignore other origins, it doesn't really know for sure that the rows we are copying originated on `beta`. Let's insert a row here on `alpha`:

```
INSERT INTO support.tickets (content) VALUES ('third');
INSERT 0 1

SELECT id, content FROM support.tickets;
 id | content
----+----------
  1 | first
  2 | second
  3 | third
(3 rows)
```

And let's check that it arrived on beta:

```
SELECT id, content FROM support.tickets;
 id | content
----+----------
  1 | first
  2 | second
  3 | third
(3 rows)
```

We now have bi-directional logical replication established, and we can write to both nodes, so let's also insert a row on beta:

```
INSERT INTO support.tickets (content) VALUES ('fourth');
ERROR:  duplicate key value violates unique constraint "tickets_pkey"
DETAIL:  Key (id)=(1) already exists.
```

Oops. What happened here? It looks like beta tried to insert a row, but the sequence generating the primary key was still at 1, and we already had that key in the table because it was inserted by node alpha. For logical replication, you generally need a primary key or other unique constraint, and these tend to get values from sequences. You need to make sure that no node reuses sequence numbers from another node because, as we just saw, that creates a data conflict.

Sequence synchronization is a complicated problem; you have to either keep the whole cluster in sync with every write (which is going to be disastrous for performance) or pre-allocate ranges to each node, which is a large administrative burden to manage manually. How do you divide the ranges, what happens when those ranges run out, and how do you deal with new nodes added?

Let's see what happens when we try something different, which you are bound to do in the real world: change the schema of the database. Still on beta, we change the name of column opened_at to logged_at:

```
ALTER TABLE support.tickets RENAME opened_at TO logged_at;
ALTER TABLE
```

Meanwhile, some unaware user on alpha inserts a row:

```
INSERT INTO support.tickets (content) VALUES ('fourth');
INSERT 0 1
```

```
SELECT id, content, opened_at FROM support.tickets WHERE content='fourth';
 id | content |         opened_at
----+---------+---------------------------------
  4 | fourth  | 2024-02-01 19:24:09.162218+00
(1 row)
```

All right so far. Let's check on beta:

```
SELECT id, content, logged_at FROM support.tickets WHERE content='fourth';
 id | content | logged_at
----+---------+-----------
(0 rows)
```

The row didn't make it over. Checking the PostgreSQL log on beta reveals

```
Feb  1 19:24:10 beta postgres[22139]: [2] ERROR:  logical replication target
 relation "support.tickets" is missing replicated column: "opened_at"
Feb  1 19:24:10 beta postgres[22139]: [3] CONTEXT:  processing remote data
 for replication origin "pg_16596" during message type "INSERT" in
 transaction 879, finished at 0/1DB9628
Feb  1 19:24:10 beta postgres[21848]: [9] LOG:  background worker "logical
 replication worker" (PID 22139) exited with exit code 1
```

So, by allowing the schema to become inconsistent, even for a short while, we not only broke data consistency across our cluster, but we also threw the PostgreSQL logical replication worker process in a crash/restart loop.

The lack of provision for consistent DDL replication is a very important blocker for rolling your own multi-master distributed Postgres cluster. Factoring in the orchestration needed to introduce schema changes increases complexity significantly, as the procedure has to be managed carefully to avoid generating conflicts and breaking replication, and it also needs to be balanced against uptime requirements.

Historically, there have been attempts to offer PostgreSQL multi-master solutions, but they focused on higher levels than the actual database, such as the two replication tools originally released in 2007: Londiste, implemented in Python, and Bucardo, written in Perl (the horror!).

Practically speaking, for any enterprise usage requiring full PostgreSQL performance, you would want to go with a native PostgreSQL system performing the replication at the database level. The most advanced and proven solution is EnterpriseDB's Postgres Distributed (PGD), originally developed as 2ndQuadrant's BDR, which is, at the time of writing, proprietary software. A new contender is the source-available Spock solution developed by pgEdge, also forked from 2ndQuadrant's pglogical code.

However, what you should do is spend some time to consider whether you actually need multi-master replication. The ability for the application to write "on any node" may sound good on paper, but it usually comes with baggage that the user has not considered, with implications both on the database administration side and from the application aspect because it needs to be multi-master aware. The only valid use cases I can think of are

- *Extreme availability*—Derived from the instantly available redundancy and the ability to perform minor- and major-version upgrades with no downtime
- *Geo-distribution of data with minimal latency*—Derived from the fact that both reads and writes to the database are local to each physical location

5.6   *Homemade distributed systems*

A distributed system doesn't have to be multi-master. I believe that the normal clustering capabilities of PostgreSQL via streaming and logical replication qualify as being distributed systems in their own right. Therefore, the CAP and PACELC theorems that we read about previously still apply.

I can assure you that attempts to write your own replication mechanism or, even worse, using external Extract/Transform/Load (ETL and ELT) systems or Change Data Capture (CDC) tools to implement replication, are not going to result in a better feature set or better performance than native PostgreSQL replication.

But even when using these reliable and performant methods, you can still get into trouble. For this example, we have already configured streaming replication between the primary host `alpha` and standby host `beta`. On `alpha`, we create a table and insert some data:

```
CREATE TABLE test.accounts (
    id bigint PRIMARY KEY GENERATED ALWAYS AS IDENTITY,
    balance numeric NOT NULL,
    updated_at timestamp with time zone DEFAULT CURRENT_TIMESTAMP
);
CREATE TABLE

INSERT INTO test.accounts (balance) VALUES (100);
TABLE test.accounts;
INSERT 0 1
 id | balance |          updated_at
----+---------+-----------------------------
  1 |     100 | 2024-01-17 19:08:31.0284+00
(1 row)
```

A very common pattern, witnessed many times in the field, is for the application to read from one of the read replicas (PostgreSQL standbys) and write to the primary. We are simulating a minute's worth of replication lag between the two nodes by setting the configuration parameter `recovery_min_apply_delay` to `60000` (milliseconds) on the standby `beta`. The application now reads the account balance from the standby to charge the account and updates it on the primary (as the standby is read-only).

On the standby node `beta`, we read the balance:

```
SELECT balance FROM test.accounts WHERE id=1;
 balance
---------
     100
(1 row)
```

On the primary node `alpha`, we update the balance:

```
UPDATE test.accounts SET balance=90, updated_at=now() WHERE id=1;
TABLE test.accounts;
UPDATE 1
 id | balance |          updated_at
----+---------+------------------------------
  1 |      90 | 2024-02-17 19:09:03.172174+00
(1 row)
```

Meanwhile, another part of the application tries to read the balance to apply the annual bonus gift to the account. On the standby `beta`:

```
SELECT balance FROM test.accounts WHERE id=1;
 balance
---------
     100
(1 row)
```

Based on the inconsistent view of the data, the application mistakenly thinks that the account balance is 100 and applies the gift of +50 to that amount on `alpha`:

```
UPDATE test.accounts SET balance=150, updated_at=now() WHERE id=1;
TABLE test.accounts;
UPDATE 1
 id | balance |          updated_at
----+---------+------------------------------
  1 |     150 | 2024-01-17 19:09:34.442339+00
(1 row)
```

The business has lost 10 monies, and the customer received an unexpected gift due to a violation of the Consistency property of the ACID compliance requirements for databases (**A**tomicity, **C**onsistency, **I**solation, **D**urability).

If PostgreSQL is ACID compliant, what has gone wrong here? Well, the PostgreSQL database server guarantees ACID safety, but what we had here was the application trying to perform *atomic* (or indivisible) transactions across two different database nodes—a *distributed transaction.*

We can see that distributed transactions are not so simple to deal with. What is needed in this case is a transaction with two phases that applies the Two-Phase Commit (2PC) protocol using `PREPARE TRANSACTION` and its associated commands. However, prepared transactions are complicated and hard to implement on systems with latency or replication lag because they should be short-lived. Then they would have to be run exclusively on the primary, negating the benefit of having a read replica. Additionally, they cause the locking of objects in the database, which can cause delays in the application and are very often left behind incomplete (e.g., when an application component crashes or is restarted and loses its state).

On the primary `alpha`

```
TRUNCATE test.accounts;
TRUNCATE TABLE
```

```
INSERT INTO test.accounts (balance) SELECT generate_series(1,100000000);
INSERT 0 100000000
```

Now let's go and run a long-running report query on the standby `beta`:

```
SELECT sum(balance) FROM test.accounts
UNION
SELECT avg(balance) FROM test.accounts;
```

Meanwhile, users keep using the database. Some data changes are made on `alpha`:

```
DELETE FROM test.accounts WHERE id BETWEEN 40000001 AND 40000020;
DELETE 20

VACUUM test.accounts;
VACUUM
```

This deleted a few accounts and cleaned up afterward with VACUUM. But this is what is happening now on `beta`—our query has failed:

```
SELECT sum(balance) FROM test.accounts
UNION SELECT avg(balance)
FROM test.accounts;
ERROR:  canceling statement due to conflict with recovery
DETAIL:  User query might have needed to see row versions that must be removed.
```

Why has this happened? What we have just seen is what's known as a *(distributed) serialization anomaly* or a violation of the ACID transaction Isolation property. Specifically, this is a type of *read-write conflict* or *unrepeatable read*, where a transaction has read the data while a second transaction overwrote some of the data before the first one got the chance to complete.

You can probably prevent this from happening in most cases by enforcing synchronous replication, but that is a horrendous tradeoff and a huge sacrifice of performance that should be considered only when extreme correctness and consistency requirements trump everything else. It is self-evident that the round-trip time required for synchronicity, even with the fastest networks, will result in latency that will bottleneck database performance much sooner than network or PostgreSQL replication performance limits can be reached. The extreme in the other direction is accepting the possibility of *stale reads* or retrieving out-of-date data in a tradeoff for low latency.

These conditions apply to multi-master systems as well. The problem lies with the fact that the application-side logical "transactions" are executed spread across multiple database nodes. If the application is using one node at a time to complete the atomic operation, that's fine because it can be handled using normal conflict management techniques. However, when the application tries to use multiple nodes within the same transaction, we need strong consistency and isolation requirements, which brings us back to PACELC.

Using read replicas to offload some of the work is fine and perfectly valid but not within an application atomic operation that forms a distributed transaction. There is no good or easy way to avoid these types of problems without an authoritative global transaction manager. Global transaction managers necessarily form performance bottlenecks, and they can become a single point of failure.

In closing, building distributed databases is no simple feat because of the limitations of the laws of physics. The industry has struggled for a long time to create solutions that balance competing priorities. Unless your use case is extremely narrow (such as one table, with defined protections and conflict management rules), you will probably not do a good job improvising a distributed solution. The effort required to implement or troubleshoot it will probably inflate the scope of your project to many times what it would have been before.

Summary

- SQL_ASCII is not a character encoding so much as the absence of one. If you don't want to risk mixing encodings irreversibly and you enjoy the ease of automatic character set conversion, make sure you use UTF-8 for your database.
- PostgreSQL RULEs are not related to rules as defined in other DBMSs. RULEs are complicated to understand and are mainly there as Postgres internal machinery. In most cases, they don't behave as the user expects them to, and TRIGGERs are best used instead.
- Using JSON(B) values with relational access patterns makes for less efficient SQL, which is harder to read and might not perform as well. It's better not to mix the SQL and NoSQL paradigms but use each facility for what it's best at doing.
- uuids take up more storage space than even bigints, and indexing them is less efficient. They may guarantee a range of values that you simply don't require for your use case, and an integer index might be enough to guarantee uniqueness.
- Bi-directional or multi-master replication is more complex than what appears at first sight. For practical use in a production system, there is a very long list of prerequisites, considerations, and caveats. If your use case indeed justifies setting up a multi-master system, you are better off using an established multi-master solution whose developers have given thought to these concerns rather than re-inventing the wheel.
- All of the previous points apply to homemade distributed systems as well, and it is not recommended to set out building them unless your scope is very narrowly focused. You need to consider the potential for distributed serialization anomalies and the very real tradeoffs laid out in the CAP and PACELC theorems.

Performance bad practices

This chapter covers
- Going to production with the default PostgreSQL configuration
- Managing connection limits and life cycle
- Letting transactions go on for too long
- Turning off autovacuum may help (for a short while)
- Explicit locking and its associated risks
- Having too few or too many indexes and the effect this has on performance

We know by this point in the book that PostgreSQL is a database powerhouse—a flexible database suited for many uses that can perform extremely well when you ask it nicely. And by asking it nicely, I mean being aware of how it does things so that we can avoid entering code, configuration, and usage patterns that lead to sub-optimal outcomes. It's now time to start discussing some really common ways of hurting performance in Postgres. These may seem obvious to some but surprising to others, so they're well worth exploring.

6.1 Default configuration in production

Let's start at the top: you've just freshly installed PostgreSQL on your shiny new cloud compute instance, memory-optimized with 16 GB of RAM, all set for database awesomeness. You decide to restore your database into this instance from the latest dump of the data you have.

Let's generate a decent-sized database using our old friend `pgbench`—the utility that comes with Postgres for running benchmark tests. First, we create it from the command line, as user `postgres`:

```
createdb pgbench
```

We now have an empty database to populate:

```
pgbench -i -s 1000 pgbench
dropping old tables...
NOTICE:  table "pgbench_accounts" does not exist, skipping
NOTICE:  table "pgbench_branches" does not exist, skipping
NOTICE:  table "pgbench_history" does not exist, skipping
NOTICE:  table "pgbench_tellers" does not exist, skipping
creating tables...
generating data (client-side)...
100000000 of 100000000 tuples (100%) done (elapsed 548.92 s, remaining
0.00 s)
vacuuming...
creating primary keys...
done in 761.00 s (drop tables 0.00 s, create tables 0.03 s, client-side
generate 549.59 s, vacuum 0.74 s, primary keys 210.64 s).
```

> **NOTE** The execution time here isn't really important, as we are just running this to have some data to dump and restore and see how long it takes to restore.

After populating, we perform a dump:

```
pg_dump pgbench > /tmp/pgbench.dump
ls -lah /tmp/pgbench.dump
-rw-rw-r-- 1 postgres postgres 9.9G May 12 19:16 /tmp/pgbench.dump
```

And now we have our dataset in `pgbench.dump`. Let's wipe and restore:

```
dropdb pgbench
createdb pgbench
```

This time, we want to time how long it takes to restore:

```
time psql pgbench < /tmp/pgbench.dump
SET
SET
SET
SET
SET
```

```
    set_config
    -----------

    (1 row)

    SET
    SET
    SET
    SET
    SET
    SET
    CREATE TABLE
    ALTER TABLE
    CREATE TABLE
    ALTER TABLE
    CREATE TABLE
    ALTER TABLE
    CREATE TABLE
    ALTER TABLE
    COPY 100000000
    COPY 1000
    COPY 0
    COPY 10000
    ALTER TABLE
    ALTER TABLE
    ALTER TABLE

    real    44m15.279s
    user    0m13.108s
    sys     0m20.280s
```

Okay, that is certainly a number. Is it good? Is it bad?

Let's change some configuration settings and try again to see whether we can improve upon this. In `postgresql.conf`, we change some selected parameter values to

```
shared_buffers = 3GB            ⟵┘ Default: 128MB ┐
work_mem = 128MB                      ⟵┘ Default: 4MB ┐
maintenance_work_mem = 512MB                ⟵┘ Default: 64MB
```

We need to restart PostgreSQL for the `shared_buffers` change to take effect. After doing that, let's see if we can make a difference:

```
dropdb pgbench
createdb pgbench
time psql pgbench < /tmp/pgbench.dump

...

real    26m17.669s
user    0m12.229s
sys     0m19.520s
```

This is a significant difference: it takes less than 60% of the time we needed with the default `postgresql.conf` values.

So, isn't the default configuration made up of the most commonly used values or those that have empirically given the best results?

No. Unlike other bloated database systems you may be familiar with, the basic idea behind the default configuration of PostgreSQL is to have a baseline system that will "just work" in any machine (within reasonable bounds—your 486SX/25 from 1994 with 24 MB RAM will be below the minimum requirements, but only just). As we can see in the documentation, the default memory allocation for things such as `shared_buffers` is only 128 MB, and `work_mem` just 4 MB, so you have to understand that the default configuration is geared toward simply getting up and running on just about any system, no matter how small.

What we've just done here isn't really "database tuning"—it's basic due diligence when you're testing or staging a PostgreSQL server for production usage. The new `shared_buffers` value increased the memory available to Postgres for buffers (blocks read from disk and/or used in operations), `work_mem` increased the amount of non-shared memory available to individual operations, and `maintenance_work_mem` increased the memory available for operations like CREATE INDEX or VACUUM.

By all means, it doesn't mean that you have to choose some parameter values and stick with them for good, but it does mean that the default configuration will be woefully inadequate for most kinds of production workloads. Additionally, there are many more knobs to tweak than just memory settings.

When you're performing special operations such as data loads, it may even be beneficial to forgo some of the good conventions for running PostgreSQL in production and optimize it for all-out performance at the expense of reliability or crash tolerance (because you don't care about that during a maintenance window that you're using to load a bunch of data into the database).

Obviously, there are other much more varied database workloads besides loading data, and other factors, such as concurrency, come into play. However, as we demonstrated through this example, and as you will find in the following sections in this chapter, there are ways to adapt your system to better suit them. Just don't trust the default configuration to be sufficient for any sort of realistic workload.

6.2   *Improper memory allocation*

So now we have awareness of the fact that you shouldn't take PostgreSQL into production usage with the default settings. Specifically, in the previous section, we allocated more RAM for certain uses, and that helped improve performance.

Let's run a baseline standard `pgbench` test for 5 minutes (300 seconds) with the database we've just restored to see what sort of performance figures we get:

```
pgbench -U postgres -h test01 -c 100 -j 24 -T 300 pgbench
pgbench (17.0 (Ubuntu 17.0-1.pgdg24.04+1))
starting vacuum...end.
transaction type: <builtin: TPC-B (sort of)>
```

```
scaling factor: 1000
query mode: simple
number of clients: 100
number of threads: 24
maximum number of tries: 1
duration: 300 s
number of transactions actually processed: 323961
number of failed transactions: 0 (0.000%)
latency average = 92.347 ms
latency stddev = 60.183 ms
initial connection time = 824.391 ms
tps = 1082.342941 (without initial connection time)
```

> **TIP** Make sure you run benchmarks from another host in order to avoid overloading the database server with too much work. Ideally, the host you run the tests from should be powerful enough to be able to oversaturate the database server with requests.

On this system, with the configuration settings we selected before, we're getting 1,082 transactions per second (TPS) with a concurrency of 100 clients. We want to give our queries the best chance of executing smoothly and successfully, so we ramp up `shared_buffers` and `work_mem` to see if this will improve our performance further:

```
shared_buffers = 12GB                    ←┐  Previous
work_mem = 2GB           ←┐  Previous        value: 3GB
                          │  value: 128MB
```

We restart Postgres for the change to take effect and re-run our `pgbench` test:

```
pgbench -U postgres -h test01 -c 100 -j 24 -T 300 pgbench
pgbench (17.0 (Ubuntu 17.0-1.pgdg24.04+1))
starting vacuum...end.
transaction type: <builtin: TPC-B (sort of)>
scaling factor: 1000
query mode: simple
number of clients: 100
number of threads: 24
maximum number of tries: 1
duration: 300 s
number of transactions actually processed: 319069
number of failed transactions: 0 (0.000%)
latency average = 93.930 ms
latency stddev = 65.995 ms
initial connection time = 297.914 ms
tps = 1062.819169 (without initial connection time)
```

We can see that the TPS stayed roughly the same, if not a little worse. It therefore looks like we may have been tuning our parameters in the wrong direction!

Now let's find out what would happen if 1000—10 times as many—clients hit the database with these same settings by setting `max_connections = 1000`, restarting the cluster for the change to come into effect, and simulating a heavy workload:

```
pgbench -U postgres -h test01 -c 1000 -j 24 -T 300 -P 10 pgbench
pgbench (17.0 (Ubuntu 17.0-1.pgdg24.04+1))
starting vacuum...end.
progress: 10.0 s, 147.8 tps, lat 2532.664 ms stddev 1511.880, 0 failed
^C
```

After the first 10 seconds, the test hangs, and we can see that there is something wrong. We cancel with `Ctrl+C`, and by looking at the system logs on the database server, we find

```
kernel: Out of memory: Killed process 15255 (postgres) total-vm:1674628kB,
anon-rss:3208kB, file-rss:5760kB, shmem-rss:0kB, UID:107 pgtables:152kB
oom_score_adj:0
kernel: systemd-journald[436]: /dev/kmsg buffer overrun, some messages lost.
kernel: systemd-journald[436]: Under memory pressure, flushing caches.
systemd[1]: postgresql@17-main.service: A process of this unit has been
killed by the OOM killer.
systemd[1]: postgresql@17-main.service: Failed with result 'oom-kill'.
systemd[1]: postgresql@17-main.service: Consumed 1min 18.570s CPU time.
```

> **WARNING** Running a heavy workload such as the previous stress test, especially when PostgreSQL's memory allocation hasn't been properly configured, can crash your system in unpredictable ways.

This `oom-killer` is Linux's Out-of-Memory (OOM) killer, run by the Linux kernel to recover memory when the system is critically low on memory. It chooses processes to terminate based on their OOM score (found in `/proc/<PID>/oom_score`). What this means is that there is a possibility that it may not choose the fresh PostgreSQL backend process, which is using lots of RAM, but some other necessary process or application on your system that happens to use a lot of memory.

But why did we run out of memory? Remember, we allocated 12 GB of `shared_buffers` and 2 GB of `work_mem`. This means that we potentially allocated 2 GB of RAM for *each node* of the execution plan *for each* running query. Keep in mind that each of the 1,000 connected sessions may run a query utilizing many nodes. It's obvious that we don't have enough available RAM to do that, and we need to be aware that things can get out of hand quickly if we have complex queries with many plan nodes and/or parallel execution.

> **NOTE** It is important to avoid the OOM killer because when a backend process gets killed, PostgreSQL terminates all other active backends to avoid operating with shared memory that may have potentially been corrupted. Postgres will then go into crash recovery mode, which means that this may trigger a failover to a replica or other ugliness.

You should only allocate enough `work_mem` to cover your queries' needs and no more. As with many things in this book, this is entirely dependent on the workload. If you choose a small amount of `work_mem`, more complex queries such as those involving sorting and aggregation may run out of RAM for their operations and spill over into temporary files on disk, which is many orders of magnitude slower than in-memory operation. However, we saw firsthand that choosing a work_mem size that is too big can jeopardize your queries because the system may run out of memory and kill their processes or, even worse, PostgreSQL itself or some other critical process. Fortunately, work_mem can be SET at the session level, so we can configure the system with some sensible default and only increase work_mem for those queries that actually need the extra memory to run.

Similarly, there are recommendations out there that the ideal amount of shared_buffers is 25% of available RAM, or any number of other formulas to calculate it. You should probably not follow these blindly as the right value is again workload dependent: OLTP usage may benefit from having a large shared memory that can fit the part of the dataset that's in use, whereas the same large shared_buffers may be wasted on an OLAP workload that only visits each buffer once. You may even have mixed use, which will require you to take a careful look at balancing the memory allocation. In this case, our shared_buffers choice is clearly excessive because it doesn't help with our workload at all.

> **WARNING**   Be careful to always include the unit used after your value. If you don't, the default unit used for shared_buffers is the buffer (8,192 bytes), so you're specifying how many buffers to allocate; therefore, there's a very big difference between 1024MB and 1024 (buffers), which is just 8 megabytes. Confusingly, in other places, such as work_mem and maintenance_work_mem, Postgres uses kB as the unit; for min_wal_size and max_wal_size it uses MB; and so on.

Proper memory allocation is important, and you're stuck between a rock and a hard place because the defaults will most likely be insufficient for your workload, but bumping them up significantly may cause even worse performance and stability problems. Oftentimes, you can't avoid trial and error as your workload is what's going to dictate how much you need for each value. As a reminder, you should never try things out in production, but rather on staging systems with similar data and running similar workloads.

6.3   *Having too many connections*

It is quite common to see PostgreSQL configurations with large connection limits, such as max_connections = 2000. In my experience, it seems to be widely believed by developers that the more connections the database can handle, the better it will be for the application.

Let us try out an experiment to see how PostgreSQL will hold up to large numbers of connections. As we saw in the previous section, our memory allocation strategy proved dangerous, so we are now going to choose some more reasonable values for our server. By allocating a more conservative value for shared_buffers and especially work_mem, as it is relevant to the number of queries we're running, we are reducing the possibility of running out of memory. We will also change the connection limit to allow 2,000 clients:

```
shared_buffers = 1GB
work_mem = 4MB
max_connections = 2000
```

After a Postgres restart, which is necessary for our changes to take effect, we bring out pgbench again and run a series of tests with different numbers of clients, starting with 2,000:

```
pgbench -U postgres -h test01 -c 2000 -j 24 -T 300 pgbench
pgbench (17.0 (Ubuntu 17.0-1.pgdg24.04+1))
starting vacuum...end.
transaction type: <builtin: TPC-B (sort of)>
scaling factor: 1000
query mode: simple
number of clients: 2000
number of threads: 24
maximum number of tries: 1
duration: 300 s
number of transactions actually processed: 84835
number of failed transactions: 0 (0.000%)
latency average = 5535.267 ms
latency stddev = 13696.921 ms
initial connection time = 69772.527 ms
tps = 352.083626 (without initial connection time)
```

We next try 1,500, 1,000, 500, and so on. The results are shown in table 6.1.

Table 6.1 Test results showing TPS and latency with various numbers of clients

Number of clients	TPS	Latency average
2,000	352.1	5,535.267 ms
1,500	506.8	2,869.986 ms
1,000	586.1	1,694.616 ms
500	628.4	794.688 ms
250	635.7	392.554 ms
125	556.9	224.411 ms
63	613.0	102.758 ms
32	572.3	55.907 ms
16	301.8	53.009 ms

Let's plot this table out onto a chart and examine the results. Looking at the plot, we see that the TPS roughly plateaus between 1,500 and 32 clients with low values at the extremes of 2,000 and 16 clients.

The latency, though, shows a clear logarithmic trend, going from a very bad 5.5 seconds to stabilizing around 53 ms below 32 clients, as shown in figure 6.1.

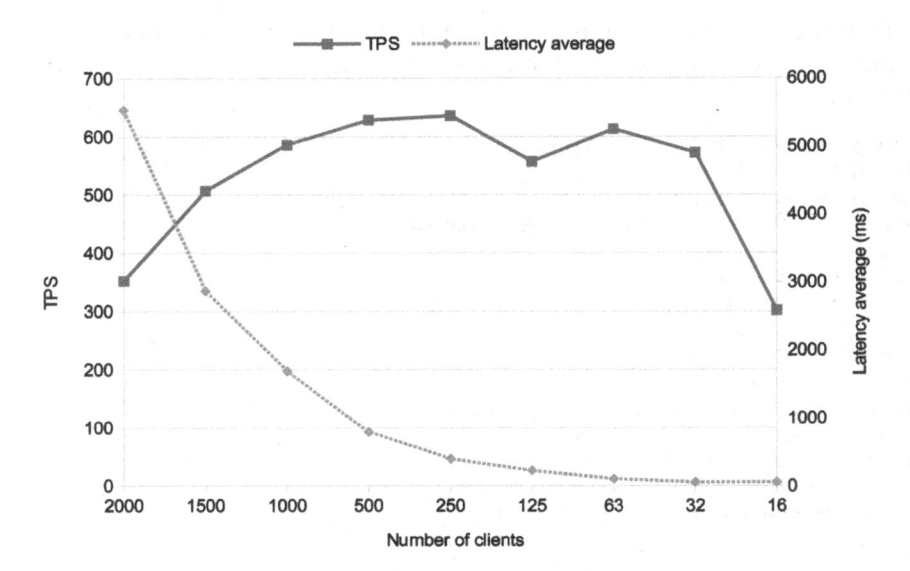

Figure 6.1   TPS and latency test result plot with various numbers of clients

What does this all tell us? It tells us that we requested excessive concurrency, which was too much for our modestly sized server. When serving 2,000 clients the server was struggling, which is reflected by the low TPS and high latency. Nonetheless, does it seem like it was more able to deal with the workload between 1,500 and 32 clients?

Yes, at first glance, it does, but the latency values tell the whole story of how overloaded the server was, with it only recovering at 32 clients and below. It was only able to sustain this TPS plateau by trading latency for higher concurrency, which, incidentally, is also how you can get around network latency because multiple connections make it less relevant for total throughput. The low TPS value at 16 clients just means that we weren't giving the server as much work as it could perform.

Multitasking aside, a computer can only do as much as it's got the resources for. If you're asking for 2,000 things to be done at the same time and don't have 2,000 CPU cores, you should understand that this is unreasonable. As an empirical rule of thumb, you shouldn't have more PostgreSQL connections than four times the number of your cores. But again, don't use my guidance as canon because your optimal ratio is bound to be workload specific.

Lightweight Lock contention

Accessing the same objects from multiple connections may incur many Lightweight Locks (`LWLocks` or "latches" as they are known in other database systems). Those are part of PostgreSQL's Multi-Version Concurrency Control (MVCC) mechanism and protect data in shared memory to ensure consistent reads and writes. Under high concurrency, a `LWLock` may become heavily contended, and there is no fair queuing for `LWLocks`; it's more or less random. Therefore, lots of lockers can slow each other down and reduce overall query throughput. A good indication that you may have excessive concurrency is lots of `wait_event_type: LWLock` appearing in the `pg_stat_activity` monitoring view.

For PostgreSQL to have a performance headroom to better deal with increases or spikes in usage, you should trade off application-side latency for overall database server health. Instead of immediately opening as many client connections as the application requires, restrict the number of clients and make the application requests queue (hopefully not for long) for an available connection. This means that the application should be able to wait, so you may have to increase timeouts on that end.

If you cannot restrict the number of connections the application requests, a good solution is to use connection pooling. A connection pooler such as PgBouncer can be inserted between the application and database and implement this nicely for you. It can accept thousands of connections from the application but only allow as many clients as you specify through to PostgreSQL and make the rest wait for their turn. When you give this a try, and if you monitor database activity via `pg_stat_activity`, you may find that the real concurrency (i.e., how many things your application is actually trying to do at the same time inside the database versus how many connections it wants to open) is much lower than what you expected. In the wild, applications with 5,000 connections have been seen only running about 15 to 30 active tasks concurrently in the database.

Regarding excessive concurrency, remember that PostgreSQL is a multiprocess system with a "process per user" model. This means that every client connects to a backend process, and all this is coordinated by the postmaster supervisor process. PostgreSQL's inter-process communication (IPC) is via semaphores and shared memory.

This tells us that if we have too many processes running in our system, this incurs operating system overhead and brings the risk of excessive CPU context switching. Needless to say, this is bad for server performance.

NOTE *Process thrashing* is when you have too many processes for them to get scheduled effectively, and each one gets a tiny slice of execution time, progressing very slowly as the system spends more time performing context switches than it does executing the actual processes. Additionally, the excessive memory usage caused by too many backends may cause thrashing of memory in and out of swap, and we remember that disk access is vastly slower than RAM.

To wrap up, while you may think that you are making your application run faster by parallelizing, you may actually be hampering its performance by swamping your database server with too much work. "Throttle" it, or introduce latency on the application side, to save your DB server's performance. It sounds counterintuitive, but it doesn't necessarily slow anything down—your queries will execute faster on a server that's not overloaded!

6.4   Having Idle connections

Let's now examine why you shouldn't keep idle connections around on your PostgreSQL server.

6.4.1   What Is MVCC?

It's worth our while to briefly discuss PostgreSQL's transactions and its concurrency control at this point. PostgreSQL uses Multi-Version Concurrency Control (MVCC) rather than locking to enable high concurrency and achieve high performance. With MVCC, reading from the database never has to wait. Writing to the DB doesn't block reading, and reading doesn't block writing. As you may have guessed from the name, the way the MVCC system works is that each write creates a new version of a tuple (row). We, therefore, have what's called *snapshot isolation*: each transaction has a point-in-time consistent view (or snapshot) of the data. Postgres uses timestamps and transaction IDs (XIDs) to enable the activity tracking that makes enforcing these consistent views possible—that is, determine which tuples are visible from each transaction. A snapshot, which contains the earliest still-active transaction, the first as-yet-unassigned transaction, and the list of active transactions, is obtained by each transaction from the Transaction Manager. You can get a fresh snapshot via the function `pg_current_snapshot()`. Figure 6.2 shows what the timeline of PostgreSQL transactions looks like.

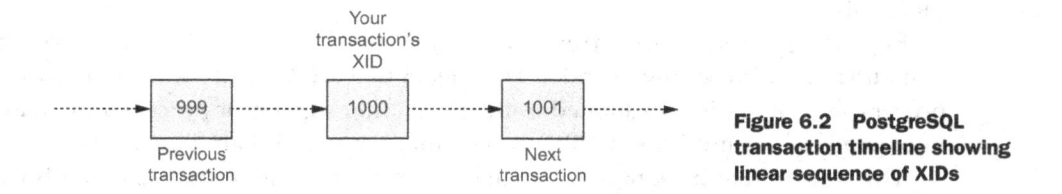

Figure 6.2   PostgreSQL transaction timeline showing linear sequence of XIDs

From within transaction 1000, you may or may not be able to see the results of transactions 999 and 1001, depending on whether they were committed or aborted before transaction 1000 completes.

6.4.2   The problem with Idle connections

It's easy to think that idle sessions are innocuous. After all, they're not performing any task in the database, so it should logically follow that they don't affect the database's performance.

It is quite common to see systems in production with thousands of idle connections, especially when language-side connection poolers are used (those offered by the programming language or framework, as opposed to intermediary or server-side). Those then keep thousands of database sessions open in order to have a pool of connections available to hand over to the application. The worst culprits are usually Java frameworks that tend to distance developers so far away from the database through abstractions that they usually have no idea how a database operates or what they should and shouldn't do.

We do know, though, that PostgreSQL's MVCC mechanism maintains snapshots for each and every transaction. This means that every time a transaction requests a snapshot before beginning to do its work, Postgres has to examine all open connections to compile the snapshot information. This is a consequence of having to check what each session is doing—we don't know that they're idle until we check. As veteran PostgreSQL developer Tom Lane succinctly put it in an email response to the pgsql-performance mailing list, this makes the (computational) cost of taking a snapshot proportional to the total number of connections.

As a result, even when your session is sitting idle doing nothing, it is consuming system resources and slowing down subsequent connections being opened, a situation that could be described as snapshot contention.

How do we end up with idle connections? It can simply be poor application design, which may be unintentional, such as allowing many connections for no reason, or intentional, such as storing application queues or states of an application with many components or workers in a single database. Or, as we previously mentioned, it can be an attempt to maintain throughput and mitigate latency through increasing concurrency. It's also a way to deal with sudden spikes in requests (although the preferred solution would rather put a connection pooler in between the application and database).

This doesn't mean that the connections are totally unused; it is sufficient for them to remain idle most of the time (e.g., because of the application not requesting queries very often). Even so, they negatively affect the performance of those connections that are indeed active in a very real and measurable way.

Optimizations for connection handling, specifically in dealing with the process of obtaining a snapshot for a new connection, arrived in PostgreSQL 14, eliminating much of the bottleneck but not entirely. Obtaining snapshots for many incoming connections is still computationally significant, even if the situation has improved. Moreover, even if the relevant PostgreSQL internals have been optimized, you still have to remember that it's a multiprocess system—every connection requires a new backend process, and the operating system overhead of having to do process accounting, scheduling, and IPC for thousands of extra processes is certainly not negligible.

As a final note, and as a deterrent, you should also consider the possibility that the application might suddenly decide to utilize thousands of those idle connections at the same time due to a spike in usage (e.g., markets opening). After all, these connections have been made available to it. Such a scenario is bound to cause a server performance meltdown.

Using a transaction pooler, such as PgBouncer in Transaction Mode, can help if you find yourself in a situation where you need to open many connections that may be mostly idling. PgBouncer will just hand over the unused connections to some other transaction that needs them, thereby mitigating the system overhead. This is preferable to using `idle_session_timeout` to automatically close idle sessions, which may not be appreciated by unaware clients or applications.

6.5   *Allowing long-running transactions*

PostgreSQL gurus will invariably tell you to avoid having long-running transactions. But why? First of all, let's differentiate between sessions that are active and just taking a long time to complete and those that are idle, doing nothing inside a transaction. We will start by examining the latter.

6.5.1   *Idle in transaction*

Simply put, a session that is `idle in transaction`, as reported by `pg_stat_activity`, is one that has begun a transaction, is not running an active query, and has not rolled back or committed the transaction. A common case is when a client opens a connection and runs `BEGIN` to start a transaction and then lets the connection idle. Badly written applications have been known to use this access pattern. Many of us have also seen database administrators or developers initiating a connection and then leaving the client running with the connection open as they leave for the day (or for their vacation). If they happened to start a transaction before going away, their session will be left `idle in transaction`.

If you remember from our short description of MVCC, PostgreSQL determines the visibility of tuples by using transaction IDs, and this is how the Isolation property of ACID is guaranteed for compliance. If you remember, we examined ACID violations of the Isolation property in chapter 5, section 5.6.

> **Locks in PostgreSQL**
>
> The concept of locks in Postgres is not complicated: from a database user perspective, locks are obtained on the table level (e.g., ACCESS SHARE) or the row level (e.g., FOR UPDATE). These then either permit or prevent access to other transactions that are trying to "use" (i.e., obtain a lock on) the same thing. This is determined by way of lock types being conflicting with each other. So, if someone attempts to obtain an ACCESS EXCLUSIVE lock on a table, that will conflict with all other types of locks, so nobody can obtain a SHARE lock on the same table.

Now, let's explore a scenario where a client leaves a session idle in transaction:

```
Client A
-----------------------
BEGIN;
SELECT * FROM mytable;
(...)
```

The SELECT statement completes and returns results (...). Client A leaves the connection and transaction open.

Now another client connects and attempts to add a column to mytable. The table is not in use at this point, right? So the client should be able to run this DDL command:

```
Client A                       | Client B
-------------------------------+----------------------
BEGIN;                         |
SELECT * FROM mytable;         |
(...)                          |
                               | ALTER TABLE mytable
                               | ADD description text;
                               | *hangs*
```

Client B's request waits forever (or, at least, until Client A's transaction ends). Client A's transaction has taken the most innocuous of locks, an ACCESS SHARE lock, to read the table. Even though this is a lock mode that can't even block others from reading or writing to the table, it conflicts with the ACCESS EXCLUSIVE lock that the ALTER TABLE ADD (COLUMN) statement requires.

What's worse, while Client B waits its turn to obtain the lock it needs on mytable, any other transaction or query that needs to access mytable will be blocked because they have to queue behind it!

```
Client A                       | Client B                  | Client C
-------------------------------+---------------------------+--------------------------
BEGIN;                         |                           |
SELECT * FROM mytable;         |                           |
(...)                          |                           |
                               | ALTER TABLE mytable       |
                               | ADD description text;     |
                               | *hangs*                   |
                               |                           | SELECT 1 FROM mytable;
                               |                           | *hangs*
```

However, Client A simply ending the first transaction will unblock everything:

```
Client A                       | Client B                  | Client C
-------------------------------+---------------------------+--------------------------
BEGIN;                         |                           |
SELECT * FROM mytable;         |                           |
(...)                          |                           |
                               | ALTER TABLE mytable       |
                               | ADD description text;     |
                               |                           |
                               |                           | SELECT 1 FROM mytable;
                               |                           |
END;                           |                           |
COMMIT                         |                           |
                               | ALTER TABLE              |
                               |                           | ?column?
                               |                           | ----------
                               |                           | (0 rows)
```

NOTE   END is a PostgreSQL extension to the SQL language that is equivalent to COMMIT.

Let's take a brief moment to talk about VACUUM. MVCC gives you amazing write and rollback performance, but it requires maintenance operations. Namely, VACUUM is the operation that removes "dead" tuples (old row versions) that are no longer visible by any transaction and are therefore not needed. PostgreSQL runs this automatically to perform maintenance on the database from time to time, and this is what we call *auto-vacuum*. As with everything else, it needs to use locks, and it waits to obtain them.

Worryingly, idle in transaction connections can prevent (auto)vacuum from running if they have modified any data or are using an isolation level such as REPEATABLE READ or SERIALIZABLE. VACUUM will also not be able to remove recently dead rows that must remain visible by this open transaction. Forgoing VACUUM for some time can bring on bloat (dead rows left over inside the table), which has serious implications for performance and disk usage.

WARNING   Worse, autovacuum also does other things such as "freezing" old table rows. If autovacuum is prevented from running over an extended period, this can cause transaction ID wraparound, a related failure mode that we'll discuss in the following section.

One way to prevent connections from staying idle in transaction is designing your application properly (ha!). Another way is setting a value for the configuration parameter idle_in_transaction_session_timeout. This will prevent sessions from sticking around in idle in transaction state for longer than the specified number of milliseconds, thereby preventing sessions from holding on to locks or blocking VACUUM for unreasonable amounts of time. However, there is a tradeoff here: if your application needs to run processing for some time after initiating the transaction before writing back and/or closing it, the timeout needs to be sufficient to accommodate that. Moreover, your application needs to be able to tolerate these types of session timeout disconnections.

For more information on this, see the PostgreSQL documentation: https://www.postgresql.org/docs/current/runtime-config-client.html#GUC-IDLE-IN-TRANSACTION-SESSION-TIMEOUT.

6.5.2   *Long-running queries in general*

Many of the same points still hold true for long-running queries. Remember, even if you haven't explicitly started a transaction, each query will run within its own implicit transaction.

Each of these transactions will obtain a snapshot of the database, as previously mentioned, and hold it for as long as it is executing its statement. The same will be true for as long as a cursor is open.

TIP   When we're talking about queries with long execution times, we mean actively running ones, not queries that are slow to complete because, for example, they are blocked. `now() - query_start` under `pg_stat_activity` is the duration that you'll be looking for.

Autovacuum will skip the cleanup of dead tuples if a transaction is holding a snapshot obtained before those tuples were changed or deleted. Additionally, if a query needs to obtain a lock that conflicts with it, autovacuum will voluntarily give up the lock and stop what it's doing. Obviously, if the query goes on for very long, autovacuum won't get the chance to run. All of these, again, can lead to problems with bloat and XID wraparound.

Lastly, long queries can cause query conflicts in a replication scenario. For instance, when heavy updates on the primary are changing data that is simultaneously being selected on the standby server, this can lead to the queries on the standby being cancelled. The query cancellation is due to the conflict caused by needing to apply WAL that will affect the data being selected.

Long-running transactions can also cause replication lag when synchronous or logical replication is in use, as changes are only replicated after they've been committed. This can be mitigated by using asynchronous streaming replication or enabling logical replication streaming of large in-progress transactions, respectively. You can do the former by setting `synchronous_standby_names` to an empty string in `postgresql.conf`, and the latter by enabling the `streaming` parameter when setting up your logical replication connection with `CREATE SUBSCRIPTION`.

It is relatively safe (for the database, perhaps not for the client application) to `SELECT pg_cancel_backend(<PID>);` to stop long-running queries. However, as we've already seen, terminating backends—for example, by killing (`SIGKILL`) the PID of the backend—is very different and much more dangerous to use, as it may bring the entire server instance down into recovery mode when PostgreSQL detects that one of its backends has been killed. `pg_terminate_backend(<PID>)` is safer to use, but it is much less graceful than `pg_cancel_backend()` as it aborts the transaction and disconnects the user forcibly, which may cause problems in the application.

6.6 *High transaction rate*

Having the ability to process transactions at a high rate is generally desirable, but is having a sustained high transaction rate actually good for your PostgreSQL database?

6.6.1 *XID wraparound*

As we mentioned previously, PostgreSQL assigns an identifier (XID) to each transaction, and those are used as the basis for the MVCC mechanism. We just write into the main data area (or *heap*) of the table, and each tuple we write has an `xmin` (the XID that inserted it) and an `xmax` (if deleted, the XID that deleted it). Remember, updates in PostgreSQL are an insert and a delete operation.

> **TIP** You can find out the current transaction ID via `SELECT txid_current();`.

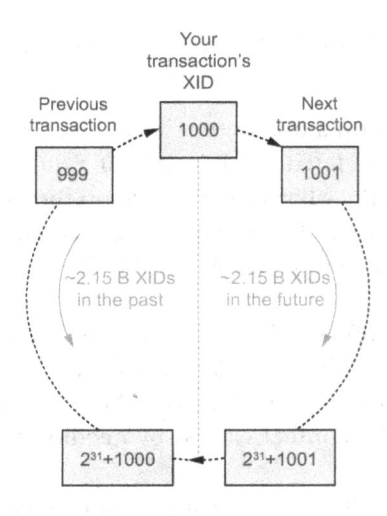

Figure 6.3 Depiction of PostgreSQL's transaction IDs as a circular space

XIDs are unsigned 32-bit integers, so they have a range of approximately 4.3 billion values.

You should think of this as a circular space, with a visibility horizon: from the perspective of your transaction, there have been ~2.15 B XIDs in the past, and there are ~2.15 B XIDs in the future, as shown in figure 6.3.

Imagine that we just zoomed out from Figure 6.2, and what appeared like a straight line was, in reality, a segment of a circle. When we next move to transaction 1001, there will still be the same number of billions of XIDs behind and ahead of it—as if `txid_current()` is the pointer on the *Wheel of Fortune!*

In the preceding section, we referred to the *XID wraparound* failure mode. This happens when you try to read a very old tuple that is more than ~2.15 billion XIDs in the past from your perspective. By looking at Figure 6.3, we can easily understand that such an XID will be in the space of future XIDs from your viewpoint and should be invisible! This precipitates an impossible situation where we don't know if the tuple is from the past or the future and can cause data inconsistency or loss. PostgreSQL tries to prevent XID wraparound at all costs by running a noninterruptible anti-wrap-around autovacuum that tries to rectify the situation. This can slow your system down to a crawl and is unavoidable once it starts. But how do we get to that point, and how do we prevent this from happening?

We prevent XID wraparound through a trick called *freezing*. VACUUM will go through each table and mark very old tuples that are known to be definitively in the past with a "frozen" flag. This marks them as being "very old" and outside our current space of XIDs, therefore making the frozen tuples safe in terms of their xmin. In a sense, it's reclaiming previously used XIDs from tuples.

The only thing we need to care about now is ensuring that this VACUUM FREEZE operation happens before XID wraparound occurs, and this is what the special anti-wraparound autovacuum is doing, albeit in a rushed manner. It kicks in when PostgreSQL believes you are close to running out of XIDs (this is configurable via `autovacuum_freeze_max_age`). As we hinted in the previous section, sessions in `idle in transaction` state can hold back the XID horizon and cause freezing of old rows to be deferred.

6.6.2 Burning through lots of XIDs

It's common for users and developers to take advantage of PostgreSQL's superior INSERT/UPDATE speed and just throw tons of data into the database with little performance consequence. Each write "uses" an XID, and it's common for heavy OLTP workloads to burn through 2 billion transactions in a short time. I have witnessed a database that went through this amount in the space of a week! This volume of activity makes it dangerously likely that our transaction burn rate will outrun autovacuum (and consequently automatic freezing), pushing us toward XID wraparound error.

So, with regard to achieving impressive transaction rates, just because you can, doesn't mean you should. What can you do when you find yourself having a high XID burn rate?

First, you should examine whether batching can help. Does your application really need to commit everything atomically? Consider the simple fact that instituting a transaction commit batch of size 1000 will bring your application down to about 1/1000th the previous XID burn rate, solving your transaction rate issue pretty much immediately. Your application developers can also try to reorganize all those incoming rows into more efficient structures that will store the results of multiple operations.

Another thing you can try is to increase the effectiveness of autovacuum by tuning the relevant configuration parameters to make it more aggressive. This will, consequently, make tuple freezing more efficient.

Check out how to tune freezing in the PostgreSQL documentation at https://www.postgresql.org/docs/current/routine-vacuuming.html.

A bit of architectural advice that is good to remember is that you don't want to be storing too much data (that you may never use) inside your database. Many organizations tend to store every bit of data that comes across their systems in case it ever becomes useful in the future for analysis purposes or otherwise. Check with stakeholders and inform them of the risks and costs of such a course of action and eliminate data nobody will ever look at from your ingestion flow.

An alternative for dealing with data that is useful but of a very high volume is to crunch or resample it right away and only store summaries, averages, or trends—if that's what you're going to need in the future anyway.

6.7 Turning off autovacuum/autoanalyze

Because of the design choice to use MVCC in Postgres, VACUUM is a necessary evil. At least, some people see it as evil because it appears to be a background process that eats resources and does nothing for their workload.

As a result, when folks who think this way find out that there's something called autovacuum running VACUUMs all the time inside their database, their response is to try to find a way to disable this pesky daemon. After all, it seems to be consuming system resources, often at the most inopportune times for their daily workload.

They often feel vindicated when turning it off results in performance gains, and there is a noticeable difference for their developers and end users to see.

Well, at least for a while. To see why this is a recipe for disaster, let's first examine what VACUUM does.

We already know that it cleans out dead tuples from our database. You can think of this as garbage collection that frees up space inside a table's data files because those tuples are not removed from the table until VACUUM is run on it. This cleared-out space can then be reused by Postgres. Next, VACUUM does the same for table indexes by performing the corresponding cleanup. We also saw that it can freeze old table rows to prevent XID wraparound. Finally, with the command VACUUM ANALYZE, we run an ANALYZE operation after the vacuum to collect useful statistics on the table's content, which helps the query planner choose suitable plans by considering the nature of data in the table.

Now let's see specifically how autovacuum operates. It's all in the name really—it pops up automatically from time to time to see if tables need vacuuming or analyzing and then performs VACUUM and/or ANALYZE on those tables. It's a way to worry less about all of the things in the previous paragraph, as it takes care of bloat prevention, query plan optimization, and XID wraparound safety.

If it isn't already obvious, these are important functions—so important that even when you choose to disable autovacuum in PostgreSQL's configuration, it still keeps an eye out for XID exhaustion situations, ready to intervene. The bottom line is that, the same as backups (more on that in a later chapter), maintenance operations should be automatic and not rely on manual intervention.

Any short-term performance gain from disabling autovacuum will soon be outweighed by the detrimental effect of bloat accumulation. From a performance aspect, having bloat simply means going through additional data on disk that is junk when scanning tables and indexes, slowing down queries that would otherwise perform better.

Letting bloat get out of hand can result in your tables ballooning in terms of size on disk, and this space is then non-reclaimable by simple VACUUM, which can't hand the space back to the operating system but just marks it as free inside the file for Postgres to use. To free up the disk space, you would then need to run a different command called VACUUM FULL, which is slow, requires even more disk space, and is highly disruptive to database operation, as it totally locks out any use of that table. This means that you should never call VACUUM FULL on a table that's in use unless you fully understand the implications.

Also, by overlooking the importance of gathering optimizer statistics, you can run the risk of reduced query performance. The optimizer needs to know data characteristics such as cardinality, number of distinct values, and other histograms in order to choose the best plan for executing a query.

Much of the same holds true for just leaving autovacuum with its very conservative defaults, which will be ineffective for production workloads—remember how we saw that PostgreSQL out-of-the-box defaults are too conservative for real-world usage in the first section of this chapter. Simply reducing autovacuum's potency by turning down those parameters will also have the same detrimental effects on bloat and statistics gathering.

The recommendation here, counterintuitively, is to *increase* autovacuum's effectiveness the more write-intensive your workload becomes instead of decreasing it to balance out resource consumption. You should bite the bullet and accept that a portion of system resources will be dedicated to this MVCC maintenance operation that keeps your database running properly under the demanding conditions that you are imposing on it. For the time being—meaning until PostgreSQL gets additional storage backends—you can't avoid VACUUM.

If your server can't cope with both your workload and the autovacuum that this requires, you may need to look into scaling up your system, scaling down your workload by identifying costly queries, or adjusting your database architecture (e.g., by splitting the data, using replication, etc.).

> **TIP** Keep in mind that you can override autovacuum settings on individual tables if the defaults are not suitable for a subset of your tables.

Autovacuum configuration parameters, including how to tune it up or down using cost-based delays and sleep time, are documented here: https://www.postgresql.org/docs/current/runtime-config-autovacuum.html.

6.8 Not using EXPLAIN (ANALYZE)

You'd be surprised to find out how few people EXPLAIN and EXPLAIN ANALYZE their queries to find out how they get executed by the database. It might be because of the weird output format that many find hard to read at first or because they don't know what a Recheck Cond on a Bitmap Heap Scan is and where to look it up. However, judging from other DBMSs, PostgreSQL's query plans are very detailed and well-documented by comparison.

It is surprising because in most cases where the complaint is "my query is too slow," EXPLAIN can help you figure out why it is taking so long to execute. The planner/optimizer generates a multitude of possible execution plans for the query; costs them according to its internal logic, previously gathered statistics, and configuration; and finally chooses the one with the lowest cost because it will have the best chance of being the fastest to run. This is why, in the previous section, we saw how important it is to allow autovacuum/autoanalyze to gather the aforementioned planner statistics.

EXPLAIN ANALYZE goes a step further than showing you the chosen query plan. It tells you the actual timings of how long each component of the statement took to run.

> **WARNING** EXPLAIN ANALYZE actually *runs* the SQL statement, as opposed to simple EXPLAIN, which only plans it. This means that if your statement changes data, EXPLAIN ANALYZE <query>; will apply those changes! Consider putting EXPLAIN ANALYZE between BEGIN and ROLLBACK commands but be aware that your ROLLBACK may incur the need for vacuuming (e.g., if you insert a lot of rows and then roll back).

The auto_explain extension allows you to automatically include execution plans for slow-running queries in the PostgreSQL log. However, be careful: running EXPLAIN on lots of queries can affect performance.

There are numerous examples of the use of EXPLAIN (ANALYZE) throughout this book to help demystify query performance and execution logic and further aid us in understanding why a particular course of action is a mistake. There's also another example in section 6.10.

Supplementing the official documentation, there are numerous tutorials available online that go over the process of reading and understanding EXPLAIN output, as well as visualizers that organize query nodes and concepts in a way that some will find more user-friendly.

6.9   *Locking explicitly*

The lock modes that PostgreSQL provides can be used by applications to control concurrent access to table data where MVCC's default behavior is not sufficient. By locking objects explicitly, applications can ensure data consistency, that actions won't be executed out of order, or that application-side objects won't get out of sync with each other.

However, locking explicitly is a bad paradigm and should generally be avoided. These explicit locks, also known as *heavyweight locks*, can block statements' read and write access completely, leading to waits.

As we saw in the example from section 6.5, the situation where we inadvertently locked access to a table could have proved disastrous for application performance. The statement there was waiting indefinitely for the lock it needed to be released, and other statements were getting queued behind it, also waiting.

It's easy to look at part of the problem and focus on, let's say, the synchronization of objects in the application, and explicit locks may seem like the ideal solution. In reality, it's more likely that, eventually, sessions will block other sessions unless your application is exquisitely crafted (hint: it isn't). The likely result will be longer run times for queries and increased latency or waits visible to interactive users of the application.

To be on the safe side, avoid using this kind of locking in your code. The alternative is to make clients try to obtain access to an object, and if that isn't available, notify them immediately with an error so they can retry later. This involves making the application tolerant so it can be allowed to fail and retry.

Luckily, there's a PostgreSQL isolation level that does exactly that. The SERIALIZABLE isolation level implements *Serializable Snapshot Isolation* (SSI), which detects and prevents *anti-dependency* cycles (when a transaction writes a new version of a row while an older version is being observed by another transaction).

> **Anti-dependency cycle (*rw-dependency*)**
> Transaction T1 reads three rows from a table WHERE active = true, transaction T2 updates one of these rows with SET active = false, and then transaction T1 tries to calculate an average value WHERE active = true, which only averages across the two rows. This is also known as *write skew on predicate read* or *G2 serialization anomaly*.

SERIALIZABLE is the strictest transaction isolation level, and when a serialization failure is detected, it will throw errors such as ERROR: could not serialize access due to read/write dependencies among transactions. Due to the overhead of anomaly detection, it may allow for slightly reduced concurrency, but the benefit is that there is nothing that can block queries, and explicit locks are not required. For some application types, serializable will be the best choice for achieving high performance.

> **TIP** An example of how to use SERIALIZABLE can be found in the PostgreSQL documentation here: https://www.postgresql.org/docs/current/transaction-iso.html#XACT-SERIALIZABLE.

Alternatively, you may want to handle synchronization inside your application. In this case, you can use advisory locks, a feature provided by PostgreSQL for developers to define locks that hold a meaning for the application but are not enforced by the DBMS. More information on advisory locks can be found at https://www.postgresql.org/docs/current/explicit-locking.html#ADVISORY-LOCKS.

6.10 Having no indexes

This one is kind of self-explanatory, I would hope, and not 100% specific to PostgreSQL. Indexes can make a very significant difference in query performance in conjunction with predicates by offering fast scan times. The different index types on offer (B-Tree, Hash, GIN, BRIN, GiST, SP-GiST, and Bloom filter) cover many varied use cases, and yet we always see slow queries that could have been made blazing fast through the use of an index.

However, coming from other DBMSs, you may assume that an index will automatically be created under some conditions. In a recent real-world case, developers had trusted that because they were querying a column that was using a foreign key, PostgreSQL would have created an index on the referencing table.

Let's see what that looked like, using two tables from our Frogge Emporium database. Frogge has a table of invoices where the column customer references the table customers. They have a query to find how many invoices they have from a specific customer:

```
SELECT count(*)
FROM erp.invoices
JOIN erp.customers c
ON customer = c.id
WHERE first_name = 'Aiden'
AND last_name = 'Kowalski';
```

With SET max_parallel_workers_per_gather=0;, the EXPLAIN ANALYZE output for this is

```
                              QUERY PLAN
-----------------------------------------------------------------------------
Aggregate  (cost=6054.51..6054.52 rows=1 width=8) (actual
  time=28.057..28.060 rows=1 loops=1)
    -> Hash Join  (cost=306.01..6054.46 rows=18 width=0) (actual
    time=2.681..28.053 rows=18 loops=1)
        Hash Cond: (invoices.customer = c.id)
        -> Seq Scan on invoices  (cost=0.00..5092.00 rows=250000 width=8)
          (actual time=0.004..12.098 rows=250000 loops=1)
```

```
        -> Hash  (cost=306.00..306.00 rows=1 width=8) (actual
    time=0.953..0.954 rows=1 loops=1)
            Buckets: 1024  Batches: 1  Memory Usage: 9kB
            -> Seq Scan on customers c  (cost=0.00..306.00 rows=1
        width=8) (actual time=0.122..0.950 rows=1 loops=1)
                Filter: ((first_name = 'Aiden'::text) AND (last_name =
            'Kowalski'::text))
                Rows Removed by Filter: 13999
 Planning Time: 0.139 ms
 Execution Time: 28.083 ms
(11 rows)
```

We can see that even though we are querying on a foreign key that's referencing the primary key on the `customers` table and is therefore indexed there, the `Gather` for our `count()` is performing a `Seq Scan` on table `invoices`. PostgreSQL doesn't create an index on the referencing table automatically, so none is used. However, the query still manages to complete in just 28 ms.

After `CREATE INDEX ON erp.invoices(customer);`, we get this plan:

```
                              QUERY PLAN
----------------------------------------------------------------------------
 Aggregate  (cost=314.84..314.85 rows=1 width=8) (actual time=0.957..0.957
    rows=1 loops=1)
    -> Nested Loop  (cost=0.29..314.79 rows=18 width=0) (actual
    time=0.121..0.954 rows=18 loops=1)
        -> Seq Scan on customers c  (cost=0.00..306.00 rows=1 width=8)
        (actual time=0.107..0.938 rows=1 loops=1)
                Filter: ((first_name = 'Aiden'::text) AND (last_name =
            'Kowalski'::text))
                Rows Removed by Filter: 13999
        -> Index Only Scan using invoices_customer_idx on invoices
        (cost=0.29..8.61 rows=18 width=8) (actual time=0.012..0.014 rows=18
        loops=1)
                Index Cond: (customer = c.id)
                Heap Fetches: 0
 Planning Time: 1.511 ms
 Execution Time: 1.338 ms
(10 rows)
```

This turned the `invoices` table access into an `Index Only Scan` that only takes 1.3 ms in total! Big deal? We were also in the milliseconds before.

However, it made our query run 20 times faster. Imagine that this kind of query gets executed thousands of times an hour or a minute. In this case, milliseconds that you would usually ignore can make a world of difference in total system throughput.

A few sections back, we talked about the importance of taking advantage of the `EXPLAIN` command. Here, we tried it to see whether an index was being used and whether the index we created helped things by comparing execution plans before and after indexing.

If you see that you get full table scan accesses, consider the nature of that column and the `WHERE` clause you're using, and it's more than likely that you will find an index type that will speed up your SQL statement.

6.11 Having unused indexes

At the other end of the scale, just mindlessly creating indexes on every column can seriously undermine the performance of INSERT, UPDATE, and DELETE operations. Also, you can end up wasting a lot of disk space on indexes that you will never need.

In one memorable case, a table had an index on each table column, an index grouping all columns together, and indexes for every combination of columns! Needless to say, almost none of them served a purpose.

There's no point in repeating the EXPLAIN song and dance here. Try it and see for yourself how much slower you can make writing to a large table by adding more indexes to its columns.

As we said in the previous section, when you have very heavy query traffic where you update a table all the time, just shaving tenths or hundreds of a millisecond off of each UPDATE will make for a significant throughput improvement.

Finally, an index will only be needed when you have a WHERE clause and, even then, only for time-critical queries. If you're going to index something that you query only once a day and it takes a couple of seconds, it may not be worth the effort of maintaining this index. Additionally, when you're selecting a significant portion of the table, scanning an index may be slower than actually going through the table sequentially. PostgreSQL knows this and will elect to do a Seq Scan instead.

You can identify unused indexes and DROP them by examining the view pg_stat_all_indexes to see which ones have idx_scan = 0. It means they have never been used in an index scan, so there is no reason to keep them around.

> **TIP** Use caution *not* to run index or constraint creation commands such as CREATE INDEX ON invoices(customer); more than once. Without explicitly specifying the index or constraint name, a duplicate index (with a unique, system-generated name) will be created. Duplicate indexes waste database space, slow down DML operations (INSERT, UPDATE, and DELETE), and increase maintenance time (such as for the aforementioned autovacuum) while providing no actual query performance benefit.

6.12 Removing indexes used elsewhere

Following the advice from the preceding section, you remove every index you find with a zero idx_scan value. Naturally, you feel smug because you applied some sound advice from a PostgreSQL book and, as a result, improved the state of your database. A few minutes later, your phone rings unexpectedly, and you pick up to find that Ashley from Accounting is livid. Their reporting queries have slowed to a crawl, and they are demanding to know what happened to the database.

How could this be possible? It turns out that Accounting is using a standby node, connected via streaming replication, for their queries as a read replica. If you had checked pg_stat_all_indexes on that node, you would have seen that it showed quite a large number of index scans, meaning that the index was heavily used for some queries. These kinds of statistics are instance specific and not for the entire cluster. And, of course, as there's physical replication between the Postgres instances, when the index was dropped on the primary, it also disappeared from the standby.

When you have standby nodes, always check to see that indexes are not used on any of those nodes before you decide to remove them.

Summary

- PostgreSQL's default configuration is very conservative and, in most cases, will not be optimal for a real-world workload. This can mean that you are leaving your system resources underutilized and leaving potential performance gains on the table.
- You can shoot yourself in the foot by calculating memory allocation settings incorrectly. You need to take your workload into account, including what types of queries you are running and how memory hungry they are, along with what level of client concurrency you are expecting.
- Excessive concurrency can kill your performance rather than allow more work to be performed in parallel because of the way Multi-Version Concurrency Control (MVCC) works. You need to be aware of the risks associated with opening too many sessions inside PostgreSQL, the nature of your workload, and the limitations of your particular database host.
- Connections that are mostly or entirely idle don't come for free; they are associated with computational overhead that may affect PostgreSQL's, and your operating system's, performance in general. You should try to avoid having connections around that don't do much actual work. If you can't, you should use a connection pooler that's aware of these connection semantics, such as PgBouncer in Transaction Mode.
- Idle in transaction sessions and sessions with long-running queries can cause unexpected blocking of other queries, leading to application delays or errors. They can also postpone or altogether block autovacuum, and this can lead to performance degradation because of bloat or more serious errors.
- If you let your transaction rate get out of control, it can outrun the efforts of autovacuum to prevent XID wraparound failure and bring down your database. You can mitigate this by batching, reorganizing, and summarizing data—or even skipping the ingestion of data you aren't likely to use again.
- Autovacuum is essential for the correct operation of your database. Lowering its effectiveness or disabling it altogether to save system resources is a fallacy because any performance gains will be undone in time by bloat accumulation, inaccurate optimizer statistics, and forced anti-wraparound prevention.
- Where there's evidence that a query is running slowly, checking its EXPLAIN is a quick and accurate way to identify the reasons why and help troubleshoot it.
- Locking objects explicitly can lead to read/write blocking that can make your application feel sluggish or broken. Where synchronization is needed, try to use the SERIALIZABLE isolation level and make your application able to retry actions.

- Indexes can make or break your queries' performance, and PostgreSQL has lots of index types. Examine your query plans and take advantage of indexing to boost performance for your WHEREs. Sequential scans are bad because they become linearly slower as the table grows.
- Having indexes that you don't need can slow down your table for writing and consume valuable disk space. Identify those that aren't in use from `pg_stat_all_indexes` and remove them.
- Be careful when dropping indexes that appear unused, as this statistic is for the local node only, and those indexes may be in use on another node you are physically replicating to.

Administration bad practices

In this chapter

- Letting disk usage get out of hand
- Missing hints of danger by not looking at logs
- Collecting and analyzing statistics
- Upgrading is not optional

After all the exciting development and optimization topics we've discussed, when the time comes to take the database into production, the comparatively mundane task of administration may feel like a chore. However, how you administer the database is an integral part of PostgreSQL's robustness and reliability. It determines the success of your Postgres deployment and can make or break critical systems. We'll now look at some mistakes database administrators (DBAs) may make, either through lack of familiarity or inexperience, when managing Postgres.

7.1 Not tracking disk usage

It seems hard to believe, yet it's still one of the top problems faced by people who support PostgreSQL installations. Inevitably, one day, someone will contact them requesting their help in solving the dreaded "No space left on device" error. This section could have been named "Running Out of Disk Space," but instead, what I want to emphasize here and now is that if you aren't tracking your disk space usage, you are taking a huge risk.

Let's take a step back and look at what happens when your PostgreSQL deployment runs out of disk space. First off, which disk are we talking about? The risks associated with space exhaustion in your operating system disk are well known. Hopefully, your PostgreSQL data directory is on a different drive or partition, and let's assume that this is what's run out of space.

You are likely to notice something similar to this:

```
ERROR:  could not extend file "base/12609/16048": No space left on device
HINT:  Check free disk space.
```

What happens when this harrowing error appears?

It really depends on where you keep your data files and the Write-Ahead Log and if they're on the same disk volume or not. Just filling up your data disk is not a fatal error in itself, but it can certainly prevent your application from performing its usual database activities. However, if the disk where your WAL resides runs out of space, journaling and committing data changes will no longer be possible, and this can lead to PostgreSQL going into panic and shutting down.

This is most undesirable, so people will try to prevent it at all costs. Unfortunately, knee-jerk reactions may lead to missteps that can even compound the error and make matters worse.

A lifeline many may reach for at this time is to delete some old data to free up disk space. Unfortunately, because of PostgreSQL's MVCC model, this won't yield immediate results or may not work at all. Postgres needs to write WAL for every change to the data, so you effectively need disk space in order to delete data! If you have enough disk space to run DELETE or TRUNCATE, the dead rows left behind will still require a VACUUM to reclaim the space. However, even then, the space won't be returned to the OS but will just be marked as free space within the table's data files. VACUUM FULL, which can relinquish the free space back to the OS, obtains an ACCESS EXCLUSIVE lock on the table while rewriting it, making the table unusable during the operation—this also qualifies as a Very Bad Thing.

Opting to resize the disk volume can also turn out to be the wrong move in production, as many cloud providers and filesystems need to pause all disk operations until the volume expansion operation has been completed. This may potentially cause unexpected downtime for your database. Also, be aware that the resize operation may take a very long time, so you may be better off restoring the database to a fresh server or cloud instance with more disk space.

Another quick thought will be to look for logs to delete. This has led many an inexperienced PostgreSQL user to one of the most common ways to shoot themselves in the foot.

7.1.1 Deleting the Write-Ahead Log

In the days of yore, the PostgreSQL data directory contained directories named `pg_log`, `pg_clog`, and `pg_xlog`. If you know that `pg_log` contains logs that you want to delete, it's easy to assume that you can also blow away those "c"-logs and those "x"-logs as well. Unfortunately, `pg_clog` was the directory that contained the Commit Log, which keeps track of the state of all transactions and is an integral part of the MVCC mechanism. `pg_xlog` was the directory for the Write-Ahead Log, and by this point in the book, you should already know how important the transaction log for the database is. Effectively, removing those directories nuked the Postgres installation, making it unusable instantly, and the only remaining choice would be to rebuild the database cluster from a backup.

When the PostgreSQL project realized that this was starting to happen all too often, `pg_log` was renamed to `log` to make it somewhat unambiguous, `pg_clog` was renamed to `pg_xact`, and `pg_xlog` was renamed to `pg_wal` to stop people thinking that these are "logs" that can be removed at will. Even though these directories were intentionally renamed, still to this day, people manage to delete files from inside them, which is truly one of the biggest mistakes you can make with a PostgreSQL installation.

Honestly, it seems that there's just no way to stop people from deleting files that appear useless to them because they don't understand their function. You could say that the only thing we can do is write books about these mistakes and hope that one day these pages will get read!

7.1.2 What can eat up your disk space?

Moving on, let's discuss what can consume your disk space gradually or suddenly. Obviously, tables and indexes will grow over time as you add more data to them, but this can be greatly exacerbated by bloat. If dead rows aren't removed promptly, this can cause table file size to balloon out of control, and this disk space will be lost to the filesystem until it is reclaimed. Temporary files, normally used only for the duration of an operation that doesn't fit in memory, such as a large sort or hash join, can also persist on disk after an improper Postgres shutdown. These temp files will then need to be manually cleaned up.

We previously mentioned that the WAL is essential to the operation of the database; however, you may be generating and accumulating too much of it on disk. If your `max_wal_size` and `wal_keep_size` settings are not optimal, this may lead Postgres to use up more disk space than is necessary. Also, if there is replication lag or failure of a standby server using replication slots, the WAL produced will accumulate locally until the standby server can receive and consume this WAL. If this goes unnoticed (and this is more common than you may think), it can exhaust all disk space where the WAL directory resides. Finally, a failure of the archive_command will also lead to keeping around on disk the WAL that is supposed to get archived until it can get archived successfully.

7.1.3 What can you do?

As a mitigation strategy, you can keep your database and the WAL on separate volumes (and, of course, keep a very close eye on disk usage on those volumes). Moreover, *tablespaces* in PostgreSQL allow you to define the storage locations for database objects, so you are effectively free to create any table or index in any directory or volume on your filesystem. Besides the obvious performance or cost-saving optimizations you can perform with the flexibility to move things around to faster or cheaper disk storage, this allows you greater control over the disk layout of your PostgreSQL installation. Finally, you can add tablespaces at will, so you can use them temporarily until you can resolve the situation with your main disk.

Arguably, the most important monitoring task of a database administrator is to ensure that the disk doesn't become full ("You Had One Job"). Now that you know how your Postgres deployment can find itself filling up its drive—and what kinds of reactions to this eventuality can make things worse—you're hopefully more aware of the importance of monitoring disk usage at all times. Use monitoring tools of any type, set up alerts well ahead of the panic threshold, and regularly check manually for anything that looks out of place before the alerts trigger.

> **TIP** Some filesystems suffer performance degradation as they fill up to capacity, so it's important to take action before your disk is almost full.

7.2 Logging to PGDATA

You may think that letting your database run out of disk space is quite a banal error, but hey, if it wasn't something that happens out there, it wouldn't be in this book. In case you do think that, here's a less obvious and insidious mistake.

By default, PostgreSQL writes its log files to the same filesystem as the database itself (we call the data directory PGDATA for short). This may seem like a convenient default choice, but it can also lead to trouble if logs start growing unchecked. If they consume too much disk space, they can make the database run out of room, as we saw in the previous section. If you monitor your database properly, you can catch this, but what if this happens faster than the DBAs can react? One could even argue that it can form an attack vector for a denial-of-service (DoS) attack through the intentional generation of excessive logging to purposely fill up the disk.

Let us demonstrate, assuming that somehow the following code manages to slip past application testing and QA. The developer who works for Frogge Emporium has written a simple routine—with error checking, mind you—to calculate the total energy use from all branches for the previous day and log it to the audit log. This uses a query that calculates the totals per branch with window functions and then sums up everything and writes an entry to the audit table. The code has a built-in retry capability.

Listing 7.1   Routine to log the sum of the previous day's energy use

```python
import psycopg
from datetime import date, timedelta as td

with psycopg.connect("dbname=frogge user=frogge") as conn:
    try:
        while True:
            with conn.cursor() as cur:
                try:
                    # I have learned my lesson about using BETWEEN!
                    cur.execute('''WITH
                                yesterday AS (
                                    SELECT *
                                    FROM erp.energy_use
                                    WHERE reading_time >=
                                        date_trunc('d', now())
                                        - interval '1d'
                                    AND reading_time <
                                        date_trunc('d', now())),
                                perbranch AS (
                                    SELECT first_value(reading) OVER w,
                                        last_value(reading) OVER w,
                                        row_number() OVER w
                                    FROM yesterday
                                    WINDOW w AS (
                                        PARTITION BY branch_id
                                        ORDER BY reading_time
                                        RANGE BETWEEN UNBOUNDED PRECEDING
                                        AND UNBOUNDED FOLLOWING))
                                SELECT sum(last_value - first_value)
                                FROM perbranch
                                WHERE row_number=1''')
                    total = cur.fetchone()[0]

                    cur.execute('''INSERT INTO audit.audit_log
                                    (what, who, tstamp)
                                VALUES (%s, %s, now())''',
                        (f"Energy usage for {date.today() - td(days=1)}: "
                        + f"{total} kWh", "Frogge Emporium"))

                    conn.commit()
                    break
                # If this goes wrong, something must be keeping the DB busy
                # and we can just retry
                except psycopg.errors.Error:
                    conn.rollback()
    finally:
        conn.close()
```

So, our Frogge developer runs this, and a few seconds later, the database logs are riddled with

```
2024-09-20 12:26:19.606 BST [3055342] frogge@frogge ERROR:  relation
"erp.energy_use" does not exist at character 148
2024-09-20 12:26:19.606 BST [3055342] frogge@frogge STATEMENT:  WITH
                            yesterday AS (
                                SELECT *
                                FROM erp.energy_use
                                WHERE reading_time >=
                                    date_trunc('d', now())
                                    - interval '1d'
                                AND reading_time <
                                    date_trunc('d', now())),
                            perbranch AS (
                                SELECT first_value(reading) OVER w,
                                    last_value(reading) OVER w,
                                    row_number() OVER w
                                FROM yesterday
                                WINDOW w AS (
                                    PARTITION BY branch_id
                                    ORDER BY reading_time
                                    RANGE BETWEEN UNBOUNDED PRECEDING
                                    AND UNBOUNDED FOLLOWING))
                            SELECT sum(last_value - first_value)
                            FROM perbranch
                            WHERE row_number=1
2024-09-20 12:26:19.606 BST [3055342] frogge@frogge ERROR:  relation
"erp.energy_use" does not exist at character 148
2024-09-20 12:26:19.606 BST [3055342] frogge@frogge STATEMENT:  WITH
[...]
```

Ouch, it seems that instead of energy_usage, which is the proper table name, they wrote energy_use. In this scenario, this causes the code to run indefinitely, sending a query to the database that will always fail because it will always try the wrong table name. Every time this occurs, the error is logged to the PostgreSQL log.

If we look at the timings, there are multiple entries during the same millisecond with this same error, which makes our code a very efficient endless loop. Unfortunately, this is particularly bad for us, as something that writes to the log so fast can rapidly fill up the disk containing the logs. If the process running this query is not interrupted, it will continue until disk space is exhausted. So, if you have your database on the same disk as your logs, this can cause the database to crash, as we previously saw.

However unlikely the previous scenario is, it underscores the importance of keeping the logs on a separate filesystem or partition from the main database storage. This way, you can mitigate the risk of log production eating up all the disk space from your database. As additional safety measures, you should also make sure that your installation implements log rotation and enforces size limits for your logs. If you're not using your operating system's log management and rotation facilities, you can manage the size of the logs by adjusting parameters such as log_rotation_size, log_rotation_age, and log_truncate_on_rotation. Subsequently, you will need to find the balance point between accumulating too many logs, which consume a lot of disk space and are harder to scan through, and risking the deletion of logs with useful error history and details that you may need later.

7.3 Ignoring the logs

Many believe that database logs are something you look at only if something goes wrong. Wrong! PostgreSQL's logs are not there just for post-mortem analysis; they can inform you in near real-time of what's taking place inside your database. By ignoring them, you will be missing out on crucial insights that may help you prevent serious problems down the line.

Let's look at a few things you may miss if you don't examine your logs regularly.

7.3.1 Bad configuration

First off, you may catch configuration errors. For example, if you find something like this in the logs, it may mean that you aren't currently replicating to a standby or taking streaming backups properly:

```
2024-09-21 13:41:10.692 BST [3214372] replicator@[unknown] FATAL:  number of
requested standby connections exceeds max_wal_senders (currently 10)
```

This is probably not noticeable in the application, yet it's something that requires your immediate attention—in this case, checking what actual replication connections are coming into your DB server and the `max_wal_senders` limit in the configuration.

Similarly, you may find errors in the log complaining of an insufficient number of available connections:

```
2024-09-21 13:49:39.821 BST [3219655] frogge@frogge FATAL:  remaining
connection slots are reserved for roles with the SUPERUSER attribute
```

This points to the fact that either you're not giving the application the number of connections that it legitimately needs or potentially that the application is requesting an excessive number of connections. If you remember what we talked about in chapter 6, this may be the time to start investigating adding a connection pooler, such as PgBouncer, to your setup.

It's not just `FATAL` level errors that you need to worry about, though. Here are a few cases that aren't errors but may reveal underlying problems, such as memory configuration errors. If you have `log_temp_files` enabled, you may notice a lot of log entries that look like this:

```
2024-09-21 13:51:15.133 BST [3226458] frogge@frogge LOG:  temporary file:
path "base/pgsql_tmp/pgsql_tmp3226458.0", size 8437760
2024-09-21 13:51:15.133 BST [3226458] frogge@frogge STATEMENT:  SELECT *
FROM erp.payments WHERE tstamp >= date_trunc('y', now()) ORDER BY
amount;
```

This may mean that your `work_mem` value is set too low, and the database is having to resort to writing temporary files on disk in order to run your queries that don't fit in memory. As we know, this can severely affect performance because of the sheer disparity in speed and latency between memory and disk.

7.3.2 Performance Issues

Slow-running queries are also something to keep an eye out for, as they may point to inefficiencies causing performance problems, such as badly written SQL, missing indexes, or progressive problems such as gradual performance degradation. Setting your `log_min_duration_statement` parameter to a value like 100 ms will allow you to log slow query executions similar to this:

```
2024-09-21 14:17:41.763 BST [3232957] frogge@frogge STATEMENT:  SELECT *
 FROM erp.payments WHERE tstamp >= date_trunc('y', now()) ORDER BY
 amount;
2024-09-21 14:17:41.764 BST [3232957] frogge@frogge LOG:  duration:
 157.096 ms  statement: SELECT * FROM erp.payments WHERE tstamp >=
 date_trunc('y', now()) ORDER BY amount;
```

As this query ran for 157 ms, it crossed our reporting threshold and was subsequently captured in the log. We discussed extensively in the previous chapter how long-running queries can seriously affect your deployment's performance and reliability.

Additionally, your workload may be causing issues to surface in the logs that may assist you in troubleshooting your database and application's performance. For example, if you find evidence in the log that checkpoints occur too frequently, this will indicate that Postgres is flushing data to disk way too often, which will hurt your performance:

```
2024-09-21 14:20:27.920 BST [3260055] LOG:  checkpoints are occurring too
 frequently (2 seconds apart)
2024-09-21 14:20:27.920 BST [3260055] HINT:  Consider increasing the
 configuration parameter "max_wal_size".
2024-09-21 14:20:27.920 BST [3260055] LOG:  checkpoint starting: wal
2024-09-21 14:20:27.963 BST [3260055] LOG:  checkpoint complete: wrote 1359
 buffers (8.3%); 0 WAL file(s) added, 2 removed, 0 recycled; write=0.155
 s, sync=0.019 s, total=0.201 s; sync files=2, longest=0.019 s,
 average=0.010 s; distance=33073 kB, estimate=37487 kB; lsn=11/8371F2D0,
 redo lsn=11/81A37E70
```

In this case, the HINT is spot on; you should probably increase `max_wal_size`, but you should also investigate the reason for the disk write spike elsewhere in your system. As previously mentioned, other workload problems, such as an excessively high transaction rate, can also be betrayed by the presence of anti-wraparound VACUUM mentions in the log.

7.3.3 Locks

Locking issues captured in the log, such as deadlock errors, can also be a telltale sign of current or impending performance problems. Instead of waiting indefinitely, Postgres will terminate one of the two conflicting queries to break the deadlock. You'll then spot something like this in the log file:

```
2024-09-21 14:40:24.541 BST [3279275] frogge@frogge ERROR:  deadlock
detected
2024-09-21 14:40:24.541 BST [3279275] frogge@frogge DETAIL:  Process 3279275
waits for ShareLock on transaction 3810; blocked by process 3279214.
Process 3279214 waits for ShareLock on transaction 3811; blocked by process
3279275.
Process 3279275: UPDATE audit.audit_log SET tstamp=now() WHERE id=99925;
Process 3279214: UPDATE audit.audit_log SET tstamp=now() WHERE id=500002;
2024-09-21 14:40:24.541 BST [3279275] frogge@frogge HINT:  See server log
for query details.
2024-09-21 14:40:24.541 BST [3279275] frogge@frogge CONTEXT:  while updating
tuple (1868,57) in relation "audit_log"
2024-09-21 14:40:24.541 BST [3279275] frogge@frogge STATEMENT:  UPDATE
audit.audit_log SET tstamp=now() WHERE id=99925;
2024-09-21 14:40:24.747 BST [3279214] frogge@frogge LOG:  duration:
20217.150 ms  statement: UPDATE audit.audit_log SET tstamp=now() WHERE
id=500002;
```

As no "magic bullet" PostgreSQL configuration parameter can stop deadlocks, what you can do is check your application logic to find where deadlocks are possible so that you can potentially prevent them from occurring.

7.3.4   *Corruption*

One of the more serious consequences of ignoring your logs can affect your data integrity—mentions of errors such as the one below may reveal filesystem- or even hardware-related problems that may initially pass unnoticed in the application:

```
2024-09-21 14:45:11.172 BST [3281235] ERROR:  could not read block 8185 in
file "base/16384/2613": read only 0 of 8192 bytes
2024-09-21 14:45:11.172 BST [3281235] CONTEXT:  while reading block 8185 of
relation base/16384/2613
2024-09-21 14:45:11.172 BST [3281235] STATEMENT:  SELECT * FROM
audit.audit_log WHERE tstamp > '2024-09-21';
2024-09-21 14:45:11.173 BST [3281235] LOG:  invalid page in block 8185 of
relation base/16384/2613
2024-09-21 14:45:11.173 BST [3281235] HINT:  This could be a corruption
issue caused by hardware problems or a software bug. Check for hardware
issues and consider running pg_checksums or other diagnostic tools.
```

In this case, the log may have revealed the early signs of data corruption. This can give you a heads-up, which will allow you to address the problem before it can escalate into a major data loss incident.

7.3.5   *Security*

Scanning the logs can help you catch security incidents, too. The appearance of repeated failed authentication attempts may indicate brute-force login attempts:

```
2024-09-21 14:49:34.300 BST [3306179] frogge@frogge FATAL:  password
authentication failed for user "frogge"
2024-09-21 14:49:34.300 BST [3306179] frogge@frogge DETAIL:  Connection
matched file "/etc/postgresql/17/main/pg_hba.conf" line 123: "local
all             all                             scram-sha-256"
```

Moreover, things such as irregular login patterns or suspicious queries, such as SQL injection attempts or unusual interest in tables that hold sensitive data, can point to an attempted or in-progress security breach.

As the volume of logging that can be output by a database in a production environment can be very large, in some cases, it's simply not practical to review everything manually. A tool that can help out with this is a log analyzer such as pgBadger, which can summarize the data for specific periods and create nice HTML-formatted reports for us. It can capture the things we previously mentioned, as well as report on resource usage, and you can configure specific thresholds or patterns that will trigger pgBadger to alert you.

> **NOTE** You can find pgBadger at https://github.com/darold/pgbadger.

Even without such a specialized tool, you can still perform due diligence and scan your log files with blazing-fast UNIX utilities such as `grep`, for example, by writing something like this, which scours the log for lines denoting ERROR or FATAL error conditions:

```
grep -E 'ERROR|FATAL' /var/log/postgresql/postgresql-17-main.log
```

To sum up, it is essential to actively monitor PostgreSQL logs to have a full up-to-date picture of your DB instance's health when it comes to configuration, performance, data integrity and security, and dealing with all other sorts of unexpected events.

7.4 Not monitoring the database

One would assume that any competent person or team in charge of a PostgreSQL database would have a monitoring setup. However, it has been shown time and again that this cannot be stated enough, so here we go:

- If you don't monitor your database appropriately, things *will* go wrong, and even worse, you will get no advance warning or clue that things have gone wrong. In a database that's used in a production environment, this should be simply unthinkable because of the risk to operations that it entails, yet you can still come across databases where basic monitoring tasks have been overlooked.
- If monitoring is neglected, you may not notice that your queries are slowing down and identify and resolve the performance bottlenecks that are causing this. You need to be immediately informed about usage spikes, as these can cause slowdowns that may impact user experience and subsequently lead to reputational damage.
- Similarly, you should also track PostgreSQL's resource utilization because inefficiencies or, simply, increasing loads can lead to operating near or at the limit. This again brings the risk of degraded performance or even of your database becoming unresponsive.
- Monitoring is also about detecting unusual activity, such as excessive resource usage, either inadvertently or purposefully, and other things mentioned in section 7.3 that can be early warnings of security threats or malicious activity.

- Finally, monitoring can alert you to the need to perform maintenance tasks such as VACUUM and ANALYZE or can highlight that your current autovacuum settings are inadequate.

Let's talk about which things you should track to ensure that your installation is adequately monitored. PostgreSQL itself offers a wealth of information, but you need to know where to look. Most monitoring tools, even if they don't come with PostgreSQL monitoring configured out of the box, will allow you to define metrics, checks, and dashboards, either through customization or via plugins. Good things to track are

- (Naturally) disk and temporary file usage
- Table and index-related metrics from pg_stat_user_tables and pg_stat_user_indexes
- Number and total size of WAL files, from pg_stat_wal and with pg_ls_waldir()
- Connections, running queries, their duration, and whether they are blocked (pg_stat_activity)
- Replication status, with pg_stat_replication and relevant WAL-related functions
- Database transaction age, from pg_stat_database
- Backup status

More involved things that you can monitor are

- The detailed query statistics collected by the extension pg_stat_statements
- Buffer, checkpointer, and background writer statistics
- Locks and waits in your server
- Lower-level I/O statistics such as those provided by the pg_statio_*_tables and pg_stat_io views (available since Postgres 16)

Some general-purpose open source monitoring tools that people use are

- RRDtool and Cacti
- Nagios/Icinga
- Munin Monitoring
- Zabbix
- Percona Monitoring and Management (PMM)
- Prometheus for more cloud-native settings
- PGWatch
- Even pgAdmin for real-time viewing

These are all easy to find with your preferred search engine. There are also proprietary solutions like EDB's Postgres Enterprise Manager (PEM) and SaaS offerings from DataDog and SolarWinds.

PostgreSQL's built-in pg_monitor role has access to most, if not all, important metrics. Some tools and platforms may require access to more restricted things, such as everything that's in `pg_stat_activity`. Before granting access, you should weigh the benefits of monitoring against the interests of your system's security.

From dealing with performance problems and preventing resource starvation to checking for backup failures and security intrusions, it is clear that monitoring is all about effectively managing the risk to your database. Murphy's law ("Anything that can go wrong will go wrong") and the culture of monitoring need to be embedded in you, your team, and your organization. Don't wait until something goes very wrong to start monitoring for that eventuality because it may be too late.

7.5 *No tracking of statistics over time*

Database monitoring isn't only about notifying you of current problems to fix. Don't get me wrong, that's fine, but it can only tell you so much about your database's overall "look" over time unless you tend to keep the data around and create reports about long periods. Most monitoring tools are focused on displaying the current state and alerting and aren't optimized for long-term reporting that can let you "zoom out" and give you access to the bigger picture of how your database is performing in the grand scheme of things.

If you don't keep tabs on your PostgreSQL statistics, you may miss out on insights that can help you prepare for your database's future growth. Having a view of performance trends, usage patterns, and other metrics over time can help you perform analyses and projections to make your capacity planning and scaling decisions easier and more informed.

For example, let's say that Frogge Emporium's customer base keeps steadily expanding. Without access to historical data about how the system has responded to this gradual change, it may be hard for Frogge to predict database architecture changes or infrastructure changes that may be necessary to deal with this growth.

You may find a monitoring tool that allows you to track important metrics over time, but keeping around a lot of data may bring about massive storage requirements where the tool resides. In the case of proprietary tools and SaaS platforms, there are almost certainly cost factors associated with tracking many systems and accumulating lots of data from them for a long time. You may also be a fan of simplicity and use custom scripts and standard utilities for monitoring instead of complicated tools with features you may not need.

With these in mind, I developed an extension called `pg_statviz`. It can take snapshots of important PostgreSQL cumulative and dynamic statistics so you can track their evolution over time, perform analyses, and produce visualizations to aid your understanding of your server's workload. The key benefit of the extension is that it's very lightweight and does not require a module to be loaded in `shared_preload_libraries`, which means that installation doesn't even require a server restart. Second, it enables you to perform this analysis without the overhead of external tools or storage, such as Prometheus, Logstash, or Elasticsearch, or intrusive agents, such as those employed by a certain Dog of Data and others.

You can set up any job scheduler to take these periodic snapshots. With a reasonable snapshot interval of 1 minute (which is the shortest one offered by `cron`), the amount of data generated is very little, so why not keep it inside the database itself? This is exactly what `pg_statviz` does by storing the timestamped snapshots in tables under the `pgstatviz` schema. It currently collects statistics on the background writer, checkpointer, cache hit ratio, connection count, I/O, number of tuples read/written, locks, wait events, WAL generation, transactions, configuration, and others. By implementing resampling, it enables unlimited data analysis by allowing you to downsample thousands, potentially millions, of snapshots down to an arbitrary number of plot points (100 by default).

The accompanying visualization utility it comes with reads from these tables and can produce graphs (output to disk as `.png` images) to let you analyze this time-series data at a glance, as shown in figure 7.1.

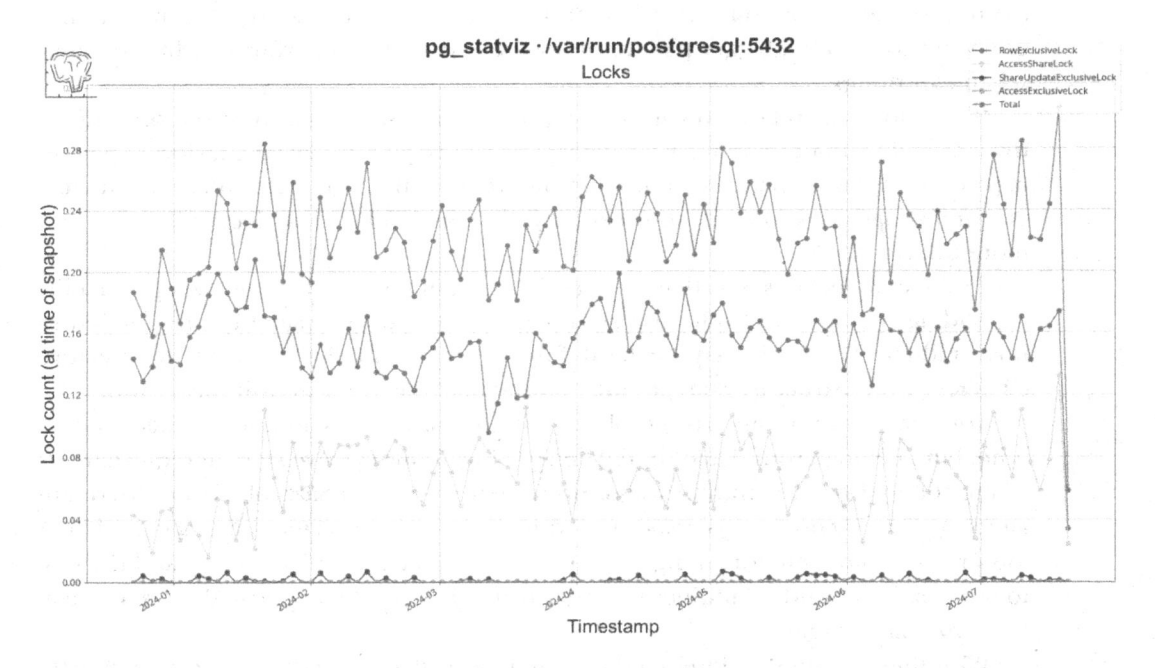

Figure 7.1 `pg_statviz` **locks analysis output. This visualization displays the mean number and type of locks in the database, with snapshots taken every minute over a period of several months in 2024.**

You can download the `pg_statviz` extension from the PostgreSQL community repositories by installing the package `pg_statviz_extension` for Red Hat–based systems or `postgresql-statviz` for Debian-based systems. Alternatively, you can install it from *PGXN* (the PostgreSQL Extension Network). Installing it manually from the source is also an option, as it requires no compilation.

You can enable the extension in the desired database by running (as a superuser):

```
CREATE EXTENSION pg_statviz;
```

As soon as the extension has been enabled, users with the appropriate privileges can immediately start taking snapshots using

```
SELECT pgstatviz.snapshot();

NOTICE:  created pg_statviz snapshot
            snapshot
---------------------------------
 2024-06-27 11:04:58.055453+00
(1 row)
```

As mentioned previously, taking regularly scheduled snapshots is recommended and can be done with any OS or database scheduling tool, including pg_cron.

The visualization utility can be installed from the PostgreSQL community repos as the package pg_statviz for Red Hat–based systems or pg-statviz for Debian-based systems. It can also be downloaded from *PyPI* (the Python Package Index) as follows:

```
pip install pg_statviz
```

Its usage is as simple as

```
pg_statviz buf --host froggeserver -d frogge -U frogge -D 2024-06-24T23:00
 2024-06-26
```

This will connect to host froggeserver's frogge database as the user frogge and generate a visualization for the buffer statistics spanning from 23:00 on 2024-06-24 to 00:00 on 2024-06-26.

NOTE The source code and documentation can be found at https://github.com/vyruss/pg_statviz.

7.6 *Not upgrading Postgres*

Which PostgreSQL version are *you* on? PostgreSQL's development spans over three decades and boasts both minor and major releases. *Minor* releases happen roughly quarterly, and they are the last part of your version number (i.e., 16.*4*). They fix bugs, security, and data corruption problems. They never add features or change the internal format, and the Postgres community considers not upgrading to them to be riskier than upgrading. *Major* releases are the first part in the versioning scheme (i.e., *16*.4). These bring thoroughly vetted new features and can change the internal format of system tables and data files. As such, they don't have compatibility with the data stored by a previous major release (but you can upgrade it). In short, new major releases are what keep Postgres moving forward. Each major version is typically supported for a period of five years, during which patches and security updates are provided.

Feature-wise, backward compatibility is almost a given. SQL is SQL, and something that was written for Postgres 9.3 will usually work with Postgres 17. The upgrade path from version to version has proven to be very reliable.

This then brings us to the burning question: Why are people wary of upgrading?

First of all, the dreaded "It works fine now." You can be lulled into a false sense of stability by adhering to the tired adage, "A tested and monitored system is stable." In reality, what works today may not work tomorrow if your users discover a latent bug or if the application triggers unexpected behaviors through changing workloads or data access patterns. Also, don't forget about new security vulnerabilities that can always crop up. You should not rely solely on your own testing to ensure that the system is secure.

Closely associated is the fear of an upgrade potentially introducing problems, such as bugs, performance regressions, and incompatibilities. A lack of familiarity with PostgreSQL can also be a causal factor, as DBAs may worry that they don't have sufficient knowledge to execute the upgrade without jeopardizing the system.

Finally, there are organizational reasons that may contribute to upgrade avoidance. Bureaucracy in the approval process, the need to coordinate with multiple departments, and the need for—and reluctance to schedule—downtime can all discourage upgrades.

By failing to upgrade your Postgres installation regularly, you are exposing it to significant risks. Critically, you will miss out on security-related patches. As an open source project, PostgreSQL has the ability to issue updates to eliminate security threats, sometimes within a matter of hours, which is unheard of in proprietary software. However, if you stay on an outdated version or, even worse, one that's fallen out of support, you won't get the benefit of any of that.

The second reason why you should upgrade regularly is that bug fixes keep streaming in. Both newly introduced regressions and long-standing bugs (which can lay undetected for years) are continuously addressed. By not upgrading, you are increasing the likelihood of encountering a bug that has already been fixed in a later version.

Third, you will be missing out on the newer features and performance enhancements that every new major release brings. Those that stayed on PostgreSQL 9.6 didn't get native (declarative) partitioning and logical replication. Those that stayed on version 11 didn't get `pg_checksums` or generated columns, and those that stuck with Postgres 13 didn't get throughput improvement for large numbers of connections and advanced features like the streaming of large transactions and `libpq` pipelining.

Finally, the longer you stay on an older release, the more difficult it becomes to maintain and the more complicated the upgrade path becomes.

Speaking of upgrade paths, PostgreSQL is great in that you can upgrade from one major version to another without having to upgrade to the intervening versions.

However, when you do this, it is vitally important to read the release notes of every single intervening major version.

You should always read the release notes for every upgrade, even for minor version upgrades! A good reminder of why is that while release 14.4 fixed an index corruption bug, the fix required a REINDEX for some cases. Similarly, this release addressed a security vulnerability, but the resolution could affect users of the extension pg_trgm.

On the subject of extensions, remember that those come with their own bug fixes and release schedules, too. You should always check that the new extension version is compatible with your current PostgreSQL version.

Upgrades aren't as risky or disruptive as they are made out to be. Especially minor release upgrades involve little risk and are a good way to stay on top of the latest improvements. For major release upgrades, there are tools, such as pg_upgrade, that have been refined over time to the point of being considered extremely reliable (and they also have dry-run modes for sanity checking). Alternate upgrade methods, such as using logical replication for near-zero downtime upgrades, may involve more work to pull off but can also significantly reduce disruption to the deployment.

Finally, the commitment of the PostgreSQL project and its community to the reliability of the platform ensures that the upgrade path is made robust, is well-tested, and is very well documented in the accompanying release notes.

> **TIP** Make sure to check out the "Version and Platform Compatibility" section of the PostgreSQL documentation for breaking changes at https://www.postgresql.org/docs/current/runtime-config-compatible.html.

7.7 Not upgrading your system

Hopefully, the benefits of keeping your PostgreSQL installation up to date are clear by now. What's slightly less obvious is that you may upgrade your Postgres regularly but leave your operating system stuck on the same release due to inertia or reluctance on the part of system administrators. It's not uncommon for production environments to stay on the same operating system major version for four or five years. Sometimes they avoid the upgrade for as long as they can get away with, only upgrading just before— or, in some cases, even just after—all support for the OS has been withdrawn. Extreme bad examples of this are Debian, Red Hat, and Ubuntu's commercial offerings for support of ancient releases for up to 10 years, which is far longer than is comprehensible or reasonable.

Let us examine a real-world case where following this trend ended up affecting a production PostgreSQL deployment. A database used with the PostGIS extension for geospatial queries was exhibiting a performance slowdown that nobody could explain or account for because it seemed to be restricted to specific values of the geospatial data being processed!

For instance, wildly inconsistent performance was observed for a PostGIS function such as ST_DistanceSphere, which returns the distance in meters between two points on the globe. The function seemed to be massively slower for certain pairs of data points compared to nearly identical ones, like these:

```
SELECT ST_DistanceSphere('POINT(-150 33)',
                         'POINT(-120.120120 42.488888)');
```

The query inexplicably took more than 50 times as long to run as the following one:

```
SELECT ST_DistanceSphere('POINT(-150 33)',
                         'POINT(-120.120120 42.4888881)');
```

What's worse is that it was not possible for anyone investigating this edge case to reproduce the behavior, even when using the exact same combination of PostgreSQL and PostGIS versions. After much trial and error, someone on the team managed to trigger this condition on a test system but only for these exact data values. This was good enough to start investigating, and profiling tools like `perf` were put to use to analyze this on a system level.

It was determined that the Postgres backend process was spending most of its time in the `libm` math library function `__mul`:

```
+    62.78%    61.29%  postgres  libm-2.23.so              [.] __mul
```

This means that the culprit was a multiplication?!

`libm` is part of the broader GNU C library `glibc`, and a quick check confirmed that this behavior wasn't present on systems employing different `glibc` versions. Further investigation uncovered that some slow paths for trigonometric sine and cosine functions had been found in `glibc`. This performance problem had already been eliminated from the mathematical functions *two* years previously. However, the system in question had been using a `glibc` version that was *four* years old.

Because a significantly outdated version was still in use, it contained these inefficient paths and had missed out on this critical optimization. This was the cause of the hard-to-pinpoint dramatic slowdown in the geospatial math.

This underlines the importance of keeping system libraries up to date as a vital safeguard against obscure problems like this. Even when PostgreSQL and its extensions appeared to be working fine, the system library that formed the underlying dependency ended up triggering a performance bug further down the line in the software stack, making it much harder to troubleshoot.

System administrators' reluctance to update system components or Postgres itself often manifests as a misguided attempt to "maintain stability" in production environments. It is perceived that by not upgrading, the risk of introducing new bugs or downtime is reduced, as the system currently appears to be working fine. However, as shown by our example, this is a dangerous mindset because users may be exposed to lurking bugs that can manifest with new use cases or larger datasets.

Locking down dependencies for fear of potential breakages doesn't pay off, as the risk of not receiving critical bug fixes and security updates outweighs the risk of introducing a new unintended behavior that will be easy to detect and fix. Moreover, the longer updates are postponed, the more tangled the dependency chain becomes. Subsequently, it becomes harder to apply all the accumulated updates, and more things have to be tested. Skipping minor version updates, which usually entail no functionality change or contain breaking changes, is especially unforgivable in a modern database environment.

Summary

- Running out of disk space can cause serious problems, so monitor your usage closely. Rash decisions like deleting what looks like logs or unnecessary files or resizing volumes can make the situation worse. Identify what's consuming your space and mitigate by employing multiple volumes.
- Storing PostgreSQL logs on a separate filesystem from the database helps you reduce the risk of excessive logging filling up your disk. You should also implement log rotation and enforce log size limits.
- Regularly checking PostgreSQL logs is crucial for identifying and addressing configuration errors, performance bottlenecks, data integrity concerns, and security incidents in near real-time. This can allow you to deal with problems before they escalate, and you can use pgBadger to help with the task.
- Not monitoring your PostgreSQL database can lead to undetected performance problems, security threats, and resource exhaustion that could impact its operation. By using the appropriate tools and metrics to look out for slowdowns, resource spikes, and maintenance needs, you can ensure optimal performance and mitigate risk.
- Long-term tracking of PostgreSQL statistics is important for understanding performance trends and making informed capacity planning decisions. You can use the usual monitoring tools or the lightweight `pg_statviz` extension to capture and visualize these statistics over time without the need for heavy tooling or storage overhead.
- If you don't regularly upgrade Postgres with minor releases, you can incur security risks or run into bugs that have been fixed. By not upgrading to the next major release, you can miss out on new features and enhancements. Upgrading is made safe and reliable by well-tested tools and thorough documentation. Don't fear the upgrade; fear the alternative.
- Failing to upgrade the operating system, and dependency libraries as well, can lead to obscure PostgreSQL performance problems, bugs, and vulnerabilities, negating the perceived stability in pursuit of which you avoided upgrading.

Security bad practices

In this chapter

- Being careless with command-line password use
- Inadvertently exposing your database to outside actors
- Granting more access than necessary
- Writing and using functions insecurely

As a well-respected piece of software, PostgreSQL is renowned for taking security seriously and its security-by-default posture. The project's Security Team is comprised of experienced contributors who assess and react to threats rapidly through the issue of minor releases that contain the vulnerability fixes.

However, unfortunately, the majority of IT security breaches are not attributable to obscure exploits and vulnerabilities but rather more mundane reasons, such as the system administrator not changing the default credentials in the production server. When security best practices are not adhered to, there can be severe consequences like attacks using privilege escalation, data breaches, and worse. What we address in this chapter is operator error (i.e., how sloppiness can affect Postgres security) and what you can do to prevent this.

8.1   *Specifying psql -W or --password*

Most PostgreSQL command-line tools, like `psql`, accept the same options, such as `-h` or `--host=` for specifying the hostname of the database server to connect to or `-U/` `--username=` for the user to connect as. It's very common for users to use the `-W` or `--password` switch when connecting to specify the password for the user.

Our database administrator needs to connect to Frogge Emporium's server to perform some activities. It's something they have already done dozens of times today and are starting to find it tedious because, to connect, they've had to type in their password a lot, each time issuing this command:

```
psql -h froggeserver -U frogge -W
```

It's getting late in the day, and they can feel their typing getting sloppy because of the tedium. While they're almost certain they mistyped their password, `psql` connects to the server successfully. Surprised, they think they must be a better typist than they believed they were, even when tired.

What's happened in reality, though? They had indeed entered the wrong password, yet the server let them through and accepted the connection. How can that be? Didn't they specifically ask `psql` to prompt them for a password?

This is why using the `-W` option is what we, in PostgreSQL circles, call a *footgun* or a feature that's likely to let the user shoot themselves in the foot. Using it can be misleading and detrimental to security. Why is it wrong then?

First, by using `--password`, you are telling whatever Postgres utility you are calling to prompt you for a password—regardless of whether one is needed by the server. To elaborate, the database server may be configured (some would say *mis*configured) to accept incoming connections without requiring a password.

As a result, our DBA is lulled into a false sense of security. Since the client is asking for a password, it's easy to assume that the server is running in password-protected mode, whereas it really isn't. This means that anyone in their place could just as easily connect passwordless, and they are none the wiser because they think they are authenticating properly by entering their password.

What's more, specifying the `-W` or `--password` option is completely redundant! If PostgreSQL's authentication settings are configured to require a password to connect, the server will automatically ask for one even if you don't pass this option in the command line.

Fortunately, `-W` doesn't allow you to specify a password in the `psql` command line, as that is a significant security oversight. If you could do that, the cleartext password you typed in would be visible in the system's processes as listed by `top` or `ps faux`. Even worse, it would be recorded in the shell's command history. However, even though Postgres protects you against making this mistake, you should be really careful never to include cleartext passwords in connection strings in configuration or script files.

An additional problem with requiring the client to prompt for a password even when one isn't necessary is that wrong passwords also work. Since the server doesn't need one, it simply ignores the password sent by the client.

Finally, getting into the habit of using -W can result in unpleasant surprises for the user when connecting from a different workstation or client. If password-based authentication is enforced for that connection, they may be blindsided when the password they previously thought was accepted by the server no longer works. If the password wasn't being checked by the server on their other connection, they would have thought it was correct even if it was invalid.

What's best is to basically forget about the existence of this switch and rely on the automatic password prompt that is triggered by PostgreSQL whenever one is required. If the server is not configured to be protected with a password, this is definitely something you should be aware of.

8.2   Setting listen_addresses = '*'

Since we mentioned configuration, it's time to look at one of the most commonly misused parameters in `postgresql.conf`, namely `listen_addresses`. It specifies the IP addresses on which the PostgreSQL server should listen for incoming connection requests. The default value for that is quite restrictive because it's set to `localhost`. So, when our proverbial developer stops experimenting locally on their laptop and wants to try out their code on an actual database server, they find that what worked locally doesn't let them connect over the network.

What's the easiest way to make the server let you connect? Simple, just set `listen_addresses` to the wildcard value "*", which means "any address"; restart the server process; and presto, you can connect. Great, right? Well, no.

The reason this scenario is not great is that this configuration change allows the database instance to accept connections coming on any of the DB server's IPs—that is, any one of its configured network interfaces.

Why is this bad? Typically, your databases will only need to be accessible from specific private networks, such as a secure intranet or a VPN connection. However, if the server has other network connections configured, such as one that is connected to the Internet, this setting will make Postgres accessible through all interfaces, including the public Internet connection. Needless to say, if your server responds to connection requests coming from a network it's not meant to listen on, this creates a larger attack surface and forms a security risk.

`listen_addresses = 'localhost'` is one of the predefined choices that are included when we are talking about PostgreSQL adopting "security by default." The configuration should default to the most secure setting possible, which, in this case, is only allowing local connections on the loopback hostname and ignoring anything coming in from the network. This way, network connectivity to the database has to be explicitly enabled by the DBA.

Using security by default

Specifying `listen_addresses = '*'` effectively negates the default security built into the product. For a real-world example of why opting for security by default is a good idea, you should know that in 2020, security researchers found that a staggering *3.6 million MySQL and MariaDB servers were exposed to the Internet*. Needless to say, you don't want your server open to potential attackers who can easily perform port scans to discover open database instances on insecure networks such as the Internet.

Instead, make sure that you are restricting `listen_addresses` to only those interfaces and networks from which clients are actually supposed to be able to connect. For instance, if Postgres should only be accessible from a private network, specify just the database server's IP on the interface connected to that network in `postgresql.conf`:

```
listen_addresses = '10.10.10.56'
```

It's also good practice to set up firewall rules that restrict access to the server instance to only trusted subnets and IPs. Many firewalls also implement logging, which can help with intrusion detection.

8.3   *trust-ing in pg_hba.conf*

The infamous `pg_hba.conf` is one of the most confusing and, unfortunately, feared beasts in the PostgreSQL configuration jungle. It contains the *Host-Based Authentication* (HBA) rules for the database server instance, which control who can connect, where they can connect from, what they can connect to, and how they need to authenticate for that. Its syntax is well-defined for what it's supposed to do but, sadly, uses a format that few will understand nowadays. This can lead to developers and administrators struggling because they have to fiddle with the entries in this file a lot to make Postgres finally accept their connections:

```
psql -h froggeserver -U frogge
Password for user frogge:
psql: error: connection to server at "froggeserver" (10.10.10.56), port 5432
failed: FATAL:  password authentication failed for user "frogge"
```

Sometimes, out of frustration and desperation after having tried lots of combinations and seen the previous message for the hundredth time, DBAs will configure the server to just `trust` them for this connection. This has the consequence of making the server accept their connection without the use of a password, which is frankly "fine for now," as they are finally able to connect.

Other times, there is much less drama, and the choice to do this turns into a learned behavior and habit for developers. To avoid dealing with passwords, `.pgpass` files, certificates, etc., they will take the easy option to allow connections with `trust` in `pg_hba.conf` to speed things along, as follows:

```
host    all    all    10.10.10.0/24    trust
```

The previous entry means that *any* user defined in Postgres can connect to *any* of the cluster's databases *without a password* from the entire *network subnet* 10.10.10.x.

"Okay, so why is this a problem?", you will say. After all, the Frogge Emporium intranet on 10.10.10.0/24 is private, and only authorized persons have access to it.

What happens, though, if another device, application, or piece of software on another server in this subnet is compromised? Then, as Postgres is trusting all connections from that network, it will allow full access to any potential attacker with no authentication.

pg_hba.conf is called that for a reason. Host-based authentication ensures that only trusted clients from trusted hosts can connect to the server and defines how they must authenticate to connect to specific databases.

trust is not an authentication method: it means "let them in with no authentication". It's dangerous and should not be used under any circumstances on machines in, or connected to, production environments as it constitutes a serious security vulnerability. Even if you use trust for local connections only, can you guarantee the security of every other bit of software that's running on that server?

The answer is easy: HBA trust should be avoided entirely. At a minimum, you should use the scram-sha-256 password-based challenge-and-response authentication method to secure access to your databases, like this:

```
hostssl frogge  frogge  10.10.10.29/32  scram-sha-256
```

And while you're at it, it's not a bad idea to enforce SSL encryption and only allow access from specific users on specific hosts to specific databases, as in the previous example.

trust is rarely safe in any environment, let alone in production, as it bypasses essential security layers, and it can end up putting your data at risk.

8.4 *Database owned by a superuser*

It's super common to find clusters that contain databases owned by the postgres user or some other user that has been granted superuser privileges. This is not surprising, as many create those databases by simply following instructions from a post they found on StackOverflow or poor online tutorials. Alternatively, echoing a familiar theme from the two previous sections, some developer or DBA gets fed up with not being able to run all the nice DDL commands they prepared. They then end up doing everything as a superuser, including creating and owning databases. As a PostgreSQL superuser has unrestricted privileges, they can create and manage schemas, tables, and all other types of database objects.

Sooner or later, someone creates a new database and makes it be owned by the superuser:

```
CREATE DATABASE frogge_next OWNER postgres;
```

Before you know it, other people are using it, too, and this arrangement achieves a certain degree of permanence. Unfortunately, while you wouldn't expect to see it on production systems, it is very common to find operational databases owned by a superuser (or, even worse, to find user tables and objects in production use living inside the default `postgres` database). Sometimes, you'll even find the application connecting to the database using the default `postgres` superuser account. Let's see why this is an ill-thought-out strategy.

PostgreSQL's design is meant to encourage the application of the *Principle of Least Privilege* which advocates for granting only those permissions necessary to perform particular tasks. If you make the database and the objects contained within owned by a superuser, for most actions, it will be necessary to access them as a superuser. Therefore, it's easy to assume that people will try to connect to this database using correspondingly privileged accounts.

The problem with this is that, in Postgres, the superuser is omnipotent and can bypass pretty much every security check. This makes using superuser accounts for regular database ownership and operations very dangerous. I can illustrate.

At some point down the road, Frogge's new developer connects to the database with their unprivileged account `jettrodriguez`. Somehow, they manage to run a stored function called `reset_schema()`, a function that cleans out the database so a fresh copy can be restored in its place. However, it was designed by the DBA for developers to use with their unprivileged accounts in development environments only. `reset_schema` proceeds to `DROP` all tables in the current schema, and this now has disastrous consequences for the production database, as the only option is to restore the data from backup, causing significant downtime and reputational damage to Frogge.

You ask, how was this allowed to happen? The function was created by a superuser, and that superuser bestowed the rights to execute it as a superuser to anyone who uses it. As such, the function ran with superuser privileges and proceeded to wreak havoc. The unprivileged developer account *did* have permission to execute functions in that database, and this function *was* visible to the account, so it was easy for disaster to strike.

As the function was created with a privileged account, allowed to run with the corresponding permissions, and provided to unprivileged users, all of the privileges pictured in figure 8.1 became available to the unprivileged user during the execution of this function.

We'll see in the next section how it is possible to expose yourself to malicious actions simply through improper ownership of stored functions or procedures. Even if the stored code is not supposed to be dangerous, executing a buggy procedure with superuser privileges can make the consequences much worse.

Another example: the organization has implemented Row-Level Security (RLS) policies on all their tables. A user connects with an unprivileged account that, through RLS restrictions, is not supposed to see any rows of data in those tables. The user proceeds to `SELECT` from a `VIEW`, and surprisingly, the query does return rows of data. That view is owned by a superuser, and if you remember, we said that superusers bypass most permission checks. Therefore, the RLS `POLICY` will not be taken into account, and the view will return rows to whoever selects it.

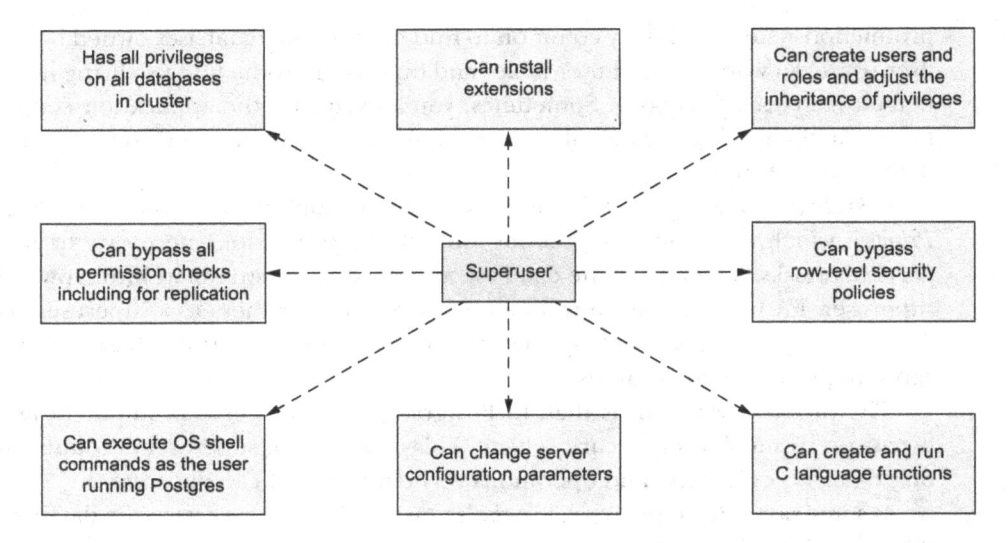

Figure 8.1   A superuser, analogous to the `root` user in UNIX, can bypass all privilege checks and do more things that no other user can. It is far more dangerous than simply having all privileges on all databases.

> **TIP** Look up another way to protect VIEWs against data leaks with the (security_barrier) attribute in the PostgreSQL documentation: https://www.postgresql.org/docs/current/rules-privileges.html.

Therefore, you need to take a step back and ask: Do you really need the superuser to be involved in your database's ownership, given all the privileges a superuser has? Consider the dual risks of people connecting as a superuser to use this database and of objects having superuser privileges attached that effectively allow privilege escalation by unprivileged users. By bypassing the proper use of Postgres ROLEs, you are incurring the unnecessary risk of unauthorized data access and of destructive actions being performed accidentally.

Additionally, if everyone connects with the superuser account, auditing and accountability become difficult, as it's hard to track who performed what actions. Many regulatory frameworks require the enforcement of role-based access control (RBAC) and audit trails, so make sure that you use the built-in role system provided by PostgreSQL.

Most common tasks do not require superuser privileges. You should restrict the use of superuser accounts to only those administration tasks that require the added privileges and create databases and objects owned by nonprivileged accounts. For every new database, you can create a dedicated database role that has just the necessary privileges to own and manage the database. Afterward, you can GRANT the appropriate privileges on this database's objects to the accounts that need them.

8.5 *Setting SECURITY DEFINER carelessly*

In PostgreSQL, you can write code into the database backend with functions, triggers, and RLS policies. As we saw, this code can be executed unintentionally, so it can become a Trojan horse of sorts.

A developer at Frogge Emporium with the username `marionjohnson` is asked by the Sales and Finance departments to create a function that returns the running total of sales income for the month and is granted authorization to access this data. They write the function as follows:

```
CREATE OR REPLACE FUNCTION erp.current_month_sales()
RETURNS numeric AS $$
SELECT sum(amount)
FROM erp.payments
WHERE tstamp BETWEEN date_trunc('month', now()) AND now()
$$ LANGUAGE SQL SECURITY DEFINER;
```

The declaration `SECURITY INVOKER`, which is the default, means that the function will be executed with the privileges of the user that calls it. As the developer wants users from Sales and Finance to be able to execute the function, they choose to specify `SECURITY DEFINER` so that they'll be able to execute it with `marionjohnson`'s (the owner's) privileges.

It works as designed, and the departments in question are pleased, until one morning when the developer receives an angry phone call asking how everyone in the company seems to know the sales figures. You see, Frogge treated this as privileged information, and they were not expecting unauthorized employees to be able to access it. By using `SECURITY DEFINER` and not enforcing checks on who could execute this function, carte blanche was effectively given to anyone who came across it.

`SECURITY DEFINER` works like the `setuid` bit in UNIX file access control. When set, it allows a file to be executed with the permissions of whoever owns the file instead of the permissions of the user executing it. It has legitimate uses for providing access to functionality that certain roles cannot perform directly themselves—for example, a trigger function that writes to the table `audit_log` (that users aren't permitted to touch) when specific actions are performed.

This is why it makes sense to keep `SECURITY DEFINER` functions as straightforward as possible to ensure that they only serve their single purpose and can't be repurposed through parameter use, side effects, or injection of logic.

> **NOTE** Another relevant cool concept is the `LEAKPROOF` declaration in function definitions, which indicates that the function has no side effects. This means that it cannot reveal information about its arguments except through its return value. Therefore, a function that throws an exception for some argument values but not for others can be considered "leaky."

To mitigate these risks, first, ensure that only the roles who are supposed to can execute any functions declared as `SECURITY DEFINER`. You may do this by revoking the default execution privileges from PUBLIC and selectively granting the privileges to run the function, like so:

```
BEGIN;
    CREATE OR REPLACE FUNCTION erp.current_month_sales()
        ...
    REVOKE ALL ON FUNCTION erp.current_month_sales() FROM PUBLIC;
    GRANT EXECUTE ON FUNCTION erp.current_month_sales() TO sales_role;
    GRANT EXECUTE ON FUNCTION erp.current_month_sales() TO finance_role;
COMMIT;
```

Wrapping everything inside the same transaction ensures nobody unauthorized can use the function before the permissions are set correctly.

Second, make sure that any SECURITY DEFINER functions are well-written, tested, and reviewed and that they validate their inputs properly. Otherwise, they may be exploited to cause data leaks or for privilege-escalation purposes.

Additionally, always SET the search_path on a SECURITY DEFINER function to a value with a safe order (see the next section for more details on why), like this:

```
ALTER FUNCTION erp.current_month_sales()
SET search_path = pg_catalog, erp, pg_temp;
```

Last, use SECURITY DEFINER only where it's strictly necessary, as you may end up creating complicated permission tracking scenarios, which make managing your system's security harder.

> **WARNING** As stated in the docs, "Functions run inside the backend server process with the operating system permissions of the database server daemon." This means that if we write a function in a programming language that permits unchecked memory access, we can write code that changes the PostgreSQL server's internal data structures. This is why languages in this category are labeled "untrusted" by Postgres, and only superusers are permitted to create functions using them.

8.6 *Choosing an insecure search path*

In order to save us all some typing, PostgreSQL allows us to specify unqualified object names without having to include the schema name, so we can type in the table name customers instead of erp.customers. The schema search path (search_path) is what makes this possible, as it is the list of schema names that Postgres goes through to find the object that we're referring to.

The schemas (or schemata) are searched in their order of appearance in the search_path. Even if there is a table with the name customers in another schema that is not part of the search path, it will not match, and Postgres will say that no objects with that name were found. The default looks like this:

```
SHOW search_path;
   search_path
-----------------
 "$user", public
(1 row)
```

This signifies that, first, we'll look for that object in a schema with the same name as the current user. If one is not found there, we move on to the next entry, which is the public schema.

Unfortunately, this ordered search, paired with the matching of the first item found, means that you can interfere with the behavior of users' queries by accident or on purpose. To elaborate, if you have permission to create objects in a schema that is found in someone else's search_path, you may place your own object before the one they would normally use due to the search path order.

At the very least, this can cause confusion—for example, if a well-known function name is reused so that now(), which is, in fact, pg_catalog.now(), gets overridden by erp.now(), which gets called in its place.

At worst, someone with malicious intent could create an object in a schema that's ahead of the usual one in your search path to hijack the order in which that object name is encountered. This can trick you into accidentally reading from or inserting into their table or executing their code with your privileges. Because of the extensibility of PostgreSQL, this risk can extend to unexpected objects, such as operators, sequences, etc. For instance, say you have a search path that looks like this:

```
SHOW search_path;
     search_path
--------------------
 "$user", public, erp
(1 row)
```

Someone acting in bad faith could create a function public.current_month_sales(), and that would be chosen over erp.current_month_sales(), causing you to execute their arbitrary code instead of what you were expecting to run.

This is why users nowadays don't have permission by default to create objects in the public schema. But *beware*! Before PostgreSQL 14, all users had CREATE privileges in the schema public. This means that any database upgraded from PostgreSQL 14 or earlier will retain this privilege. To remove it, you can run

```
REVOKE CREATE ON SCHEMA public FROM PUBLIC;
```

The strongest degree of protection against abuse like this can be afforded by restricting who can define objects. Users cannot access objects in a schema that doesn't belong to them unless they are granted USAGE privileges on that schema by the owner. They will also need CREATE privileges on the schema to create objects, and so on. Use roles to control which schemas each user is allowed to access and which they are allowed to CREATE in. In case that's not feasible, remove from the search_path any schemas that allow untrusted users to create stuff and make your queries refer explicitly to objects whose owners you trust.

You should also avoid overuse of the public schema. If you have a complicated system, you should probably create separate schemas for each application component or team. If you have multiple tenants, their data can also reside in different schemas.

In general, while the `public` schema and the `search_path` offer convenience, you need to control their use carefully to avoid the risks of query hijacking and privilege escalation through object name override.

Summary

- Using `psql -W` or `--password` can be confusing and lead to lapses in security. Rely on PostgreSQL's automatic built-in password prompt mechanism instead.
- Setting `listen_addresses = '*'` can expose your database server to insecure networks, so you should only enable the trusted network interfaces that are necessary for database connectivity.
- Using the `trust` method in `pg_hba.conf` in production environments is unacceptable. You should always enforce proper authentication to your server and restrict access as much as is practical.
- Having your databases and their contents owned by a superuser can lead to security problems and accidental damage to your data. Instead, create roles that have only the relevant permissions to own and manage these databases and grant permissions selectively to other roles.
- Declaring functions as `SECURITY DEFINER` can cause data leaks and enable privilege escalation. To reduce risk, use it sparingly and with a safe `search_path` and prefer the combination of `SECURITY INVOKER` with explicit `GRANT`s.
- Not securing your `search_path` can let others hijack queries and escalate their privileges. Apply tight control over object creation in schemas and reference objects owned by trusted users only in queries.

High availability
bad practices

In this chapter

- Neglecting proper backup hygiene
- Forgoing PostgreSQL recovery features
- Being unprepared for database failure
- Using the wrong tools for the job

Another thing for which PostgreSQL has gained a reputation in the industry is its famed resilience. However, this resilience is predicated upon following best practices and using the proper tools. Dangerous situations can arise if complacency takes hold due to "Postgres being a resilient database" and high availability (HA) is relegated to an afterthought. Instead, HA should be central to the deployment plan of any production database cluster.

When I refer to *high availability* in this chapter, I am encompassing the techniques and methods that can keep your database accessible to its users throughout failure scenarios, from minor to catastrophic, and allow it to recover from these failures. The goal of HA is to guarantee the minimum amount of downtime or data loss, being fully aware that the requirements and acceptable limits can differ for each organization.

Unfortunately, out there in the real world, we can find Postgres installations whose keepers neglect some (or all!) of the tenets of HA. This may be due to misconceptions, overconfidence in hardware and software, misplaced cost-saving measures, or just an outright lack of awareness of the importance of the topic. If your database suffers downtime or data loss, it will already be too late to start worrying about HA. This means that the only way to ensure that your data remains safe is to be prepared, vigilant, and proactive. Let's take a look at how things can start to go wrong.

9.1 Not taking backups

Our friendly system administrator at some other company (not at Frogge Emporium; they have suffered enough!) is aware of the risks associated with losing their organization's data. In order to make this outcome less likely, they have opted to go with standard solutions: the disks holding their database implement mirroring with RAID level 1 so that even if they suffer a hard disk crash, there will be a backup drive to fall back on.

> **RAID**
>
> *RAID*, or Redundant Array of Independent Disks, is a storage technique that distributes the data across multiple disk devices to improve performance, achieve increased redundancy, or do both at the same time. The various disk arrangements that also specify what responsibilities each disk has in the scheme are called RAID levels.
>
> There are various levels specifying striping, mirroring, and data parity arrangements, and these levels can also be combined via nesting them. In our case, RAID1 (mirroring) stores a byte-for-byte copy of the data on other disks, so it needs a minimum of two devices.

Apart from RAID, to be extra safe, the administrator has set up a standby server with PostgreSQL streaming replication. They've got double redundancy now, as shown in figure 9.1. So, everything is rosy, right?

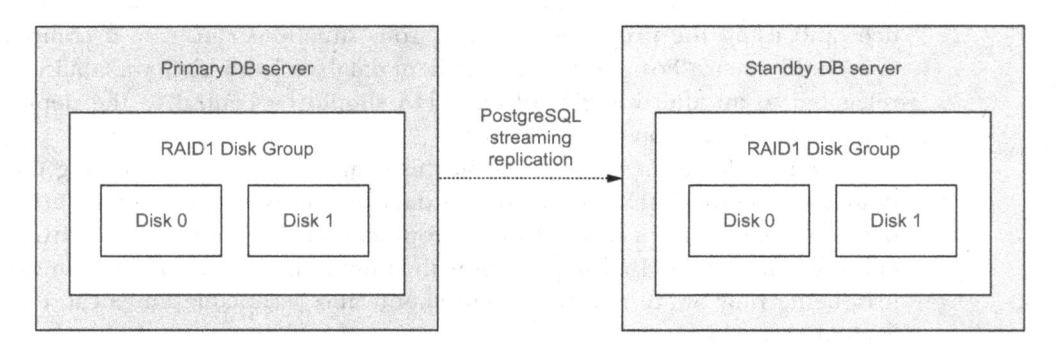

Figure 9.1 A PostgreSQL installation layout demonstrating the double physical redundancy of having a standby server but also RAID1 mirrored disks in each of the servers.

Let's see why they are not as protected as they think they are. First, RAID cannot protect you against filesystem corruption. If the logical file structure or data within is damaged, this corruption gets perfectly duplicated onto the redundant disks, and now you have two (or more) identical bad disks.

What if they had also enabled, through some virtualized or physical implementation, filesystem snapshots? Well, in the case of some software, snapshots may be enough to be able to restore the system to a safe state. PostgreSQL, though, is a complex system with its own write-ahead log, buffers, transaction states, segmented data files, and so on. Its data integrity, as we know, depends on the WAL and data files being in a state of synchronization. It is therefore unsafe to take a file-level copy unless the snapshot is guaranteed to be atomic (i.e., a flashbulb goes off and we take an instantaneous photograph of the entire filesystem). But, even then, the result is not great because when we restore this disk snapshot and start Postgres, it is just as if we had suffered a crash. So, upon startup, Postgres goes into crash recovery and proceeds to replay any committed transactions from the WAL.

You should be aware that restoring the snapshotted filesystem on top of the data directory of a running PostgreSQL instance is a recipe for disaster because of the near-certainty of inconsistencies that will corrupt your data. So, don't do that. We saw that if Postgres is stopped before restoring the filesystem, it behaves as if after a crash when it starts back up, but at least any inconsistencies are taken care of. Realistically, the only safe way to take a snapshot is for the database to be shut down cleanly before taking the snapshot (or quiesced by calling `pg_backup_start()` before and `pg_backup_stop()` after it). However, for many users, this involves an amount of downtime that they can't afford.

> **WARNING** If the data is in multiple tablespaces, then filesystem snapshots are not safe to use unless the snapshot is atomic for the sum of the filesystems in use, which is quite a tall order technically.

Moving on, let's examine why the redundancy of having a physical replica is also insufficient to protect them. Take the super-simple example of the following user error taking place on the primary server:

```
DROP TABLE patient_data;
```

Some careless soul has dropped an important table in production. This immediately gets replicated to the standby server, and now the table is gone from there, too. Even with superhuman speed, there is realistically no way to prevent this from propagating to the other server in time. The only way for them to get it back is to restore it from the backup that they don't have.

Even if there is no errant SQL command, replication is not a guarantee for data safety. Annoyingly, some types of corruption on the primary server (such as corruption of the WAL through a disk or memory error or managing to run two Postgres instances on the same PGDATA) can be replicated to the standby. If the data is corrupted before it is streamed, the replica will receive the bad data.

Delayed replicas are not a solution for this class of problem. Even if you set up an 8- or 24-hour replication delay, what tells you that the realization that something bad has taken place won't happen 8 hours and 1 second after the event or 24 hours and 1 millisecond, for that matter? Remember that the mistake, corruption, or malicious action may not be as immediately obvious as `DROP TABLE patient_data`. The mistake of this organization was that since they had RAID1 disks, server snapshots, and a redundant standby server, they felt they did not need to also take backups.

To recap, solutions at the hardware level like RAID cannot protect you against corruption occurring at any level above the hardware. Block- or file-level solutions such as snapshots are also not a satisfactory backup strategy for PostgreSQL as they need to be managed and synchronized carefully in conjunction with the server process. Ideally, you need to use suitable tools to take backups that are aware of PostgreSQL's process, data file, and WAL semantics so that they don't inadvertently destroy your data integrity. `pg_basebackup` is a safe backup tool that comes with Postgres for the explicit purpose of taking safe data directory snapshots without needing to stop the database.

NOTE   You can find the official documentation for `pg_basebackup` at https://www.postgresql.org/docs/current/app-pgbasebackup.html.

Finally, it is a misconception that snapshots or replication are appropriate or adequate substitutes for having proper backups, and in the following section, we will see more reasons why this is the case. Backups give you the ability to recover your data regardless of your hardware or replication setup. Because of the high risk posed to operations, any experienced DBA should find the lack of explicit backups unforgivable.

9.2   *No Point-In-Time Recovery*

Our DBA has seen the light and has decided to begin backing up immediately. The time investment is seen as worthwhile, and everyone is pleased to hear that their database will be made safer. The traditional concept of a database backup involves "dumping" the data and then storing it somewhere safe, so they decide to use `pg_dump`. According to the documentation, this is "a utility for backing up a PostgreSQL database," so, as it comes with Postgres, it seems to fit the bill well.

Backups are made. `pg_dump` can only dump one database at a time, so, one by one, each database in the cluster is successfully backed up. These backups are guaranteed to be consistent as `pg_dump` obtains a snapshot to extract the data, and there's no need to interrupt database operations. A point of note, though: backup consistency across two interdependent databases cannot be guaranteed while they are both running.

The `pg_dumpall` utility extends the backup scope across the cluster by essentially looping through and performing a `pg_dump` of each database. While this is convenient and ensures that global objects common to all databases are included, the backups are still not consistent between databases.

Let's assess where we stand now. We have safe dumps of the data that can be perfectly restored to an empty database. Great! Let's look at the problems that we mentioned in the previous section one by one.

Are we protected against losing all our data? Yes, mostly. We can restore it at will, irrespective of what happens to our servers. The reason why it's "mostly yes" is because we only have the data up to the point of the last backup, so while we may lose some of the most recent transactions, not all is lost. Are we safe against data corruption? Eh, again, yes and no. We have a snapshot of the data, but only up to the point of the last verified safe backup. The same goes for accidental or malicious damage to the data. Even if you can pinpoint exactly when it happened, you can only roll back to the point where the last known safe backup was taken by restoring it.

This means that even if they back up their DB every day, a proverbial DROP TABLE executed in the afternoon would result in the loss of all data from that morning with no way to recover it. The same is true for filesystem snapshots and any full backup method, not just pg_dump.

This is exactly why the late, great Simon Riggs introduced *Point-in-Time Recovery* (PITR) to the PostgreSQL code base some 20 years before the writing of these pages. PITR allows you to effectively roll your database back to the *precise* transaction you require. This means restoring to the exact point *before* the damage occurred because, with PITR, you are not limited to the state captured in the last full backup of the database. It can achieve this by taking advantage of the write-ahead log; after all, we do have a perfect and replayable record of each and every transaction.

To perform PITR, we use the combination of *base backups* (produced by the Postgres utility program pg_basebackup) with archived WAL files. The base backups are full binary-perfect snapshot copies of the entire database cluster, not just individual databases. WAL archival is also known as *continuous backup* because if you keep around all the WAL that's been constantly produced by Postgres since your base backup, it allows you to restore to any point in time after the base backup was taken.

All you need to do to take advantage of this is to set up WAL archiving by defining a custom archive_command in postgresql.conf and then taking a full backup with pg_basebackup. Remember that base backups are snapshots in essence, so it's important to note that, for PITR, you also need all the WAL generated from the moment you start the backup until it completes. Restoring is as simple as setting the recovery_target_time parameter to the moment you want to recover up to and then pointing Postgres to a restored data directory. In PostgreSQL 17, a feature to facilitate backing up huge databases was introduced: incremental backups using pg_basebackup. These can be combined with older base backups to create full backups.

> **TIP** You can read about *timelines* in the "Continuous Archiving and Point-in-Time Recovery" section of the PostgreSQL documentation (https://www.postgresql.org/docs/current/continuous-archiving.html#BACKUP-TIMELINES). It explains how you can travel back in time to before a transaction was committed and branch off into different timelines as many times as needed to pinpoint the correct moment to return to, all without overwriting or losing any data.

To return for a moment to the topic of pg_dump, there are other serious problems with using it as a backup tool. pg_dump performs *logical*, not *physical*, backups. This means that it stores the description of how to re-create the database as opposed to the actual bytes of data. As a consequence, when you restore from a `pg_dump`, PostgreSQL needs to re-create the binary structure of every object you are recovering on disk. This includes indexes, which are not copied over and get re-created on the fly, so the restore operation can end up being quite time-consuming. Additionally, your old cluster's internal Postgres stats are lost (since this is a fresh cluster), and table statistics need to be re-created from scratch.

If you don't take advantage of PITR, you are exposing yourself to the danger of easily avoidable data loss and possibly painstaking re-creation of the missing data. PITR and continuous archival may require significant storage space because of the need to store full backups alongside any WAL generated since they were taken. Nevertheless, it is regarded as an essential feature for heavy-workload systems and enterprise usage where high reliability is critical.

9.3   *Backing up manually*

So, following on from the previous sections, the diligent DBA has resolved to back up the database every day, taking control of the situation personally as it's such an important process. However, it's one of the facts of life that everyone needs a day off eventually. One Monday morning comes around, and the administrator isn't there to take a backup. Instead, they are basking in the warm sun at the beach on a well-deserved vacation.

Is this the mistake?

No! The diligent DBA has dutifully delegated this deed to a developer. Said developer indeed comes in on Monday morning and proceeds to take a database backup every day for the rest of the week while the DBA is away.

When the DBA comes back the following week feeling all refreshed, they take a look at the server and are horrified to discover that the developer had saved the backups of the PGDATA location `/mnt/pgdata` inside a directory called `/mnt/pgdata/backups`! Not only is this not the proper backup location, but even worse, it's on the same filesystem and physical drive as the database. Disaster was averted, but only narrowly, because the organization was lucky enough not to suffer a server failure during the DBA's absence.

This should teach us two things. First, don't keep the backup on the same physical hardware as the database; we all know that hardware eventually fails. Some would take this further and mandate that there should always be an offsite copy of the backups in case the whole site catches on fire or otherwise.

The second lesson here is that nobody should rely on manual processes to safeguard their data. Humans make mistakes, they get distracted or forget, they miss work, or they leave on holiday or for another job. They may take the backup at a different time every day or even skip a day. Worst of all, sometimes they tend to keep all the knowledge of the backup procedure in their head, so it isn't written down anywhere. I think we'll all agree that all this variability and uncertainty has no place inside an IT system.

The key to good backup hygiene is to remove the human factor and rely on automation. The ideal here is to have a non-interactive system that automatically takes regular backups of the database. Of course, this should be monitored in case it also fails for some reason. At the same time, you should take advantage of continuous WAL archiving for PITR purposes.

WARNING Beware that you can't mix and match logical and physical backups. You can't perform PITR with a `pg_dump` backup and a bunch of WAL files.

You can use any tool that comes with PostgreSQL and set up an automatic schedule for your backups using a reliable task scheduler such as `cron`, which is available on any UNIX system. The two most popular dedicated open source tools are Barman (Backup and Recovery Manager) and pgBackRest (Postgres Backup and Restore). These make PITR easy and support advanced scenarios such as complex schedules, backing up multiple servers, multiple locations for redundancy, retention policies, a choice of transfer methods, and parallelization. Setting them up is as simple as installing the packages and adding a couple of lines in their respective configuration files.

You could craft a backup architecture that looks something like figure 9.2. So, you could back up your cluster with Barman automatically using `pg_basebackup` to pull base backups and a replication connection to pull in WAL for PITR. Alternatively, Barman could set up an `archive_command` that sends the WAL using `rsync`, which allows the parallel transfer of multiple files, as a way to deal with huge WAL production.

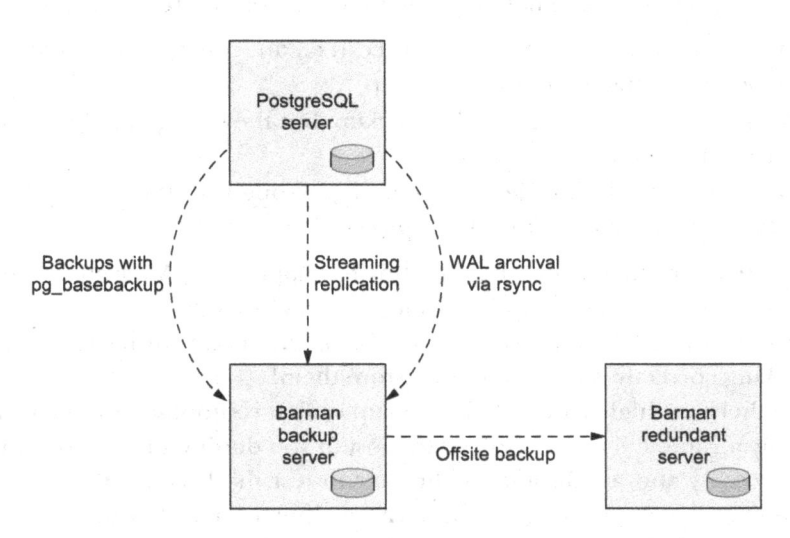

Figure 9.2 A sample PostgreSQL backup setup with a dedicated Barman server and geographical redundancy showing the possible transfer paths

NOTE You can find these PostgreSQL backup tools and their documentation at https://pgbarman.org/ (Barman) and https://pgbackrest.org/ (pgBackRest).

Finally, besides being error-prone, manual processes don't scale well; you can't reasonably expect someone to perform frequent backups of dozens or hundreds of database servers, which is a realistic number for large operations these days. Now, admittedly, this mistake is not PostgreSQL specific or even database specific, but it happens in the industry more than you would like to think. It's simply inexcusable to take backups manually with such an abundance of backup tools, schedulers, and facilities to automate backing up in the PostgreSQL ecosystem. You can go so far as to say, "A backup that is not automated is no backup at all."

9.4   *Not testing backups*

This one is, again, one of those that you cannot repeat enough times. There have been infamous incidents involving important names in the industry where data was lost because, even though a backup did exist, too much faith was placed in it working properly.

Let's imagine that all the previous advice from this chapter has been adhered to and that backups are being taken from Postgres in an automated fashion and stored safely in two locations, along with all the necessary WAL to enable PITR. The time comes for the server to blow up, and the DBA obligingly brings out the backup to restore the database. However, Murphy's law strikes again, and the backup doesn't work: the restore command fails. Now, the company has no database and no backup to restore one from. You could say that the situation is somewhat bad.

How can it all go so wrong? There's ample potential for failure here:

- The backup may be broken at the source (i.e., an incorrect invocation of the command producing an unusable backup).
- The backup process creates a usable backup, but the storage medium corrupts its data at some point.
- The backup succeeds, but there's something wrong with the storage location, and it loses the backup after it's been placed there.

How can you be aware that something like this has happened? After all, the backup process produces no indications or hints about these eventualities.

The answer is *testing*. The only way to make 100% sure that your backups are available and working correctly is to attempt to restore them!

The stakes here are high. After all, the backup is what is supposed to save you from data loss—only for it to fail when it's needed most. If you don't want this to happen to you, it is a necessity and an absolute no-brainer to test the backups that you make. After all, commands can go wrong, software can malfunction, disks can fail, networks can go bad, and so on.

You can test your PostgreSQL backups by using a testing environment to restore them. Alongside the backup itself, you'll be testing the recovery procedure, too, so this forms a useful "fire drill" for you and your team in the case of an actual emergency. Here is an example of how to test the backup by restoring it to a fresh Postgres instance:

1 Copy the base backup to the testing PGDATA target directory.
2 Verify the base backup's checksums with `pg_verifybackup`.
3 Copy the rest of the WAL produced since the backup into the test PGDATA.
4 Call `pg_waldump` on the WAL files to verify that they are parsable.
5 Start Postgres from the testing PGDATA directory to recover the database and verify that it can reach a consistent state.

For the ultimate peace of mind, you can go through every page in the restored database to make sure that it is correctly readable. It just involves using the `pageinspect` module to loop over every page of every relation. You read it from the disk with the `get_raw_page()` function, check its header with `page_header()`, and verify its checksum with `page_checksum()`.

NOTE You can see how to use the `pageinspect` functionality at https://www.postgresql.org/docs/current/pageinspect.html.

The backup verification procedure is also a prime candidate for automation, and you should have it alert you if any errors are encountered along the way.

I will now wrap up with a true story from the field that shows how scary things can get if you don't stick to these best practices. A company that was a market leader in its field had grown organically over many years. Since the beginning, they had been using PostgreSQL for their database, which was central to their operations. It is fair to say that the company could not exist without this database as it contained critical data for the services the company provided. One fair day, their database server blew up: the hard disk malfunctioned.

They were aghast to discover that their backup was unusable and that their last usable backup was many months old, making most data irrelevant to current company operations. Ever since they were a small startup, this company had been taking backups (good) with `pg_dump` (bad because, since then, PostgreSQL had gained the features of streaming replication, base backups, and PITR, and they should have been using those). This is another reason why you shouldn't use `pg_dump` as a backup tool, even with full automation configured. If you rely on scripts written decades ago instead of using a dedicated backup utility that gets updates and fixes, you are taking a huge risk. User-created scripts can silently fail for whatever reason; this is exactly what happened in this case. The script the company had always been using for backing up stopped working at some point, and they were none the wiser. It may be that your ever-reliable script no longer works when it is moved into a virtualized environment or when it is run inside a Docker container, Kubernetes pod, etc.

The only reason this was not an extinction event for the company was that they had at least one ancient backup, but it was surely a near-extinction event and a wake-up call. Fortunately, they were able to recover most filesystem contents from the broken disk but with no recognizable structure. Eventually, I painstakingly reconstructed their entire database with no data loss, but the rest of this story is long and for a different type of book.

In a callback to the previous section, you can go so far as to say, "A backup that is not tested is no backup at all."

9.5   *Not having redundancy*

We'll now examine the case where the backup strategy is just perfect: Frogge Emporium is using the proper PostgreSQL tools, takes regular automated backups, and tests them automatically as well. They feel pretty well-protected now, and their operation is not at risk—or so they think.

What happens if the server catches on fire? They'll have to procure a new server to restore the backup into, and that can take time. This can, of course, be mitigated by having a spare server around, and this is exactly what cloud computing resource providers do. Even if they're using a hosting service provider, they'll have to restore the whole database installation into an empty physical server or a newly created cloud instance.

Although this takes a lot less time, the downtime is still significant, and here's when we start talking about the disaster recovery terms *RPO* (Recovery Point Objective) and *RTO* (Recovery Time Objective). RPO is how much data we can afford to lose in a theoretical disaster scenario. We've got that handled pretty well, with PITR capable of restoring our data up to the last transaction that was committed in the last WAL file that we were able to save. RTO, however, is how much downtime we can afford before service is fully restored, and this is entirely dependent on our HA architecture.

PostgreSQL high-availability features and a bit of history

Replication has been a core part of PostgreSQL's HA architecture since the time of log shipping, when this was achieved with continuous archiving by copying WAL files to the other server through the `archive_command`. Starting with PostgreSQL 8.2, this introduced the concept of *warm standby* servers that were ready to take over from the primary server at the drop of a command.

With the introduction of *streaming replication* in PostgreSQL 9.0, WAL started getting automatically streamed asynchronously to the other server. This enabled warm standby servers to have more up-to-date data than was possible by copying whole WAL files and, therefore, opened the door to being able to use those servers to serve data as well. The capability of connecting to a standby server to run read-only queries is known as having a *hot standby* (another Riggs feature).

PostgreSQL 9.1 allowed *synchronous replication*. By performing the streaming of WAL synchronously, standby servers were guaranteed to always be up to date with the primary by having exactly the same transactions committed. This eliminates any potential to lose data that hasn't been streamed to the standby because of replication lag but introduces a latency penalty (because of the roundtrip to ensure the transaction is written on both sides).

In version 9.2, the ability to *cascade* replication or stream from a standby server to another standby was added. By using a standby to relay, you can offload and reduce the number of replication connections that the primary needs to handle.

Replication slots came with Postgres 9.4, and they solved the problem of WAL being removed by the primary before it can be consumed by a standby by guaranteeing that WAL remains on disk until it can be streamed to the last standby that needs it. This, however, introduces the potential problem of accumulating WAL on disk indefinitely for an unresponsive or missing standby.

Release 9.5 introduced continuous archiving in standby, so replicas could have their own separate WAL archive. Finally, PostgreSQL 10 introduced native logical replication, but this capability's main use is not for guaranteeing HA.

With a plethora of built-in HA configurations at our disposal, PostgreSQL can cater to almost every HA scenario. Restricting yourself to a single node makes no sense in a production scenario if the database is at the center of your operations. At the time of writing these words, tolerating an RTO of whole days is almost unthinkable, and most scenarios permit an RTO of minutes or seconds. For very demanding applications, there even exist solutions that allow PostgreSQL *failover* in the range of milliseconds. Remember that PostgreSQL is a single-master system, and you can't have two primary servers for your databases at the same time. Failover is the process of *promoting* a standby to become the new primary server. We will further discuss failover mechanisms in section 9.6.

By taking advantage of data replication to have server redundancy, your database is much less vulnerable to events such as power outages or damage to hardware or even the data center location where the hardware is hosted. Not having to wait for backups to be restored and being able to just switch to another server and continue as normal can make a huge difference for your organization; just imagine the amount of money a bank or trading firm can lose in seconds if their system is not available. For reference, the SWIFT banking system handles about 11.5 million international payments each day. Given an average payment size of $45,000, this means nearly $6 million is transacted *every second.* Besides revenue loss, also consider the reputational harm that an organization suffers when their service is unavailable. If you've ever been frustrated with a social media app on your phone when it says, "Sorry, something went wrong," instead of showing you wholesome pictures of cats, you've experienced downtime from the user perspective.

Depending on your requirements, this might be an HA system that you can build, as shown in figure 9.3. In the configuration pictured, we see that, instead of two, we have three database servers. If you don't want to compromise your redundancy while one server is down for maintenance or because of permanent failure, you will need a second standby. To avoid putting extra replication and backup load on our primary, we have configured cascading replication from the first standby to both the second standby and the backup server.

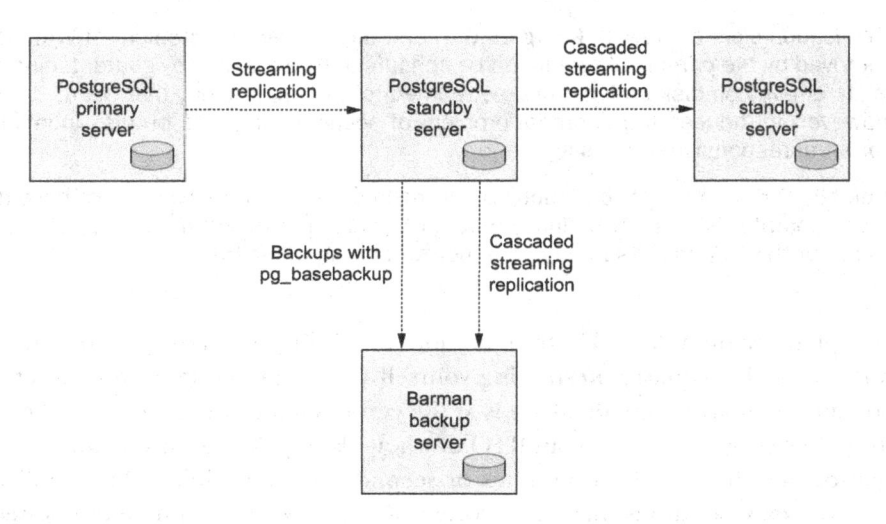

Figure 9.3   A sample PostgreSQL HA setup with a cascaded replication for redundancy and backup

Quick recovery from failure is something that almost everyone who uses PostgreSQL professionally needs, and providing redundancy is the best way to achieve this. Implement streaming replication and keep one or more standby nodes around. As a bonus, you can use them to offload your read traffic.

9.6   *Using no HA tool*

Just as with backups, your HA setup can greatly benefit from automation. Consider the following case: Frogge Emporium engineers have written custom failover scripts to automatically promote a Postgres standby server when the primary goes down for whatever reason. They've tested them extensively in the lab and have confidence in the script logic. The lab, though, isn't like the real world, and they haven't accounted for replication lag. One of the replicas may be lagging. Can you guess what will come next if the primary fails and the lagging replica happens to be the one that gets promoted?

What will happen is that the other replica(s) will have received more transactions through the WAL than the new primary has. When the lagged replica is promoted to become the new primary, it will be missing these transactions. This will necessitate a complicated procedure to extract the missing transactions from the replicas that have them and reintegrate them into the primary's timeline and data. Otherwise, the expected RPO may not be met. Even worse, this bit of extra WAL will not be compatible with the new primary's timeline, as the timelines diverged upon promotion. As a consequence, none of the other replicas will be able to follow the new primary without having their WAL *rewound* back to a point before the timeline split. By the term *follow*, we mean being able to continue to receive WAL and replay it from that point onward, and *rewinding* is simply returning to an earlier point.

This is why, instead of rolling your own HA code that needs to account for every corner case, you shouldn't reinvent the wheel but instead trust solutions written by experts who have considered every possible failure scenario and tested their HA software against it.

Let's check out another such scenario. Between the two data centers that contain the primary and standby nodes, respectively, we get a network disconnection for a few minutes (what we call a *network partition*). Frogge's promotion script on the replica node detects that the primary is down (because it is unreachable) and decides to make the replica the new primary. However, the original primary node is still working fine and accepting writes because it's just the connection between itself and the standby that has failed. When network connectivity is restored, we'll have two Postgres nodes acting as primaries, with diverging data. This phenomenon is known as a *split-brain*, and the data inconsistency between the nodes needs to be manually resolved, as in the previous example.

A dedicated HA tool is better because it can detect and handle such failures using mechanisms like witness nodes, quorum, and fencing to prevent split-brain. HA tools are aware of the entire database node cluster and every instance's state and WAL position, which is something that PostgreSQL doesn't yet do by itself. For this reason, they can effectively coordinate failover and automatically enforce the consistency of WAL timelines using tools such as pg_rewind. Some HA tools can even automatically clone standbys from the primary or a backup and integrate them into the HA cluster with a single command. Moreover, most have built-in script hooks and other facilities for monitoring, alerting, and conditional operations, such as reconfiguring PgBouncer to reflect the cluster's new state after a failover.

You can lean on solid open source solutions like RepMgr (pronounced "rep manager," short for replication manager) and Patroni (pronounced "pat-roe-knee") to set up and take care of your HA cluster with tested failover mechanisms. For the use of PostgreSQL with Kubernetes, there is the CloudNativePG operator, which uses built-in Kubernetes HA patterns to provide failover, promotion, and backup logic that is appropriate for Postgres.

Handling failover and ensuring consistency manually is difficult and susceptible to human error and may require more time than your organization can afford because of its HA requirements. Equally, custom scripts often cannot capture the nuances of proper PostgreSQL failover logic and timeline semantics or handle edge cases. Your architecture can be made more robust by taking advantage of the tested features of established HA tools, and you'll be better equipped to avoid inconsistency, downtime, and data loss.

Summary

- RAID and filesystem snapshots can't help you reliably recover from corruption, human error, or malicious activity. The best way to guarantee your data is safe is to take backups using appropriate tools like `pg_basebackup`.

- Taking full backups only makes you vulnerable to data loss between backups. Use Point-in-Time Recovery with continuous archiving to be able to restore your database to the point before it was damaged.

- Taking backups manually is not robust or reliable; you should instead schedule automated backups, preferably using dedicated software that is PostgreSQL-aware (such as Barman or pgBackRest) and ensuring that you have a redundant copy of the backups in a second location.

- Untested backups can fail when you need them the most, so to ensure that they work correctly, always attempt a full restore to test your backups. Do not rely solely on automation but verify every step. Avoid using homegrown scripts and prefer tried-and-tested solutions.

- Having a single database server with no provision for failover inevitably leads to downtime. Ensure redundancy by setting up standby nodes via replication.

- Manual failover or custom scripts are risky because of the potential for extended downtime, data divergence, or loss. Prefer proven high-availability tools such as RepMgr, Patroni, and CloudNativePG for Kubernetes to ensure reliable and effective management of your HA cluster.

Upgrade/migration bad practices

In this chapter

- Skipping upgrade versions (and their release notes)
- Not testing thoroughly before an upgrade or migration and what can happen
- Accounting for differences between different database types and versions

Upgrading PostgreSQL is pretty easy, while migrating from another Relational Database Management System (RDBMS) to PostgreSQL may be slightly trickier. Both, however, are critical steps that require careful preparation and cannot be taken lightly. If something goes wrong, the upgrade or migration can result in performance issues, outages, or even data corruption. Mistakes and oversights can come from misunderstanding the upgrade process for databases in general and PostgreSQL in particular.

10.1 Not reading all release notes

I mentioned back in chapter 7 that PostgreSQL offers great backward compatibility and that you can generally count on code written for an old Postgres release still working fine on the latest version. For this reason, as well as a conscious decision on the part of the developers, Postgres doesn't generally impose restrictions on upgrading. This means that you can usually skip versions provided there is no chasm between them, like upgrading from a release a decade older. For example, you could upgrade from version 13 to 16, and the upgrade path would usually be very reliable and worry-free.

Our proverbial DBA decides to do just this to take advantage of the new features and performance improvements offered by the latest and greatest, so an upgrade from PostgreSQL 13 to 16 is scheduled and performed. As expected, the upgrade procedure went smoothly, and even though the company arranged for a maintenance window of 30 minutes, pg_upgrade made quick work of the task, and they were able to finish the upgrade in just a handful of minutes.

All is well until strange things start appearing in the database. Specifically, the loyalty discount applied to gym subscriptions seems off since the upgrade, and the accounts team is asking why. The company offers one-third of a year free for loyal gym customers when they sign up for another full year. To illustrate, someone signing up on 2024-01-01 would get a subscription that ended on 2025-04-01. However, the account team has now noticed that the same subscription beginning on 2024-01-01 would now end on 2024-05-01, giving the customer an extra free month. The application code around loyalty discounts hadn't changed, so the DBA found the discrepancy very strange indeed and decided to investigate.

The relevant code fragment looked like this:

```
IF existing AND fullyear THEN
    expiry = expiry + '0.333 years';
END IF;
```

Just for existing customers renewing for a full year, this snippet idiomatically adds a third of a year to the subscription expiry date (don't ask—the marketing department operates in mysterious ways).

To verify the discrepancy, the DBA writes this short test:

```
DO $$
DECLARE
    existing boolean; fullyear boolean; expiry timestamptz;
BEGIN
    existing := true;
    fullyear := true;
    expiry = '2025-01-01';
    IF existing AND fullyear THEN
        RAISE NOTICE 'Expiry date: %', (expiry + '0.333 years')::text;
    END IF;
END $$;
```

This sets existing and fullyear to true, and it assumes an original expiry date of 2025-01-01. The DBA proceeds to run this on a PostgreSQL 13 instance:

```
NOTICE:  Expiry date: 2025-04-01 00:00:00+01
DO
```

This works as expected. Now the DBA runs the same code on a PostgreSQL 16 instance:

```
NOTICE:  Expiry date: 2025-05-01 00:00:00+01
DO
```

This verifies that the result has changed between Postgres 13 and 16! But how and why? After painstaking research in the documentation, the DBA finds the answer: in the section about the `interval` type, the PostgreSQL 13 documentation states,

> *Fractional parts of units greater than months are truncated to be an integer number of months*

whereas the Postgres 16 documentation says,

> *Fractional parts of units greater than months are rounded to be an integer number of months*

This single word change, from "truncated" to "rounded," makes all the difference.

To illustrate this further, the DBA runs a more granular query. First, they run it against a PostgreSQL 13 instance where they observe

```
postgres=# SELECT 1.333*12 as months, ('1.333 years'::interval) as months;
 months |    months
--------+---------------
 15.996 | 1 year 3 mons
(1 row)
```

And then, similarly, they run it against a PostgreSQL 16 instance:

```
postgres=# SELECT 1.333*12 as months, ('1.333 years'::interval) as months;
 months |    months
--------+---------------
 15.996 | 1 year 4 mons
(1 row)
```

Now the difference is obvious and aligns with the explanation in the documentation. A 15.996-month subscription was being truncated to 15 months prior to upgrade and now is being rounded to 16 months post upgrade.

The DBA read the PostgreSQL 16 release notes, but there was no warning about this! However ill-advised adding an `interval` of "a third of a year" to a `timestamptz` may be on the part of the untroubled developer, that is exactly what they were asked to do by the product manager, who, in turn, was asked by marketing.

Here, the fault lies with the DBA. What they should have done is read all the intervening major release notes to identify the changes made between Postgres 13 and 14, 14 and 15, and finally 15 and 16. Even though skip-upgrading is possible and even desirable, due diligence dictates that you should go through the entire set of release notes. If our DBA had done this, they would have discovered that this change was introduced with PostgreSQL 15, and they would have saved time and effort.

The performance and behavior of PostgreSQL features can change in subtle ways between major releases. In this case, the fractional interval specified in years was previously getting truncated, resulting in an expiry date of April 1, whereas from version 15 onward, it is getting rounded to the nearest month, giving us an expiry of May 1.

The PostgreSQL 15.0 release notes from 2022-10-13 state:

```
When interval input provides a fractional value for a unit greater than
months, round to the nearest month (Bruce Momjian)
```

> **NOTE** Fractional input to `interval` is explained here in the Postgres docs: https://www.postgresql.org/docs/current/datatype-datetime.html#DATA YPE-INTERVAL-INPUT.

What can we learn from this? Well, we can learn that ambiguity in code applying discounts can cost us money, but the more salient point is that upgrading without accounting for all the changes in behavior between two releases can result in all sorts of corner cases manifesting that are not immediately obvious after the upgrade. Bypassing the intervening release notes when you are skipping over even one version is not harmless because one of the releases in between may have introduced a breaking change that you will be unaware of. What you may have missed can take costly time to diagnose and fix later.

Take a look at the PostgreSQL release timeline in figure 10.1 and note how many minor versions are released throughout the lifetime of each major version.

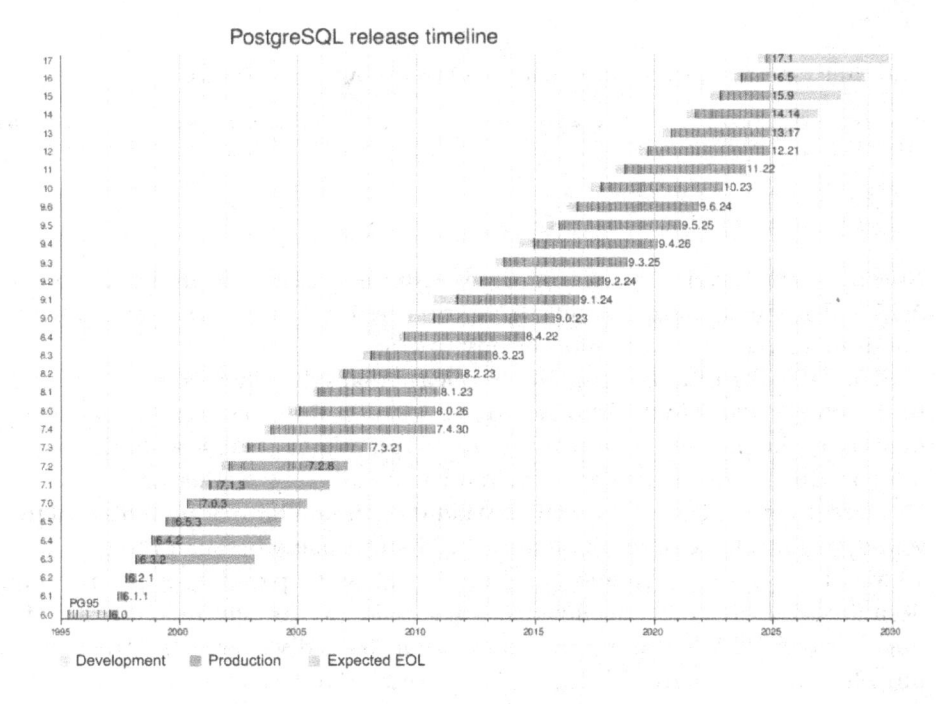

Figure 10.1 A graphical representation of the PostgreSQL release timeline. Generated from data available under the Creative Commons Attribution-ShareAlike 4.0 License using https:// en.wikipedia.org/wiki/Template:Timeline_PostgreSQL.

The bottom line is that if you have not read all the release notes between the original and target versions, you have committed a serious upgrading mistake. Make sure to pay attention to function deprecations or changes in name, changes to configuration and default settings, and SQL syntax updates.

10.2 Performing inadequate testing

The mistake in the previous section would have been caught had more rigorous testing taken place before the upgrade. Let us now look at another case where not testing enough before upgrading or migrating can catch you out.

Frogge Emporium, when upgrading from PostgreSQL 11 to 12, started noticing some performance issues. Specifically, one of their queries (that we saw in chapter 2, section 2.3) compiles a list of emails of customers who have been notified that they have an unpaid invoice for services (not purchased items). In their monitoring tool, it looks like this query is performing worse, which is a surprise. Didn't we say elsewhere in this book that code that was written for PostgreSQL 11 will work fine in PostgreSQL 12?

Frogge is intrigued and decides to investigate, so they set up one Postgres installation running on version 11 and another on version 12 to run comparative tests. They decide to run the same query through EXPLAIN ANALYZE on both instances in an attempt to detect any differences.

On the PostgreSQL 11 instance, they run

```
EXPLAIN (ANALYZE, COSTS OFF, TIMING OFF)
    WITH unp AS (
        SELECT id, customer c, order_group AS og
        FROM erp.invoices
        WHERE paid = false
    ),
    ni AS (
        SELECT og.id
        FROM erp.order_groups og
        JOIN erp.orders o ON o.order_group = og.id
        WHERE o.item IS NULL
    )
    SELECT DISTINCT email
    FROM erp.customer_contact_details ccd
    JOIN unp ON unp.c = ccd.id
    JOIN ni ON ni.id = unp.og
    JOIN erp.sent_emails se ON se.invoice = unp.id
    AND se.email_type = 'Invoice reminder';
```

The execution plan that results is as follows, somewhat abridged:

```
                              QUERY PLAN
----------------------------------------------------------------------------
 HashAggregate (actual rows=9 loops=1)
   Group Key: ccd.email
   CTE unp
     -> Gather (actual rows=1350 loops=1)
           Workers Planned: 2
           Workers Launched: 2
```

```
                    -> Parallel Seq Scan on invoices (actual rows=450 loops=3)
                          [...]
        CTE ni
          -> Gather (actual rows=1350 loops=1)
                Workers Planned: 2
                Workers Launched: 2
                -> Nested Loop (actual rows=450 loops=3)
                      -> Parallel Seq Scan on orders o (actual rows=450 loops=3)
                            [...]
                      -> Index Only Scan using order_groups_pkey on order_groups
                         og (actual rows=1 loops=1350)
                            [...]
   -> Merge Join (actual rows=9 loops=1)
        Merge Cond: (unp.og = ni.id)
        [...]
              -> Hash Join (actual rows=1350 loops=1)
                   Hash Cond: (unp.id = se.invoice)
                   -> Hash Join (actual rows=1350 loops=1)
                        Hash Cond: (unp.c = ccd.id)
                           [...]
 Planning Time: 0.216 ms
 Execution Time: 50.033 ms
```

We can see that the two common table expressions (CTEs) caused parallel table scans. Their filtered results were made available for subsequent `HashJoins` and finally a `HashAggregate` used for grouping, both of which are relatively fast operations for large datasets. The query's execution time was 50 ms.

They then run the same EXPLAIN statement on the PostgreSQL 12 instance and are surprised to see a different execution plan for the same query!

```
                            QUERY PLAN
----------------------------------------------------------------------------
 Unique (actual rows=9 loops=1)
   -> Sort (actual rows=9 loops=1)
        Sort Key: ccd.email
        Sort Method: quicksort  Memory: 25kB
        -> Nested Loop (actual rows=9 loops=1)
              -> Nested Loop (actual rows=9 loops=1)
                    [...]
                            -> Parallel Hash Join (actual rows=3 loops=3)
                                 Hash Cond: (o.order_group =
                                 invoices.order_group)
                                 -> Parallel Seq Scan on orders o (actual
                                 rows=450 loops=3)
                                       [...]
                                 -> Parallel Hash (actual rows=450 loops=3)
                                       [...]
                                       -> Parallel Index Scan using
 invoices_pk on invoices (actual rows=450 loops=3)
                                             [...]
                                 -> Sort (actual rows=1347
                                 loops=3)
                                       [...]
```

```
                                                       ->  Seq Scan on
sent_emails se (actual rows=1350 loops=3)
                                                          Filter: (email_type
= 'Invoice reminder'::email_type)
                                                          [...]
Planning Time: 0.538 ms
Execution Time: 85.025 ms
```

The PostgreSQL 12 query plan is different: there's no mention of CTEs, and there are two levels of nested loops. The inner nested loop performs an index scan, which means that the index is scanned multiple times because of the outer loop. The filtering also happens after the joins, which means that what we don't need is eliminated later, after processing more data. Finally, the results are sorted and then passed through Unique. As a result, the query now takes 85 ms to run.

It looks like Postgres has inlined the CTEs and subsequently went down a different execution path. This doesn't necessarily mean that this query plan is worse in all cases, but it so happens that, in this case, it's slower.

As we previously mentioned, the behavior of PostgreSQL features can change in subtle ways between major releases, and this is one of these cases. Starting with Postgres version 12, CTEs began to be automatically inlined when they are referenced just once in the query, as long as they are not recursive and have no side effects.

Something else that changed between releases 11 and 12 and caught out a number of people was that just-in-time (JIT) compilation was enabled by default. This caused some already fast and optimal queries to become slower by default, as Postgres needlessly spent CPU time trying to optimize them further with JIT. If regression tests are not performed with the actual queries, and using version 11 as the baseline, this sort of slowdown is hard to catch. The reason why it's needed to test the queries themselves is that they may happen to cross the `jit_above_cost` threshold that triggers the automatic JIT optimizer.

What both of these examples tell us is that instead of assuming that a successful upgrade means that everything will work as expected, you need to do the due diligence to thoroughly test your application and code with the new release. As PostgreSQL can introduce optimizations and behavior changes in the pursuit of ever faster performance, this can lead to completely different execution plans and can have a significant impact on the performance of your queries.

It's important to test your queries with real-world data (or as realistic as is feasible) to detect potential issues. Otherwise, there's simply no guarantee that everything in your upgraded system will behave the same way. Ideally, this testing should be performed in a staging environment before upgrading your production system, and it should include all your critical queries and known edge cases. `pg_upgrade` can be a useful tool for performing these testing dry runs. Finally, make sure to also test under load, as a stress test can reveal how overall performance can be affected by the upgrade.

10.3   *Succumbing to encoding chaos*

It has become common for organizations to move from other database platforms to PostgreSQL. One of the usual migrations is from MySQL or MariaDB to Postgres, and this is what the proverbial DBA has been tasked with in the following case. Their organization's database is substantial and contains years of accumulated data, including personal information with international names utilizing various special characters.

The DBA felt that this would not be a difficult migration, as the software used standard SQL and had been tested and found to be totally compatible with PostgreSQL. The DBA began by performing a dump to export the MySQL database into an SQL file. The next step, predictably, was to import this dump file into Postgres:

```
psql service=staging -f prod_dump.sql
```

They were shocked to find that the terminal started filling with errors of this sort:

```
ERROR:  invalid byte sequence for encoding "UTF8": 0xe9
```

How was that possible? Unicode (UTF-8 in this case) should be able to deal with all the names in the database, as it supports international characters. Doing a little digging by finding the data row that caused the error, the DBA determined that 0xe9 is the hex value of the "Latin 1" code for the character é.

Looking into it further, the DBA found that the MySQL release they were using when the application went live was using latin1 as the default encoding. Even though it had since been upgraded to a version that uses utf8mb4 as the default encoding, the database kept using latin1 as its tables had never been explicitly converted.

What is utf8mb4, you ask? Why is the MySQL default not utf8? It all goes back to MySQL's utf8 being a flawed UTF-8 implementation that only supports up to 3-byte characters. This means that it can't encode many international Unicode characters or emojis. As this was not a true UTF-8, eventually the utf8mb4 encoding that supports 4-byte characters was added to MySQL. Instead of fixing the bad implementation, MySQL chose to add a confusing nonstandard name for the very well-understood UTF-8 encoding, while keeping around its old unsuitable utf8 for backward compatibility.

After converting the latin1 dump into UTF-8 characters, the DBA retried the import, only to fail again with a new complaint from PostgreSQL:

```
ERROR:  invalid byte sequence for encoding "UTF8": 0x00
```

It seems that some of the data contained *null characters*, also known as the ASCII NUL character, represented by hexadecimal zero \x00 or octal \0. By referring to the PostgreSQL documentation, we can find the explanation: "The character with the code zero cannot be in a string constant."

This is another pitfall to be aware of—just because another data source or database (in this case, MySQL) accepts strings containing the NUL character, it doesn't mean that these strings will be accepted in PostgreSQL, even in the hyperflexible UTF8 encoding.

The mistake that was made here was not accounting for character set and encoding differences between MySQL and PostgreSQL. By not determining the correct source and target encodings or performing any necessary conversion during the migration, the DBA faced "invalid byte sequence" errors. Additionally, by not properly handling illegal characters in the source data, they faced more import failures.

Some of these key differences to be aware of include the following:

- PostgreSQL defaults to `UTF8` and strictly enforces valid UTF-8 encoding while rejecting characters made up of invalid byte sequences and ASCII zeros.
- Older versions of MySQL and MariaDB default to `latin1`, which is also known as `ISO-8859-1` or `Windows-1252` code page, while newer versions may default to `utf8` or `utf8mb4`. As I said, these DBMSs' `utf8` has up to 3 bytes per character, which means that it is missing support for a lot of Unicode characters.
- Oracle's `UTF8`, from version 8.1.7 onward, means only "Unicode revision 3.0," so full current UTF-8 support requires the use of yet more strangely named encodings, such as `AL32UTF8`.
- Microsoft SQL Server text support, predictably, is focused on Windows code pages. Since SQL Server 2012, Unicode support is provided via the `NVARCHAR` data type, which uses `UTF-16` encoding. `UTF-8` support was only introduced with SQL Server 2019.

Oversights of differences like these can jeopardize migration efforts, not only because they cause delays but also because they may compromise data integrity by causing unseen data corruption. For example, if the target encoding decides to accept characters that it can no longer decode correctly back to their original form, data may be lost irrevocably.

A safe data migration path would be to

1. Identify the source encoding.
2. Export the data using that same encoding.
3. Convert the data to UTF-8. An example using the UNIX tool `iconv` is

   ```
   iconv -f latin1 -t utf8 prod_dump_latin1.sql -o prod_dump_utf8.sql
   ```

4. Clean the data by removing characters that PostgreSQL cannot accept. For example, remove null bytes using UNIX tools `tr` or `sed`:

   ```
   tr -d '\000' < prod_dump_utf8.sql > prod_dump_clean.sql

   sed 's/\x0//g' prod_dump_utf8.sql > prod_dump_clean.sql
   ```

5. Ensure that the target database is configured to use the `UTF8` encoding and an appropriate collation, like so:

   ```
   ENCODING = 'UTF8'
   LC_COLLATE = 'en_US.UTF-8'
   LC_CTYPE = 'en_US.UTF-8'
   ```

6. Import the cleaned data.

Finally, and I really shouldn't have to say this again, test thoroughly using real or realistic data before proceeding with any conversion and migration.

> **TIP** Tools like `pgloader` and `ora2pg` can help with the migration task by managing character sets and converting the data automatically. You can find `pgloader` at https://github.com/dimitri/pgloader and `ora2pg` at https://github.com/darold/ora2pg.

10.4   *Not using proper BOOLEANs*

Another mistake, somewhat related to the previous one, that people often make is failing to pay attention to how boolean values are used inside their database. A quick example that parallels the migration woes we saw in the previous section would be to export a table that contains booleans from, let's say, MariaDB. The table definition is

```
CREATE TABLE Election2024 (
  VoterID INT AUTO_INCREMENT KEY,
  Voted BOOLEAN NOT NULL DEFAULT false
);
```

Our good DBA exports the table and attempts to load it into PostgreSQL. What ensues is this:

```
psql:prod_dump.sql:24: ERROR:  column "Voted" is of type boolean but
expression is of type integer
LINE 1: ... "Voting"."Election2024" ("VoterID", "Voted") VALUES (500, 0);
                                                                       ^
HINT:  You will need to rewrite or cast the expression.
```

Wait a minute: the table column `Voted` is defined as `BOOLEAN`. Let's see what MariaDB says when we ask for the table definition:

```
DESCRIBE Election2024;
+------------+------------+------+-----+---------+----------------+
| Field      | Type       | Null | Key | Default | Extra          |
+------------+------------+------+-----+---------+----------------+
| VoterID    | int(11)    | NO   | PRI | NULL    | auto_increment |
| Voted      | tinyint(1) | NO   |     | NULL    |                |
+------------+------------+------+-----+---------+----------------+
```

Oops! It turns out that MariaDB, as well as MySQL, store `BOOLEAN`s as `TINYINT(1)` internally. A quick look at these databases' documentation for types `BOOL`/`BOOLEAN` confirms it:

> *These types are synonyms for TINYINT(1). A value of zero is considered false. Non-zero values are considered true.*

This is hardly a standard boolean representation! It means that we can't import such numeric data before converting it to proper SQL `BOOLEAN` values, as PostgreSQL believes that the literal integer values exported are . . . integers.

Other database systems also have this issue:

- In Microsoft SQL Server, it's common practice to use the `bit` data type that can take values 0, 1, and NULL to represent booleans.
- IBM DB2 only started supporting BOOLEAN as a column type after version 11.1.1.1, released in 2016. However, it will happily accept the string values '0' and '1', as well as the numbers 0 and 1, in such columns.
- Historically, Oracle has lacked comprehensive support for the BOOLEAN data type. Early on, it was standard practice to use CHAR(1) to store Y and N for "yes" and "no" (Anglocentric much?). Later, most people switched to using NUMBER(1) instead. Shockingly, support for BOOLEAN was only added with version 23c, released in 2023.

PostgreSQL provides proper support for the SQL standard BOOLEAN type, making `true` and `false` first-class citizens. Its strict adherence to the standard means that other values cannot be stored in booleans.

If the column you are migrating is originally defined as BOOLEAN but holds non-standard values, you will need to convert these character or numeric values into `true` and `false` in the dump file to be loaded for the PostgreSQL native boolean type to ingest them correctly.

Even if the columns are defined as pseudo-boolean numeric or character types in the other database, there is no reason to continue this charade inside PostgreSQL. Be aware that queries that implicitly expect a boolean may fail due to the type mismatch. To ensure consistency and standard-compliant behavior, convert these columns to boolean after the data load.

Let's say the table looks like this after the migration:

```
Table "Voting.Election2024"
 Column  |  Type   | Collation | Nullable |            Default
---------+---------+-----------+----------+----------------------------
 VoterID | integer |           | not null | generated always as identity
 Voted   | integer |           | not null | 0
Indexes:
    "Election2024_pkey" PRIMARY KEY, btree ("VoterID")
```

And we have values such as the following:

```
 VoterID | Voted
---------+-------
     500 |     0
     501 |     1
```

We can then run the following conversion:

```
ALTER TABLE "Voting"."Election2024" ALTER "Voted" DROP DEFAULT;
ALTER TABLE "Voting"."Election2024" ALTER "Voted" SET DATA TYPE BOOLEAN
    USING CASE WHEN "Voted" = 1 THEN true ELSE false END;
ALTER TABLE "Voting"."Election2024" ALTER "Voted" SET DEFAULT false;
```

After the conversion has been completed, our table looks like this:

```
Table "Voting.Election2024"
 Column | Type    | Collation | Nullable |            Default
--------+---------+-----------+----------+------------------------------
 VoterID | integer |           | not null | generated always as identity
 Voted  | boolean |           | not null | false
Indexes:
    "Election2024_pkey" PRIMARY KEY, btree ("VoterID")
```

We can see that the data inside is now properly stored:

```
 VoterID | Voted
---------+-------
     500 | f
     501 | t
```

To recap, if you want to avoid problems when migrating between databases, make sure your boolean columns use standard BOOLEAN types and convert nonstandard pseudo-boolean values (like integers or characters) to `true` and `false` in the data.

10.5 *Mishandling differences in data types*

We've already discussed some of the pitfalls you can encounter when moving from one DBMS platform to another in the preceding sections, so we're going to keep this one short and sweet.

Databases like MySQL/MariaDB, SAP Sybase/Microsoft SQL Server, Informix, and others use the non-SQL-standard DATETIME type to store a date and time in a TIMESTAMP-like way. However, it's done inconsistently; for example, accuracy-wise, some databases support fractional seconds, others offer accuracy approaching "a few" milliseconds, and still others exact milliseconds or fractions thereof. Another inconsistency is that some databases accept nonsense DATETIMEs into columns of this type; for example, MySQL and MariaDB seem happy to gobble up whatever invalid date you throw at them in non-strict mode (that used to be the default for a long time).

Finally, and most damning, if you try to convert most of these DATETIMEs to PostgreSQL's SQL-compliant type TIMESTAMP WITH TIME ZONE, you will unfortunately find out that the previous implementations don't support time zones and should be treated as naive (local) timestamps. For more on why that is a bad thing and why you should not use TIMESTAMP (WITHOUT TIME ZONE), refer to chapter 3, section 3.1.

Inexplicably, some databases such as Oracle use the DATE data type to store date *and* time information, but they are restricted to an accuracy of 1 second only! (Oracle's TIMESTAMP data type also stores date *and* time information but does include fractional seconds).

This goes beyond date/time types as well. NUMBER in Oracle can store both integers and floating-point values, but PostgreSQL requires you to distinguish between `numeric`, `integer`, and `float/double precision` types explicitly. Mapping the data types improperly can result in loss of precision or incorrect calculations.

All of this tells us that you can never rely on the name to tell you what a data type stores and that there are wild inconsistencies out there among DBMSs—possibly because of (unfortunate) design choices early on in their development process. Do not assume that data types sharing the same name are directly compatible with each other and always check their definition and behavior in the relevant documentation. Use PostgreSQL's data type conversion functions to ensure compatibility and take advantage of migration tools such as `pgloader` and `ora2pg`.

Summary

- Always read the release notes for all versions between your current and target PostgreSQL versions before upgrading. Neglecting to do this can lead to unexpected behavior because of new optimizations or breaking changes that are time-consuming to diagnose and fix.
- PostgreSQL upgrades can introduce subtle changes in behavior or performance that may add up to become a problem in the end. Thoroughly test your application and queries in a staging environment before upgrading and use realistic data and workloads to uncover potential issues early.
- Neglecting to address character encoding differences and disallowed characters during a database migration can lead to import errors or even data loss. When migrating between different RDBMSs, make sure to properly specify character encodings and the corresponding conversion between them and clean the data from things such as ASCII nulls. Migration tools can help with this task.
- When migrating boolean data to PostgreSQL, ensure it uses the proper `BOOLEAN` type. Convert nonstandard representations (e.g., integers or characters) to `true` and `false` to maintain consistency and avoid type mismatch errors.
- Inconsistencies in data type naming, functionality, and precision across DBMSs can lead to migration errors. Always verify and understand data type definitions and behavior and use PostgreSQL's conversion tools and migration utilities to ensure compatibility.

PostgreSQL, best practices, and you: Final insights

In this chapter

- Exploring how common user profiles shape PostgreSQL mistakes
- Planning proactively to avoid technical debt and problem escalation
- Approaching and improving a poorly designed inherited PostgreSQL database
- Using PostgreSQL thoughtfully to improve performance and reliability

11.1 What type of user are you?

Having discussed errors and potential mishaps at length, it's now time to take a step back and look at the PostgreSQL experience from a distance for more perspective. One of the reasons why PostgreSQL means so much and is loved by so many different kinds of users is that it can cater to their varied requirements. And yes, PostgreSQL users are not all the same—this much is obvious. From professional experience and talking to people at conferences alike, it's become clear to me that there is a vast range of people doing all sorts of different stuff with our database of choice, and more use cases crop up every day!

When someone shares a Postgres success story, that is really cool because you get to learn about a new or different use case. When someone shares a story of trying and failing to make something work using Postgres, that is equally interesting because understanding the underlying reasons for the failure is important for avoiding similar scenarios and seeking alternate paths. Incidentally, that is the whole premise of reliability and safety engineering and the whole culture that surrounds the discipline.

Reliability and safety culture teaches us that mistakes can occur as a consequence of human error, failure of processes, insufficient training, or simply through misunderstanding or miscommunication. In this book, we have seen errors that can be ascribed to pretty much any of these factors. Let's recognize that not all PostgreSQL users are the same and that the user role they occupy in their organization will give them a particular alignment or bias in the way they approach database usage. This way, we can appreciate how their specific focus can lead them to fall prey to mistakes that might be otherwise caught with a multifaceted look at the problem from an objective standpoint.

The following are some kinds of users and their characteristics. It is, by no means, an exhaustive list but based on observation. PostgreSQL may be involved in the background as part of a professional picture or in an academic or home setting.

11.1.1 *The dabbler*

You are a "full-stack" developer or data engineer. As part of your passion for exploring relevant technology, you come across PostgreSQL through word of mouth or articles extolling its virtues (or books such as this one)! You may even be an enthusiast working on a personally led database project. Deciding to see what the fuss is all about, you start looking into how to use Postgres for your data retrieval or research needs, and it seems to fit the bill.

However, it doesn't seem to scale as well as you had been told it would. It also doesn't seem to integrate well with the tools you've been using so far. Two paths lay out in front of you: you can dive into PostgreSQL head first and focus on learning all you can around this technology and ecosystem to achieve your goal or give up and look for an "easier" solution that you don't have to tweak to get results.

The first path can lead to gaining deep knowledge about the database and ecosystem, and you can come out the other end a consummate professional or well-informed enthusiast who will, at least, be an expert in this specific area. The second path may indeed uncover some wonder tool that "just works," but in many cases, it leads to a technology that promises the world but only really covers two-thirds of your use case, and you have to come up with the rest through custom code or manual data munging.

What effectively determines the outcome of each path is what you really want to use PostgreSQL for. Is the use case even valid for relational or document (JSON) databases? Then, most likely, you can find a way to make everything work fine. Are you relying on a different data paradigm, such as graphs, MapReduce, or specific data formats such as Parquet and Iceberg? Then, your success may hinge on third-party code such as extensions and Change Data Capture (CDC) or other data transformation or replication tools.

Looking for "the right tool" may turn out to be the fruitless pursuit of perfection. If you know any data professionals, you'll have noticed that what they care about the most is the accuracy and correctness of their data. They do appreciate ease of use but only in a relative way. They know enough to not care about a couple of extra clicks, as long as there's a promise that at the end of the process, they'll have a stable source of truth and a method that extracts and analyzes the data reliably.

This theoretical "dabbler" may be prone to misusing PostgreSQL features or data types, forgoing SQL conventions and best practices, and misunderstanding (or even skipping entirely) the documentation in search of quick-and-dirty solutions that will yield quick results. As we saw in chapters 2 and 3, such shortcuts can lead to significant problems down the line.

11.1.2 The cautious steward

You are a stalwart database administrator and the protector of data in your realm. You know all about best practices because you were the best in your database class or because you've been successfully navigating those waters for the past several years. You may be an experienced DevOps engineer or site reliability engineer (SRE).

However, there are things that can stump you. A developer asks to use JSON(B) for nonrelational data storage, and others reach out to you about distributed technologies, event buses, and stream processing. Invariably, you put them back in their place because PostgreSQL is a relational database, and it's being used in production. Any of these newfangled things may jeopardize the integrity of the data through their lack of an ACID implementation or affect the system's performance through excessive querying or replication demands, and the list goes on. In your relentless focus on the core tenets of database administration, you may have missed out on the latest PostgreSQL features or emerging data technology trends.

This "cautious steward" may be prone to sticking with what they know through their exposure to another database system or practices that are outdated, such as relying on logical dump and restore for backups. Their reluctance to try out new or PostgreSQL-specific features (see chapter 4) may lead them to inflexibility and missing out on efficiencies and synergies with new technologies. As I pointed out in chapter 7, not keeping up with the latest and greatest, including not upgrading, can paint you into a corner.

11.1.3 The oblivious coder

You may not even know, or care, that you are using PostgreSQL underneath it all, down in the "data layer." The database is something that is provided to you and "should just work" with your platform of choice, be it language or framework. All you ask for is one database connection (or a few thousand connections, for that matter). As far as you're concerned, the database is of secondary importance to your task, and the "database people" are obliged to deal with whatever your application or object-relational mapper (ORM) throws their way.

You may be interested in AI and want to explore vectorization and embeddings. Or you may have other specialized uses in mind, like GIS using PostGIS or other types of specialized extensions that add sets of features to PostgreSQL. However, your narrow focus on these things may not let you see the bigger picture that, in the end, there's a database system out there holding and processing your data. Alternatively, you may be relying too heavily on your ORM and programming framework and not enough on the core strengths of relational databases.

Often called the *naive* (or *parametric*) end user, the "oblivious coder" can be prone to basic data retrieval or SQL language errors if the SQL interface is exposed to them, such as N+1 queries and filtering in the application. If you recall, we discussed these types of issues in chapter 6. This is the type of user who is liable to code serialization anomalies inside their application or use text strings to store dates if left to their own devices. Reestablishing context to see how everything is connected and how all components can work optimally together usually helps.

11.1.4 *The freefaller*

You have been thrust into an unenviable position: you have been dropped into the middle of the operations circle of a highly complicated system, or you are very familiar with RDBMSs but not PostgreSQL in particular. After all, how different can this system, or PostgreSQL, be from what you've encountered before?

Of course, the answer can be *very*. There's a huge variety of Postgres users out there in the industry, and through custom code, Postgres can occupy niches your average person has not even thought about. All these specializations and workflows often require particular morsels of expertise, such as knowing that tables with a high frequency of updates will require an aggressive autovacuum configuration. This means that you may be overwhelmed by the complexity of what has been set up or the PostgreSQL features and techniques that are in use. Not asking for help or clarification out of pride or the desire to show that you're on top of things can incur risks.

The "freefaller" may be prone to blindly following blog posts that roughly correspond to what has been asked of them or describing and delegating the task to an LLM, with dubious results. As with every powerful tool, LLMs can be wonderful in the right hands but can be dangerous if you don't know what you are doing. Feeling they are in freefall, they may succumb to task fixation, making them less aware of the necessity of applying best practices at all times, especially regarding security and reliability (remember chapter 9 on high-availability bad practices).

These descriptions of hypothetical users are not meant to be negative stereotypes but are rather aimed at provoking thought as starting points for self-reflection. Identifying your specific needs as a PostgreSQL user and acknowledging the expectations, restrictions, conventions, and biases tied to your organizational role or alignment are important for self-awareness. Once you know what your particular characteristics are as a database user, you can better understand what comes naturally to you and the areas that require more attention. It's not about pigeonholing yourself as a particular user type but recognizing your strengths and weaknesses when it comes to effective PostgreSQL use on your journey to achieving good outcomes.

Embracing your particulars, aligning your practices with the responsibilities of your role, and using this heightened awareness to learn more or seek guidance from peers can help you prevent mistakes.

11.2 *Be proactive: Act early*

In the world of database management, every decision you make can potentially have cascading effects on performance, reliability, and maintainability. A well-maintained PostgreSQL database does not come about as the result of frantic firefighting efforts but rather through careful examination of issues and forward-thinking planning.

If you notice that a query is a bit slow or is performing worse than before, it means something. Take it as a warning signal that has to be acted upon immediately. Don't wait until

- Performance nosedives to start optimizing queries or introducing indexes.
- You lose data to start implementing a robust backup strategy.
- Your server goes down to establish and test redundancy and high-availability measures.
- You require a feature from a newer PostgreSQL release to hastily plan an upgrade.
- You start running out of primary key IDs to start looking for a solution for your key column.
- Your table balloons to gigabytes of bloat before you assess and adjust autovacuum settings.
- You accumulate a billion rows in your table to realize that it is necessary to partition it.
- Hardware or cloud provider costs skyrocket before you think about optimizing your database.

When you see these scenarios spelled out, they seem like pretty commonsense actions that any DBA worth their salt would take. And yet, there are constantly new examples of these things getting overlooked time and time again. Often, too much focus on short-term deliverables can detract from long-term stability and performance.

Being vigilant is the first step toward being proactive:

- Review developer code to catch mistakes and inefficiencies.
- Notice data access patterns that may become future bottlenecks.
- Examine database usage patterns to identify anomalies or spots for improvement.

Plan your course of action. Test the proposed solution and apply it to a staging environment that mirrors production as closely as possible. Then, roll it out at your own pace, with plenty of time to spare. Nobody wants to see an issue potentially escalate into a disaster, and being proactive protects you against that.

When the focus is on rapid development, many considerations can be deferred or neglected. However, applying best practices and planning for scalability, performance, and maintainability are activities that start at day one. This way, you can minimize or even eliminate technical debt. By worrying about predictable challenges and acting on those early on, you can prevent them from coming back to haunt your database in the future.

You are not alone in all this. Use the PostgreSQL ecosystem to your advantage. Tools for high-availability readiness, backing up, monitoring and alerting, and statistics analysis and visualization provide numerous ways to have early warning and address potential issues before they disrupt operations.

Finally, commit to continuous learning. Stay current on PostgreSQL and adjacent technologies and allocate time for training (even in the form of informal knowledge-sharing sessions). Participate in the PostgreSQL community through public fora and events. By staying informed, you can expand your horizons and learn from other people's experiences. Isn't this part of why you are reading this book?

Spearhead and cultivate a culture that values foresight and preparation. Encourage your peers and team members to think ahead, share insights, and exchange knowledge.

11.3 All right, so you inherited a bad database

It's a common story. You join a project and discover that the state of its database leaves much to be desired. However, it's not the end of the world. Let's explore why.

11.3.1 "Historical reasons"

Sometimes, it happens that you have to manage databases designed by your predecessor. Sometimes it even happens that the team used to not have a DBA. Those "hysterical raisins" can lead to disheartening discoveries, such as finding an `SQL_ASCII` database.

The database you inherit may be a house of horrors. It might be a result of questionable decisions, rushed deadlines, or architectural arrogance. What you have to remember is that whoever built it may have been using all the tools and knowledge they had at their disposal at the time and that this mess may have developed out of an organic growth of the code base and dataset.

11.3.2 What now?

What do you do now, when there are so many things to sort out? Instead of panicking, refer back to the old adage: "Never let a good crisis go to waste." Savor the opportunity to start fixing things before they have actually imploded and learn from this journey.

There may be many things wrong with the system—bad encoding or object naming choices, overly broad tables with hundreds of columns and multiple uses, too many narrow tables, an ineffective multi-tenancy design with lots of repetition, or spaghetti code. The DBA may have ignored the basics, such as normalizing, enforcing data integrity, and creating indexes.

Take a deep breath; remember that you are not alone and that these are solvable problems. First, see if anything is on fire. Ask those working with the system for the major pain points, and they will be all too happy to share them with you. They may complain about things working slowly, running out of disk space all the time, or having to reboot frequently because the server runs out of memory.

If there is something you can do to address significant known failure points, take those easy wins and buy yourself some time to improve the system incrementally and more systematically. Remember not to fall into the trap of the XY problem, identify what's wrong, consult best practices, and refer back to database basics to fix things.

What is known as the *XY problem* is a common miscommunication where the user attempts to get someone to help them by describing what they believe is the solution to their problem (X) instead of detailing their actual problem (Y).

11.3.3 *First things first*

Set out by assessing the situation and mapping the terrain of what you are dealing with. Use `pg_dump` and other tools such as `pgAdmin` or `DBeaver` to extract, visualize, and examine the schema's structure. Then, you can start inspecting the data and its quality by running exploratory queries. This can help you further understand the nature of the database contents. Look at the PostgreSQL configuration and ask yourself if it aligns well with what you've found so far. Monitor the database's logs and performance using `pg_stat_activity`, `pg_stat_statements`, and other relevant tools. This will uncover hints that can lead you back to the source of the problem, whether it's in the application code, database design or configuration, or even the data ingestion pipeline. Break down the proposed improvements into projects of a manageable size with measurable goals instead of trying to fix everything all at once.

Inheriting a bad database isn't just about fixing what's broken; it's also about futureproofing it (see figure 11.1). To ensure that your hard work pays off,

- Document as much as you can. Keep the documentation of the schema, relationships, configurations, and key contextual notes up to date.

- Automate as many of the high-availability, disaster recovery, and maintenance processes as you can. We've gone over the importance of this, especially the chapters on administration bad practices (chapter 7) and high-availability bad practices (chapter 9).

- Share your list of guidelines and best practices when it comes to security, schema and query design, and indexing and optimization with the broader team.

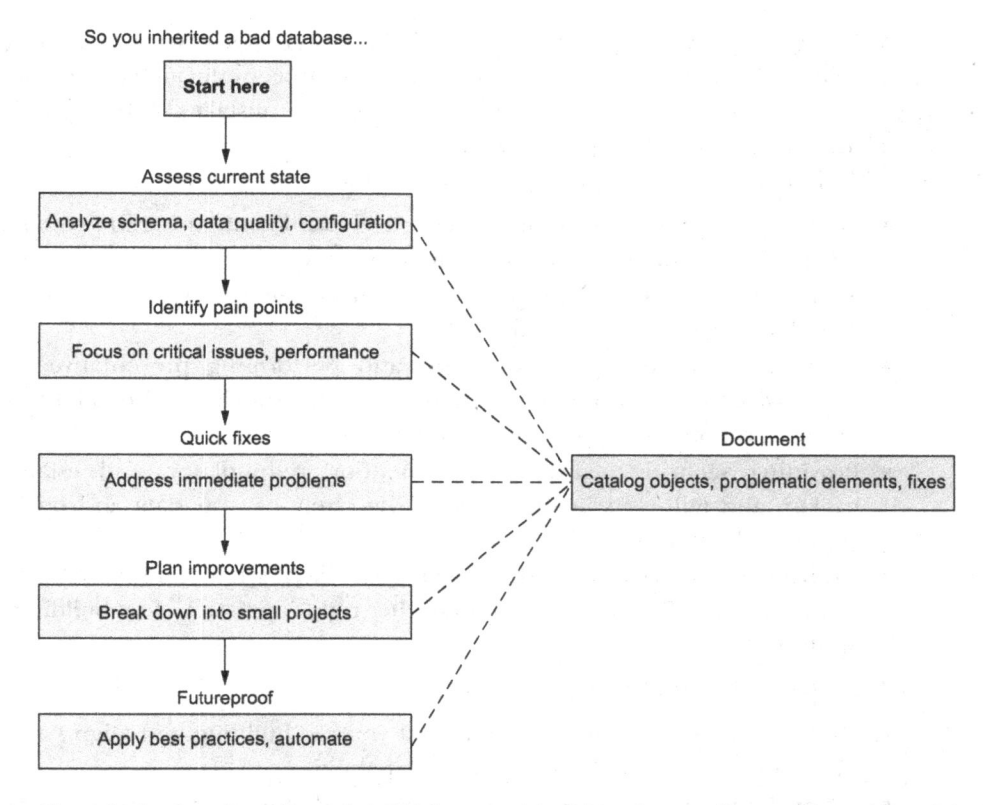

Figure 11.1   A roadmap for systematically assessing, fixing, documenting, and improving an inherited database.

The task of taking over an existing database may feel daunting, but it's also an opportunity to make a real impact. Even if you don't manage to turn it into the most enviable of data foundations, you can at least turn something that doesn't work well into a serviceable, robust, and reliable system. Prioritize repairs and take an incremental approach afterward. By being methodical, sticking to best practices, and looking ahead, you can make the database work for you and others and gain valuable experience.

11.4   *Treat Postgres well, and it will treat you well*

PostgreSQL is not just a database engine; it's a versatile powerhouse that has earned its reputation for reliability and adaptability. But, as with any tool, the key to succeeding lies in using it properly and treating it well. As a computational system, Postgres reflects how you interact with it.

This versatility makes PostgreSQL special because it can support a wide variety of use cases, from complex relational tasks on terabytes of data to blended paradigms with JSONB data or highly specialized jobs like geospatial processing. However, this power is also why it requires respect and care.

As Frogge Emporium navigated the sea of the PostgreSQL ecosystem in the pages of this book, it learned the fundamental truth of this concept through experience: it is rewarding to learn from your (and other people's) mistakes. When pitfalls are revealed, a roadmap for best practices emerges.

With thoughtful use, PostgreSQL can deliver the goods:

- Optimizing your queries, indexing effectively, and configuring the system properly lead to a responsive and performant system.
- Measuring and planning properly allow you to scale your system in accordance with data and user base growth.
- Proactively monitoring performance and performing preventative maintenance with VACUUM and other methods guarantee stability and reliability. Chapter 6 talks about the importance of autovacuum.
- Providing security measures, implementing redundancy, and establishing backup and failover strategies ensure the safety of your data and operations (refer to chapters 8 and 9).
- Utilizing Postgres's advanced and expressive SQL syntax and NoSQL features gives you the flexibility to choose the right approach for building your application.

To develop this thoughtfulness, you need to

- Understand your needs. Consider what you are building and align your goals with PostgreSQL's and its ecosystem's capabilities.
- Follow best practices. Create clean designs and schemas and architect your system to be safe.
- Keep learning. Stay updated on the latest features and extensions and stay connected with the community.

In a way, you can treat PostgreSQL like a partner in your database journey. It can help you a lot, but you have to meet it halfway and respect its idiosyncrasies. As an example, adhering to proven design patterns and vacuuming diligently will enhance performance and reliability. When you do your part, Postgres will work as hard as you do.

Closing this book isn't the end, as the journey with PostgreSQL extends far beyond these pages. Let the mistakes, solutions, concepts, and ideas we discussed inspire you to continue to explore, learn, and innovate.

Summary

- Misaligning your usage of PostgreSQL with your needs may stem from a lack of self-awareness and can lead to predictable mistakes. Recognizing your user profile and role-specific tendencies, biases, and limitations helps you focus on areas needing improvement to prevent mistakes and optimize your database interactions. Understanding what kind of user you are, following best practices, and seeking guidance allow for a more objective view of potential problems.

- Waiting until problems escalate before intervening on performance, reliability, or scalability is an unnecessary risk. Plan for future growth and optimize from the beginning to prevent technical debt. Proactive measures like code reviews and usage pattern analysis, coupled with regular monitoring and prompt attention to inefficiencies, are crucial and can save you a lot of trouble.

- Inheriting a poorly designed database means you should address major pain points as a priority before incrementally improving the system. Systematically assess the database using tools for schema inspection, data analysis, and performance monitoring. Along the way, document what you find and what you change, automate processes, share best practices, and take care to avoid the XY problem.

- Failing to recognize PostgreSQL's requirements stemming from its versatile nature can limit its effectiveness. Use it thoughtfully by optimizing queries, indexing effectively, and using preventive maintenance to have a performant, stable, and reliable system. Stay informed and treat Postgres, its ecosystem, and its community as trusted partners on your data journey. Recognizing common mistakes and adopting best practices let you harness PostgreSQL's potential to build robust, reliable systems.

appendix A
Frogge Emporium database

This appendix provides the information needed to create the Frogge Emporium database schema and populate it with sample data.

A.1 *Frogge Emporium database schema*

To re-create the Frogge Emporium database and user, run the following in `psql` as user `postgres`:

```
CREATE USER frogge PASSWORD <password>;
CREATE DATABASE frogge OWNER frogge;
```

Then you can create the schema by running the file `schema.sql` as follows from the command line:

```
psql -U frogge -f schema.sql
```

`schema.sql` can be found at https://github.com/vyruss/postgresql-mistakes/.

The content of `schema.sql` is as follows:

```
CREATE SCHEMA erp;
CREATE SCHEMA audit;
CREATE SCHEMA support;
CREATE SCHEMA test;

-- Customers go in this table.
CREATE TABLE erp.customers (
    id bigint PRIMARY KEY GENERATED ALWAYS AS IDENTITY,
    first_name text NOT NULL,
    middle_name text,
    last_name text,
    marketing_consent boolean DEFAULT false NOT NULL
);
```

```
-- This is where we hold contact details for customers.
CREATE TABLE erp.customer_contact_details (
    id bigint PRIMARY KEY REFERENCES erp.customers(id),
    email text DEFAULT '' NOT NULL,
    street_address text,
    city text,
    state text,
    country text,
    phone_no text
);
CREATE INDEX ON erp.customer_contact_details (email);

-- We represent order status by an enumeration.
CREATE TYPE erp.order_status AS ENUM (
    'Placed',
    'Fulfilled',
    'Cancelled'
);

-- Order groups aggregate large orders for multiple items.
CREATE TABLE erp.order_groups (
    id bigint PRIMARY KEY GENERATED ALWAYS AS IDENTITY,
    status erp.order_status,
    placed_at timestamptz,
    updated_at timestamptz,
    customer bigint REFERENCES erp.customers(id)
);

-- Table to hold orders for individual items or services.
CREATE TABLE erp.orders (
    id bigint PRIMARY KEY GENERATED ALWAYS AS IDENTITY,
    order_group bigint REFERENCES erp.order_groups(id),
    status erp.order_status,
    placed_at timestamptz,
    updated_at timestamptz,
    item integer,
    service integer
);

-- Each invoice for an order group goes in here.
CREATE TABLE erp.invoices (
    id bigint PRIMARY KEY GENERATED ALWAYS AS IDENTITY,
    amount numeric NOT NULL,
    customer bigint REFERENCES erp.customers(id),
    paid boolean DEFAULT false NOT NULL,
    order_group bigint REFERENCES erp.order_groups(id),
    updated_at timestamptz DEFAULT CURRENT_TIMESTAMP,
    created_at timestamptz DEFAULT CURRENT_TIMESTAMP
);

-- We hold payments for specific invoices in here.
CREATE TABLE erp.payments (
    id bigint PRIMARY KEY GENERATED ALWAYS AS IDENTITY,
    tstamp timestamptz NOT NULL,
    amount numeric NOT NULL,
```

```sql
    invoice bigint REFERENCES erp.invoices(id)
);
CREATE INDEX ON erp.payments (tstamp);

-- Our list of suppliers and their details.
CREATE TABLE erp.suppliers (
    id integer PRIMARY KEY GENERATED ALWAYS AS IDENTITY,
    company_name text,
    state text,
    country text,
    phone_no text,
    email text
);

-- We represent the type of each email sent by an enumeration.
CREATE TYPE erp.email_type AS ENUM (
    'Invoice reminder',
    'Welcome',        '
    'Account closed',
    'Happy birthday'
);

-- This table is the history of all emails sent out to customers.
CREATE TABLE erp.sent_emails (
    tstamp timestamptz PRIMARY KEY DEFAULT CURRENT_TIMESTAMP,
    customer bigint REFERENCES erp.customers(id),
    email_type erp.email_type,
    invoice bigint REFERENCES erp.invoices(id)
);

-- This table records energy usage readings for each of the branches.
CREATE TABLE erp.energy_usage (
    branch_id integer NOT NULL,
    reading_time timestamptz NOT NULL DEFAULT CURRENT_TIMESTAMP,
    reading numeric NOT NULL,
    unit varchar DEFAULT 'kWh' NOT NULL
);

-- This table holds customer service ticket details.
CREATE TABLE support.tickets (
    id integer PRIMARY KEY GENERATED ALWAYS AS IDENTITY,
    content text,
    status smallint,
    opened_at timestamptz DEFAULT CURRENT_TIMESTAMP NOT NULL,
    closed_at timestamptz
);


-- Logging of user activity for audit purposes.
CREATE TABLE audit.audit_log (
    id bigint PRIMARY KEY GENERATED ALWAYS AS IDENTITY,
    what text,
    who text,
    tstamp timestamptz
);
```

A.2   *Frogge Emporium database data*

You can populate the database with the data for customers and their contact details by loading the file `customer_dump.sql` as follows from the command line:

```
psql -U frogge -f customer_dump.sql
```

`customer_dump.sql` can be found at https://github.com/vyruss/postgresql-mistakes/.

Finally, you can create the rest of the data by running `create_data.sql` as follows from the command line:

```
psql -U frogge -f create_data.sql
```

`create_data.sql` can be found at https://github.com/vyruss/postgresql-mistakes/.

The content of `create_data.sql` is as follows:

```
-- Data for suppliers table
INSERT INTO erp.suppliers (company_name, state, country, email) VALUES
('Omni Consumer Products', 'MI', 'United States of America',
'ocp@example.com'),
('Yoyodyne',null,'Japan','yoyodyne@example.com');

-- Data for orders, order_groups, invoices, payments, sent_emails tables
DO $$
DECLARE _id bigint;
DECLARE _t1 timestamptz;
DECLARE _t2 timestamptz;
BEGIN
SELECT CURRENT_DATE - INTERVAL '1y' INTO _t1;
SELECT CURRENT_DATE INTO _t2;
FOR i IN 1 .. 50000 LOOP
    INSERT INTO erp.order_groups (status, placed_at, updated_at, customer)
    VALUES ('Fulfilled',
        (_t1 + (i * INTERVAL '1 s')),
        (_t1 + (i * INTERVAL '1 s')),
        TRUNC(RANDOM() * 14000 + 1)) RETURNING id INTO _id;
    INSERT INTO erp.orders (order_group, status, placed_at, updated_at,
        item) VALUES
        (_id, 'Fulfilled',
        (_t1 + (i * INTERVAL '1 s')),
        (_t1 + (i * INTERVAL '1 s')),
        TRUNC(RANDOM() * 1000 + 1));
    INSERT INTO erp.invoices (amount, customer, paid, order_group,
        created_at, updated_at) VALUES
        (59.95, (SELECT customer FROM erp.order_groups WHERE id=_id), 't',
        _id,
        (_t1 + (i * INTERVAL '1 s')),
        (_t1 + (i * INTERVAL '1 s')
        + INTERVAL '30 s')) RETURNING id INTO _id;
    INSERT INTO erp.payments (tstamp, amount, invoice)
    VALUES ((_t1 + (i * INTERVAL '1 s')
        + INTERVAL '30 s'), 59.95, _id);
END LOOP;
FOR i IN 1 .. 200000 LOOP
```

```
    INSERT INTO erp.order_groups (status, placed_at, updated_at, customer)
    VALUES ('Placed', _t2 - INTERVAL '2 d' + (i * INTERVAL '1 s'),
        _t2 - INTERVAL '2 d' + (i * INTERVAL '1 s'),
        TRUNC(RANDOM() * 14000 + 1)) RETURNING id INTO _id;
    INSERT INTO erp.orders (order_group, status, placed_at, updated_at,
        item) VALUES
        (_id, 'Placed', _t2 - INTERVAL '2 d' + (i * INTERVAL '1 s'),
        _t2 - INTERVAL '2 d' + (i * INTERVAL '1 s'),
        TRUNC(RANDOM() * 1000 + 1));
    INSERT INTO erp.invoices (amount, customer, paid, order_group,
        created_at, updated_at) VALUES
        (59.95, (SELECT customer FROM erp.order_groups WHERE id=_id), 't',
        _id,
        _t2 - INTERVAL '2 d' + (i * INTERVAL '1 s'),
        _t2 - INTERVAL '2 d' + (i * INTERVAL '1 s') + INTERVAL '30 s')
        RETURNING id INTO _id;
    INSERT INTO erp.payments (tstamp, amount, invoice)
    VALUES (_t2 - INTERVAL '2 d' + (i * INTERVAL '1 s') + INTERVAL '30 s',
        59.95, _id);
END LOOP;
WITH o AS (SELECT id FROM erp.orders ORDER BY RANDOM() LIMIT 1350
        FOR UPDATE)
    UPDATE erp.orders SET item = NULL, service = 21
    FROM o WHERE orders.id=o.id;
WITH i AS (SELECT id FROM erp.invoices ORDER BY RANDOM() LIMIT 1350
        FOR UPDATE)
    UPDATE erp.invoices SET paid='f' FROM i WHERE invoices.id=i.id;
WITH i AS (SELECT id, created_at, customer FROM erp.invoices
        WHERE paid='f')
    INSERT INTO erp.sent_emails (tstamp, customer, email_type, invoice)
        SELECT i.created_at + INTERVAL '1 d', i.customer,
            'Invoice reminder', i.id FROM i;
END $$ LANGUAGE plpgsql;

-- Data for tickets table
INSERT INTO support.tickets (status, content, opened_at, closed_at)
    SELECT 20, 'issue text',
    CURRENT_DATE - INTERVAL '2y' + n * (INTERVAL '1 m'),
    CURRENT_DATE - INTERVAL '2y' + n * (INTERVAL '1 m') + INTERVAL '1 d'
    FROM generate_series(1,1000000) n;
INSERT INTO support.tickets (status, content, opened_at)
    SELECT 10, 'issue text',
    CURRENT_DATE - INTERVAL '1y' + n * (INTERVAL '1 m')
    FROM generate_series(1,500) n;
```

appendix B
Cheat sheet

Table B.1   Bad SQL usage

Using NOT IN to exclude	Don't use NOT IN to exclude a list of values that can include even one null because that will return an empty result set. Consider the use of NOT EXISTS.
Selecting ranges with BETWEEN	Filtering with BETWEEN—for example, between two timestamps—can return overlapping results in subsequent queries because its ranges are inclusive.
Not using CTEs	CTEs can not only improve readability of queries but also improve performance by letting the optimizer decide to merge and reorder parts of the query.
Using uppercase identifiers	Quoting identifiers makes them case-sensitive, while the Postgres convention is for all identifiers to be case-insensitive, and this can lead to reduced usability and errors.
Dividing INTEGERS	Performing division between integers will yield an often unexpected, truncated integer result.
COUNTing NULL values	count() ignores NULL values so if you count a nullable column, you won't get the number of rows returned but the number of rows that didn't have NULL in that field.
Querying indexed columns with expressions	When you query indexed data that has had a data transformation applied to it, Postgres may not use the index at all.
Upserting NULLs in a composite unique key	Avoid using nullable columns in composite unique keys when possible. PostgreSQL 15 introduces NULLS NOT DISTINCT to address issues with upserts but you should probably use a cleaner design.
Selecting and fetching all the data	Don't slow down your queries by selecting more than strictly necessary and don't fetch more data than you need to the application side; do your filtering and data management operations on the database side.
Not taking advantage of checkers/linters or large language models	Use tools to check and lint your SQL for correctness and potential impacts to production and take advantage of generative AI to make your work easier, but be aware of the limitations and always recheck and have the final say.

Table B.2 Improper data type usage

`TIMESTAMP (WITHOUT TIME ZONE)`	There is no benefit to using `TIMESTAMP (WITHOUT TIME ZONE)`, as it can lead to time calculation errors due to lack of time zone and DST context. `TIMESTAMP WITH TIME ZONE` is the proper data type for recording timestamps as specific moments in time.
`TIME WITH TIME ZONE`	`TIMETZ` and `CURRENT_TIME` have questionable usefulness because time zones have no meaning without the context of dates. Again, it is preferable to use `TIMESTAMPTZ` even if we don't need to display the date part of the timestamp.
`MONEY`	`MONEY` doesn't store which currency and suffers from a limited and flawed implementation. It should be avoided in favor of using `NUMERIC` or other number formats that can accurately store exact values, potentially in conjunction with storing the currency as a separate column.
`SERIAL`	The two serial types `SERIAL` and `BIGSERIAL` have been effectively superseded by identity columns, which have more predictable behavior when it comes to role ownership and use of sequences, and clarity regarding which table the sequence belongs to.
`CHAR(n)`, `VARCHAR(n)`	You don't save storage space by using the limited character types `CHAR(n)` and `VARCHAR(n)`, and the whitespace stored with `CHAR(n)` can be detrimental to performance. Additionally, you run the risk of running into SQL quirks and painting yourself into a corner with maximum lengths. `TEXT` is the better choice.
`XML`	`XML` is a terrible choice for document storage unless you're just copying immutable XML data inside the database. If you intend to query/manipulate the data, you should use `JSON(B)`.

Table B.3 Table and index mistakes

Table inheritance	If you discover table inheritance and think you need it, you're probably wrong. Implement the parent–child relationships with foreign keys and triggers if needed.
Neglecting table partitioning	You can use table partitioning to make the management and maintenance of large tables easier and speed up the queries hitting those tables.
Partitioning by multiple keys	Take care when sub-partitioning because partitioning by multiple keys is not the same thing. Unfortunately, it is not obvious from the documentation what the multiple key partitioning syntax does, when best to use it, and what its implications are.
Using the wrong index type	Each index type offered in PostgreSQL has its strengths and weaknesses. By adapting your indexing plan to the type of data you have and the type of queries you need to run, you can optimize performance and storage space. When you get it right, your queries can run orders of magnitude faster.

Table B.4   Improper feature usage

Selecting `SQL_ASCII` as the encoding	`SQL_ASCII` is not a character encoding so much as the absence of one. If you don't want to risk mixing encodings irreversibly and you enjoy the ease of automatic character set conversion, make sure you use UTF-8 for your database.
`CREATE RULE`	PostgreSQL `RULE`s are not related to rules as defined in other DBMSs. `RULE`s are complicated to understand and are mainly there as Postgres internal machinery. In most cases, they don't behave as the user expects them to, and `TRIGGER`s are best used instead.
Relational JSON	Using JSON(B) values with relational access patterns makes for less efficient SQL, which is harder to read and might not perform as well. It's better not to mix the SQL and NoSQL paradigms but use each facility for what it's best at doing.
Putting UUIDs everywhere	`uuid`s take up more storage space than even `bigint`s, and indexing them is less efficient. They may guarantee a range of values that you simply don't require for your use case, and an integer index might be enough to guarantee uniqueness.
Homemade multi-master replication	Bi-directional or multi-master replication is more complex than what appears at first sight. For practical use in a production system, there is a very long list of prerequisites, considerations, and caveats. If your use case indeed justifies setting up a multi-master system, you are better off using an established multi-master solution whose developers have given thought to these concerns rather than re-inventing the wheel.
Homemade distributed systems	All of the previous points apply to homemade distributed systems as well, and it is not recommended to set out building them unless your scope is very narrowly focused. You need to consider the potential for distributed serialization anomalies and the very real tradeoffs laid out in the CAP and PACELC theorems.

Table B.5   Performance bad practices

Default configuration in production	PostgreSQL's default configuration is very conservative and, in most cases, will not be optimal for a real-world workload. This can mean that you are leaving your system resources underutilized and leaving potential performance gains on the table.
Improper memory allocation	You can shoot yourself in the foot by calculating memory allocation settings incorrectly. You need to take your workload into account, including what types of queries you are running and how memory hungry they are, along with what level of client concurrency you are expecting.
Having too many connections	Excessive concurrency can kill your performance rather than allow more work to be performed in parallel because of the way Multi-Version Concurrency Control (MVCC) works. You need to be aware of the risks associated with opening too many sessions inside PostgreSQL, the nature of your workload, and the limitations of your particular database host.

Table B.5   Performance bad practices (*continued*)

Having idle connections	Connections that are mostly or entirely idle don't come for free; they are associated with computational overhead that may affect PostgreSQL's, and your operating system's, performance in general. You should try to avoid having connections around that don't do much actual work. If you can't, you should use a connection pooler that's aware of these connection semantics, such as PgBouncer in Transaction Mode.
Allowing long-running transactions	`Idle in transaction` sessions and sessions with long-running queries can cause unexpected blocking of other queries, leading to application delays or errors. They can also postpone or altogether block autovacuum, and this can lead to performance degradation because of bloat or more serious errors.
High transaction rate	If you let your transaction rate get out of control, it can outrun the efforts of autovacuum to prevent XID wraparound failure and bring down your database. You can mitigate this by batching, reorganizing, and summarizing data—or even skipping the ingestion of data you aren't likely to use again.
Turning off autovacuum/autoanalyze	Autovacuum is essential for the correct operation of your database. Lowering its effectiveness or disabling it altogether to save system resources is a fallacy because any performance gains will be undone in time by bloat accumulation, inaccurate optimizer statistics, and forced anti-wraparound prevention.
Not using `EXPLAIN` `(ANALYZE)`	Where there's evidence that a query is running slowly, checking its `EXPLAIN` is a quick and accurate way to identify the reasons why and help troubleshoot it.
Locking explicitly	Locking objects explicitly can lead to read/write blocking that can make your application feel sluggish or broken. Where synchronization is needed, try to use the `SERIALIZABLE` isolation level and make your application able to retry actions.
Having no indexes	Indexes can make or break your queries' performance, and PostgreSQL has lots of index types. Examine your query plans and take advantage of indexing to boost performance for your `WHERE`s. Sequential scans are bad because they become linearly slower as the table grows.
Having unused indexes	Having indexes that you don't need can slow down your table for writing and consume valuable disk space. Identify those that aren't in use from `pg_stat_all_indexes` and remove them.
Removing indexes used elsewhere	Be careful when dropping indexes that appear unused, as this statistic is for the local node only, and those indexes may be in use on another node you are physically replicating to.

Table B.6   Administration bad practices

Not tracking disk usage	Running out of disk space can cause serious problems, so monitor your usage closely. Rash decisions like deleting what looks like logs or unnecessary files or resizing volumes can make the situation worse. Identify what's consuming your space and mitigate by employing multiple volumes.
Logging to PGDATA	Storing PostgreSQL logs on a separate filesystem from the database helps you reduce the risk of excessive logging filling up your disk. You should also implement log rotation and enforce log size limits.
Ignoring the logs	Regularly checking PostgreSQL logs is crucial for identifying and addressing configuration errors, performance bottlenecks, data integrity concerns, and security incidents in near real time. This can allow you to deal with problems before they escalate, and you can use pgBadger to help with the task.
Not monitoring the database	Not monitoring your PostgreSQL database can lead to undetected performance problems, security threats, and resource exhaustion that could impact its operation. By using the appropriate tools and metrics to look out for slowdowns, resource spikes, and maintenance needs, you can ensure optimal performance and mitigate risk.
No tracking of statistics over time	Long-term tracking of PostgreSQL statistics is important for understanding performance trends and making informed capacity planning decisions. You can use the usual monitoring tools or the lightweight pg_statviz extension to capture and visualize these statistics over time without the need for heavy tooling or storage overhead.
Not upgrading Postgres	If you don't regularly upgrade Postgres with minor releases, you can incur security risks or run into bugs that have been fixed. By not upgrading to the next major release, you can miss out on new features and enhancements. Upgrading is made safe and reliable by well-tested tools and thorough documentation. Don't fear the upgrade; fear the alternative.
Not upgrading your system	Failing to upgrade the operating system, and dependency libraries as well, can lead to obscure PostgreSQL performance problems, bugs, and vulnerabilities, negating the perceived stability in pursuit of which you avoided upgrading.

Table B.7   Security bad practices

Specifying psql -W or --password	Using psql -W or --password can be confusing and lead to lapses in security. Rely on PostgreSQL's automatic built-in password prompt mechanism instead.
Setting listen_addresses = '*'	Setting listen_addresses = '*' can expose your database server to insecure networks, so you should only enable the trusted network interfaces that are necessary for database connectivity.
trust-ing in pg_hba.conf	Using the trust method in pg_hba.conf in production environments is unacceptable. You should always enforce proper authentication to your server and restrict access as much as is practical.

Table B.7 Security bad practices *(continued)*

Database owned by a superuser	Having your databases and their contents owned by a superuser can lead to security problems and accidental damage to your data. Instead, create roles that have only the relevant permissions to own and manage these databases and grant permissions selectively to other roles.
Setting SECURITY DEFINER carelessly	Declaring functions as SECURITY DEFINER can cause data leaks and enable privilege escalation. To reduce risk, use it sparingly and with a safe search_path and prefer the combination of SECURITY INVOKER with explicit GRANTs.
Choosing an insecure search path	Not securing your search_path can let others hijack queries and escalate their privileges. Apply tight control over object creation in schemas and reference objects owned by trusted users only in queries.

Table B.8 High-availability bad practices

Not taking backups	RAID and filesystem snapshots can't help you reliably recover from corruption, human error, or malicious activity. The best way to guarantee your data is safe is to take backups using appropriate tools like pg_basebackup.
No Point-in-Time Recovery	Taking full backups only makes you vulnerable to data loss between backups. Use Point-in-Time Recovery with continuous archiving to be able to restore your database to the point before it was damaged.
Backing up manually	Taking backups manually is not robust or reliable; you should instead schedule automated backups, preferably using dedicated software that is PostgreSQL-aware (such as Barman or pgBackRest) and ensuring that you have a redundant copy of the backups in a second location.
Not testing backups	Untested backups can fail when you need them the most, so to ensure that they work correctly, always attempt a full restore to test your backups. Do not rely solely on automation but verify every step. Avoid using homegrown scripts and prefer tried-and-tested solutions.
Not having redundancy	Having a single database server with no provision for failover inevitably leads to downtime. Ensure redundancy by setting up standby nodes via replication.
Using no HA tool	Manual failover or custom scripts are risky because of the potential for extended downtime, data divergence, or loss. Prefer proven high-availability tools such as RepMgr, Patroni, and CloudNativePG for Kubernetes to ensure reliable and effective management of your HA cluster.

Table B.9 Upgrade/migration bad practices

Not reading all release notes	Always read the release notes for all versions between your current and target PostgreSQL versions before upgrading. Neglecting to do this can lead to unexpected behavior because of new optimizations or breaking changes that are time-consuming to diagnose and fix.

Table B.9   Upgrade/migration bad practices *(continued)*

Performing inadequate testing	PostgreSQL upgrades can introduce subtle changes in behavior or performance that may add up to become a problem in the end. Thoroughly test your application and queries in a staging environment before upgrading and use realistic data and workloads to uncover potential issues early.
Succumbing to encoding chaos	Neglecting to address character encoding differences and disallowed characters during a database migration can lead to import errors or even data loss. When migrating between different RDBMSs, make sure to properly specify character encodings and the corresponding conversion between them and clean the data from things such as ASCII nulls. Migration tools can help with this task.
Not using proper BOOLEANs	When migrating boolean data to PostgreSQL, ensure it uses the proper BOOLEAN type. Convert nonstandard representations (e.g., integers or characters) to `true` and `false` to maintain consistency and avoid type mismatch errors.
Mishandling differences in data types	Inconsistencies in data type naming, functionality, and precision across DBMSs can lead to migration errors. Always verify and understand data type definitions and behavior and use PostgreSQL's conversion tools and migration utilities to ensure compatibility.

Table B.10   PostgreSQL, best practices, and you: Final insights

What type of user are you?	Misaligning your usage of PostgreSQL with your needs may stem from a lack of self-awareness and can lead to predictable mistakes. Recognizing your user profile and role-specific tendencies, biases, and limitations helps you focus on areas needing improvement to prevent mistakes and optimize your database interactions. Understanding what kind of user you are, following best practices, and seeking guidance allow for a more objective view of potential problems.
Be proactive: Act early	Waiting until problems escalate before intervening on performance, reliability, or scalability is an unnecessary risk. Plan for future growth and optimize from the beginning to prevent technical debt. Proactive measures like code reviews and usage pattern analysis, coupled with regular monitoring and prompt attention to inefficiencies, are crucial and can save you a lot of trouble.
All right, so you inherited a bad database	Inheriting a poorly designed database means you should address major pain points as a priority before incrementally improving the system. Systematically assess the database using tools for schema inspection, data analysis, and performance monitoring. Along the way, document what you find and what you change, automate processes, share best practices, and take care to avoid the XY problem.
Treat Postgres well, and it will treat you well	Failing to recognize PostgreSQL's requirements stemming from its versatile nature can limit its effectiveness. Use it thoughtfully by optimizing queries, indexing effectively, and using preventive maintenance to have a performant, stable, and reliable system. Stay informed and treat Postgres, its ecosystem, and its community as trusted partners on your data journey. Recognizing common mistakes and adopting best practices let you harness PostgreSQL's potential to build robust, reliable systems.

index

Symbols

/ operator 25
~ operator 69

Numerics

2PC (Two-Phase Commit) protocol 95

A

ACID (Atomicity, Consistency, Isolation, Durability)
  compliance 95
  consistency 89, 93, 95
  isolation 96
administration 124–141
  database monitoring 133–135
  disk usage 125–127
    consuming disk space 126–127
    deleting WAL 126
    mitigation strategies 127
  ignoring logs 130–133
    bad configuration 130–131
    corruption 132
    locks 131–132
    performance issues 131
    security 132–133
  logging to PGDATA 127–130
  system upgrades 139–141
  upgrading Postgres 137–139
anti-dependency cycles 118
autovacuum 112, 115–117

B

B-Tree Index 69–73
backups
  HA bad practices 154–156
  manual 158–160
  testing 160–162
bad practices
  long-running transactions
    idle in transaction 110–112
    long-running queries 112–113
  missing indexes 119–120
Barman (Backup and Recovery Manager) 159
base backups 157
BETWEEN 17
BIGSERIAL 53
boolean 176–178
BPCHAR 51
BRIN (Block Range Index) 74
BST (British Summer Time) 45

C

CAP theorem 89
cascading replication 163
CDC (Change Data Capture) 94, 182
Change Data Capture (CDC) 94
CHAR(n) 47–49
character sets 76
client encoding 80
closed interval 18
CloudNativePG operator 165
code pages 76
composite unique key, upserting NULLs in 30–33

configuration, bad 130–131
connections 104–108
continuous backup 157
corruption 132
CREATE privileges 151
cron task scheduler 159
CTEs (Common Table Expressions) 19–22
CURRENT_TIME 47

D

data types 43–57
  BIGSERIAL 53
  boolean 176–178
  BPCHAR 51
  CHAR(n) 47–49
  double precision floating-point number
    type 25, 53
  JSON(B) 56–57, 83–86
  mishandling differences 178–179
  MONEY 51–53
  real floating-point number type 53
  SERIAL 53–55
  TIME WITH TIME ZONE 46
  TIMESTAMP WITH TIME ZONE 45
  TIMESTAMP WITHOUT TIME ZONE 43–46
  UUIDs (Universally Unique Identifiers) 86–89
  VARCHAR(n) 49–51
  XML 55–57
database monitoring 133–135
database owned by superuser 146–148
declarative partitioning 62
default configuration in production 99–101
DELETE operation 121
delimited identifiers 22
disk usage 125–127
distributed serialization anomaly 96
distributed transactions 95
DOCTYPE Document Type Declaration
    (DTD) 56
DOIs (Digital Object Identifiers) 72
DoS (Denial-of-Service) attack 127
double precision floating-point number type 25,
    53
DST (Daylight Savings Time) 45
DTD (DOCTYPE Document Type
    Declaration) 56

E

EAV (Entity-Attribute-Value) 84

encoding
  character 76
  client 80
EXPLAIN command 8–9, 16, 117–118
expressions, querying indexed columns with
    28–30

F

failover 163
feature usage, improper
  homemade distributed systems 94–97
  multi-master replication 89–93
  UUIDs 86–89
fetching all the data 33–35
float type 25
footgun 143
freezing 114
Frogge Emporium database 11
  data 194
  database schema 191

G

G2 serialization anomaly 118
GIN (Generalized Inverted Index) 71
GiST (Generalized Search Tree) 74
glibc library 140
GMT (Greenwich Mean Time) 44
grep utility 133

H

HBA (Host-Based Authentication) 90, 145–146
heavyweight locks 118
high availability
  backing up manually 158–160
  failover 163
  history 162–163
  Point-in-Time Recovery 156–158
  redundancy 162–164
  testing backups 160–162
  using no HA tool 164–166
homemade distributed systems 94–97
horizontal partitioning 62
hot standby 162

I

identifiers, uppercase 22–24
idle connections 108–110
  MVCC 108
  problems with 108–110

Index Only Scan 9–10, 35
index scan 35
indexed columns, querying with expressions
    28–30
indexes
    B-Tree 69–73
    BRIN 74
    expression based and partial. *See* partial index
    GIN 71–74
    GiST 73
    missing 119–120
    partitioning by multiple keys 66–68
    removing 121–122
    unused 121
    using wrong index type 68–74
inheritance. *See* table inheritance
inlined CTEs 22
insecure search path 150–152
INSERT operation 121
INTEGERs, dividing 24–26
IPC (Inter-Process Communication) 107

J

JSON, relational 83–86
JSON(B) 56–57, 83–86
jsonb operators 85

K

keys
    composite unique, upserting NULLs in 30–33
    partitioning by multiple keys 66–68

L

LEAKPROOF declaration 149
libm math library 140
libpq pipelining 138
linters 35–39
listen_addresses 144
LLMs (large language models) 39–41
locking explicitly 118–119
locks 110, 131–132
    explicit 118
    lightweight (LWLocks) 107
logs
    ignoring 130–133
        bad configuration 130–131
        corruption 132
        locks 131–132

    performance issues 131
    security 132–133
lossy index 30, 74

M

Materialize 85
memory allocation, improper 101–104
Merge Join 85
MONEY data type 51–53
multi-master replication 89–93
MVCC (Multi-Version Concurrency
    Control) 107–108

N

naive end user 183
naive timestamp 44
network partition 165
NOT IN clause 13–17
    alternative 16–17
    performance implications 16
NULL values 32–33
    COUNTing 27–28
    upserting in composite unique key 30–33
NULLS NOT DISTINCT clause 33

O

OOM-killer 103
OOP (Object-Oriented Programming) 59
opened_at column 92
ORM (Object-Relational Mapper) 60, 183

P

PACELC theorem 89
pageinspect module 161
parametric end user 183
partial index 9
partition pruning 65
partitioning
    by multiple keys 66–68
    tables, neglecting 62–66
passwords, psql -W or --password 143–144
Patroni 165
PEM (Postgres Enterprise Manager) 134
Percona Monitoring and Management
    (PMM) 134
perf tool 140
performance 98–123
    default configuration in production 99–101

performance *(continued)*
  high transaction rate 113–115
    burning through lots of XIDs 115
    XID wraparound 113–114
  idle connections 108–110
    MVCC 108
    problems with 108–110
performance bad practices
  connections 104–108
  EXPLAIN (ANALYZE) 117–118
  improper memory allocation 101–104
  locking explicitly 118–119
  long-running transactions 110–113
  missing indexes 119–120
  removing indexes used elsewhere 121–122
  unused indexes 121
pg_hba.conf 145–146
pg_statviz extension 135–137
pgBackRest (Postgres Backup and Restore) 159
pgbench utility 99
PGD (Postgres Distributed) 93
PGDATA, logging to 127–130
PGXN (PostgreSQL Extension Network) 136
PITR (Point-in-Time Recovery) 156–158
PMM (Percona Monitoring and
  Management) 134
Point-in-Time Recovery (PITR) 156–158
Postgres Enterprise Manager (PEM) 134
PostgreSQL
  avoiding pitfalls 3
  best practices 187–189
  client-server architecture figure 1.1 6
  common mistakes 196–202
    administration bad practices 200
    high-availability bad practices 201
    improper data type usage 197
    improper feature usage 198
    performance bad practices 198
    security bad practices 200
    table and index mistakes 197
    upgrade/migration bad practices 201
  inheriting bad databases 185–187
    assessing situation 186–187
    historical reasons 185
    next steps 185–186
  mistakes with
    coming with expectations from other
      databases 4
    misunderstanding documentation 5
    misunderstanding PostgreSQL 4
    not following best practices 5
    using relics from SQL Standard 5
  name xiv

release notes 168–171
upgrading 137–139
users 181–184
  cautious steward 182
  dabbler 181–182
  freefaller 183–184
  oblivious coder 183
Principle of Least Privilege 147
promoting standby 163
psql -W or --password 143–144
public schema 151–152
PyPI (Python Package Index) 137

Q

queries, long-running 112–113
query plan 8

R

RAID (Redundant Array of Independent
  Disks) 154
RBAC (Role-Based Access Control) 148
RDBMS (Relational DataBase Management
  System) 75
read-write conflict 96
real floating-point number type 53
redundancy 162–164
REINDEX command 139
relational JSON 83–86
replication
  cascading 164
  multi-master 89–93
  origins 90
  slots 163
RepMgr (replication manager) 165
Riggs, Simon 157
RLS (Row-Level Security) 147
RPO (Recovery Point Objective) 162
rsync 159
RTO (Recovery Time Objective) 162
rules, CREATE RULE 81–83

S

search path, insecure 150–152
security 132–133
  database owned by superuser 146–148
  listen_addresses 144
  psql -W or --password specifying 143–144
  SECURITY DEFINER 149–150
  trust in pg_hba.conf 145
selectivity 21

Seq Scan 8, 121
SERIAL data type 53–55
SERIALIZABLE isolation level 118
Serializable Snapshot Isolation (SSI) 118
setuid bit 149
shared buffers 100–105
snapshot isolation 108
split-brain 165
SQL (Structured Query Language) 12–42
  COUNTing NULL values 27–28
  CTEs (Common Table Expressions) 19–22
  dividing INTEGERs 24–26
  querying indexed columns with
    expressions 28–30
  selecting and fetching all data 33–35
  uppercase identifiers 22–24
  using NOT IN to exclude 13–17
    alternative 16–17
    performance implications 16
SQL Standard, using relics from 5
SQL_ASCII encoding 76–80
SSI (Serializable Snapshot Isolation) 118
stale reads 96
streaming replication 162
sub-partitioning 67
superuser 148
synchronous replication 162
system upgrades 139–141

T

tables 58–74
  inheritance of 59–62
  partitioning 62–66
    by multiple keys 66–68
    neglecting 62–66
  using wrong index type 68–74
tablespaces 65
TIME WITH TIME ZONE 46
TIMESTAMP WITH TIME ZONE 45
TIMESTAMP WITHOUT TIME ZONE 43–46
TIMESTAMPTZ data type 45–46
TOAST (The Oversized-Attribute Storage
  Technique) 88

TPS (Transactions Per Second) 102
transaction rate, high 113–115
  burning through lots of XIDs 115
  XID wraparound 113–114
transactions, long-running 110–113
  idle in transaction 110–112
  long-running queries in general 112–113
tsvector data type 71
Two-Phase Commit (2PC)
  protocol 95

U

UCS (Universal Coded Character Set) 76
unrepeatable read 96
UPDATE operation 121
uppercase identifiers 22–24
USAGE privileges 151
UTC (Universal Time Coordinate) 44
UTF-8 encoding 76, 78–80, 174–175
UUIDs (Universally Unique Identifiers) 86–89

V

VACUUM FREEZE operation 114
VARCHAR(n) 49–51
VOLATILE functions 82

W

WAL (Write-Ahead Log) 90
  deleting 126
warm standby servers 162
WHERE clause 13, 66, 69, 121
wraparound, XID 113–114
write skew on predicate read 118

X

XID wraparound 113–114
XML data type 55–57
XY problem 186

RELATED MANNING TITLES

100 SQL Server Mistakes and How to Avoid Them
by Peter A. Carter

ISBN 9781633437401
408 pages, $59.99
November 2024

Grokking Relational Database Design
by Qiang Hao and Michail Tsikerdekis

ISBN 9781633437418
280 pages, $49.99
March 2025

Learn SQL in a Month of Lunches
by Jeff Iannucci

ISBN 9781633438576
304 pages, $49.99
February 2025

Grokking Data Structures
by Marcello La Rocca
Foreword by Daniel Zingaro

ISBN 9781633436992
280 pages, $49.99
June 2024

For ordering information, go to www.manning.com